# Chasing Around Britain

# CHASING
## AROUND BRITAIN

## John Tyrrel

The Crowood Press

First published in 1990 by
THE CROWOOD PRESS
Gipsy Lane
Swindon
Wiltshire SN2 6DQ


Text © 1990 John Tyrrel
Design by Graeme Murdoch


**British Library Cataloguing in Publication Data**
Tyrrel, John
Chasing around Britain.
1. Great Britain. Steeplechasing
I. Title
789.450941


ISBN 1-85223-214-5

Typeset by Novatext Graphix Limited, Edinburgh.
Printed in England by Richard Clay Limited

*For Noël*
*My son and my racing companion.*

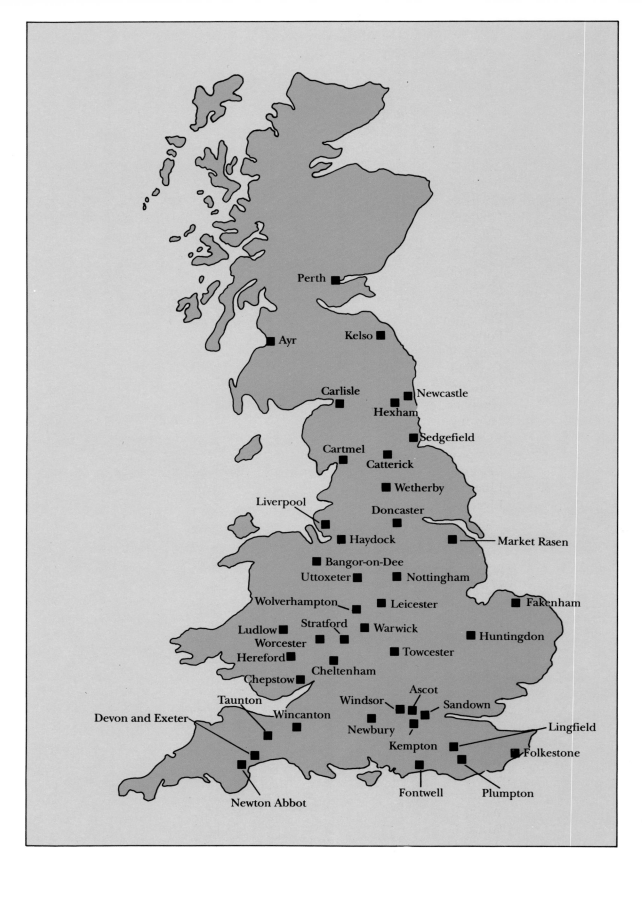

Perth

Ayr

Kelso

Carlisle

Newcastle

Hexham

Sedgefield

Cartmel

Catterick

Wetherby

Liverpool

Doncaster

Haydock

Market Rasen

Bangor-on-Dee

Uttoxeter

Nottingham

Wolverhampton

Leicester

Fakenham

Ludlow

Stratford

Warwick

Huntingdon

Worcester

Hereford

Towcester

Chepstow

Cheltenham

Ascot

Taunton

Windsor

Sandown

Devon and Exeter

Wincanton

Lingfield

Newbury

Kempton

Folkestone

Newton Abbot

Fontwell

Plumpton

# Contents

# ACKNOWLEDGEMENTS

THE author is grateful to all who have assisted in the preparation of the book, and in particular to the following: Ann Robinson, Susan Carrol and Candy Whiston of the Thoroughbred Breeders' Association; Nick Musgrave for the loan of the books from the TBA library; Dede Marks, Curator of the York Racing Museum and Library for the loan of books and much advice on steeplechasing in the North; Margaret Cresswell for the loan of books; Nick Cheyne and Michael Webster for the loan of books, material and photographs, together with advice on Sandown and Kempton; the Doncaster Museum and Art Gallery; Cynthia Sheerman for the loan of books; Bill and David McHarg for the loan of books and advice on the Scottish courses; Jackie Dennis for typing the manuscript; George Ennor for his invaluable editorial assistance, and both Christopher and Jo Forster for all their help and encouragement; Graeme Murdoch, Graham Hart and Peter and Janet Simmonett for the design and picture research; and finally Virginia, my long-suffering wife, who has spent another winter engulfed in books, papers, maps and manuscripts.

# INTRODUCTION

WHEN I was asked by Christopher Forster to write a companion volume to *Racecourses on the Flat* I was flattered, grateful and apprehensive. I was apprehensive because the history of flat racing occupies several hundred years, but National Hunt racing dates only from the mid nineteenth century and there are little more than one hundred and fifty years to record. However, as I researched the subject while travelling around Britain for Channel 4 Racing, it became clear that the jumping game was steeped in historical drama, with many colourful episodes which had long been forgotten.

As in *Racecourses* I have not attempted a purely factual or encyclopaedic recitation, but to recapture the colour of racing past, set against the changing pattern of social history.

Also as before I have not concentrated too much on recent times which are fresh in the mind and without the benefit of historical hindsight. Accordingly, Edinburgh, the absorbing history of which I described in *Racecourses* but where National Hunt racing has been staged for only three years, has been excluded; as has Southwell, which with due respect cannot claim a distinguished history and has assumed a fresh importance as an all-weather track outside the mainstream of National Hunt racing.

Racing in general is frequently labelled in the 'Play it again, Sam' tradition of amiable inaccuracy, as 'The Sport of Kings'. It was actually fox hunting which was described as such by Surtees, who wrote in *Handley Cross*: 'Unting is all that's worth living for . . . it's the sport of kings, the image of war without guilt, and only five-and-twenty per cent of its danger'.

I can think of a few battered jockeys who might disagree with the latter assertion, but it was hunting which provided the taproot of National Hunt racing, and it was from the hunt meetings that the sophisticated and organised sport that we know today originated.

Over the decades the cost has been high, in both equine and human terms, and as one of the most dangerous sports devised, 'the sticks' will continue to take a toll from brave horses, brave men and brave women.

It is the price they willingly pay as we sit cosily at our firesides before the television, shuffle around the betting shop or play the role of riders in the stand. 'Lest we forget'; and to all those who give so much for our amusement, I humbly dedicate this book.

John Tyrrel
Winchester, 1990

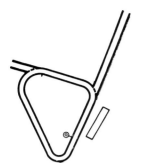

# ASCOT

U NHAPPY though she may have been in her private life, married as she was to Prince George of Denmark-'an overweight virile glutton'-who subjected her to eighteen pregnancies and sixteen children who failed to survive infancy, Her Majesty Queen Anne was fortunate to preside over one of the comparatively stable periods of English history and perhaps even more fortunate to have inherited a love of racing from her uncle, King Charles II.

No lightweight herself, the Queen followed the Royal Buckhounds seated in a small trap drawn by a sturdy pony, and although it was the Duke of Somerset who took charge of the practical aspects of the inaugural Royal Meeting in 1711, it was not long before Sir William Wyndham, Master of the Buckhounds and related by marriage to the Duke, exercised the rights of an appointment which had been served by Warwick the Kingmaker, the royal lothario Robert

SWINLEY LODGE.

THE EARL OF CORK.

THE EARL OF HARDWICKE.

Dudley, Earl of Leicester, and dated back to Edward III when the first Master was Sir Bernard Brocas, in 1362.

The early meetings at Ascot chiefly consisted of races with runners owned by members of the Royal Hunt and ridden by their servants. The Master, who was also Her Majesty's Representative, occupied an official residence, a seventeenth century building known as Swinley Lodge, where royal and other distinguished followers of the Buckhounds were entertained to massive breakfasts as the hounds patiently awaited the day's sport in the adjacent Royal Kennels.

Sir Bernard Brocas is commemorated at Ascot today along with later Masters of the Buckhounds, namely the Lords Coventry, Ribblesdale, Cork and Orrery, Hardwicke, Errol, Cornwallis, Bessborough, Chesham and Sandwich, whose grandfather invented the staple diet of most racegoers.

THE EARL OF BESSBOROUGH.

All have races named after them, thus forging a link between the soft elegance of the Royal Meeting and the more rugged pleasures of National Hunt racing, which came to Ascot in 1965.

Not everyone was happy. The Duke of Norfolk, Her Majesty's Representative from 1953 and the father of modern Ascot, was quoted as saying that steeplechasing would take place at the Royal course over his dead body; happily he survived to see it. A famous owner-breeder observed that the jumping track was like 'Blackpool with the tide out' but the author suspects that the gentleman's acquaintance with Blackpool may have been superficial.

The introduction of racing over the sticks was simply the final stage in the broadening of activity at Ascot, which before the war had been limited to the four days of the Royal meeting. It was King George VI who decided that much more use should be made of the course and it was that master administrator, Sir John Crocker Bulteel, who carried out the King's wishes to considerable effect.

Bulteel's father had won the Grand National in 1899 with the superb chaser Manifesto having bought the horse from Mr Harry Dyas who owned him for his 1897 success and it was Bulteel's policy to provide races for good stayers as an antidote to the over-production of precocious sprinters which was the fast-buck policy of many breeders in the years just after the war.

Sir John died in 1956, but surely would have approved of steeplechasing at Britain's premier course. It was an immediate success, thanks to imaginative race planning and generous sponsorship, long the saviour of National Hunt racing but unthinkable at the Royal Meeting.

First in line were the Buchanan whisky family, who sponsored the entire card on 19 November 1966, starting with a steeplechase named after the horse described by no less than Fred Darling as 'the best horse I have every trained, the best I am ever likely to train'. The animal was Hurry On, and this was no mean compliment from a man who produced nineteen classic winners.

Following the celebration of the 1916 Leger winner later races twice remembered Lord Woolavington, formerly James Buchanan, and naturally enough plugged Black and White whisky. The day ended with the Coronach Hurdle, named in honour of the Woolavington's 1926 Derby and St Leger hero.

The winner of the Black and White Gold Cup was Dicky May, trained by Tom Dreaper and ridden by Pat Taaffe.

Steeplechasing in the sixties was dominated by the Irish, and Dicky May was a mere understudy to the mighty Arkle, who won the S.G.B. Chase with the facile skill of a great champion in mid-December 1966.

Alas, it was glister and not gold. Horses, like humans, are mere beings and it was to be the last race that Arkle ever won; two weeks later the king of the winter game was the crumpled victim of a cruel injury at Kempton, and eased his way from life in honourable retirement at the age of thirteen.

The S.G.B. remains a top class three mile chase with £30,000 added to a prize supported by the sponsors to the tune of £18,000, contrasting with the £2,823 8s. won by Arkle in 1966, and the Heinz Novices' Chase displayed the talents of Three No Trumps, owned by that fine sportsman Prince Rajsinh of Rajpipla, Midnight Court and Gay Trip.

The Duke of Norfolk retired in 1972, and it was left to the Marquess of Abergavenny, who succeeded the Duke as Her Majesty's Representative, and the Clerk of the Course Captain the Hon. Nicholas Beaumont to sustain Ascot's reputation as a National Hunt track. Captain Beaumont is still in charge today, and when Lord Abergavenny, himself a good rider over country in the 1930s, was replaced by Sir Piers Bengough in 1982, the future of England's then newest jumping venue was assured.

Colonel Bengough, the finest soldier rider of recent times, rode four winners of the Grand Military Gold Cup at Sandown, on Joan's Rival in 1960 and three times with Charles Dickens in 1970, '71 and '72. Both horses were trained by Alec Kilpatrick at Collingbourne Ducis near Marlborough, and Charles Dickens finished third in the 1974 Grand National, ridden by Andy Turnell, only seven lengths and a short head behind Red Rum and L'Escargot.

Sir Piers is a man of humour and enjoys

SUN RISING LEADING IN THE BAGSHOT HANDICAP CHASE.

the story, not apocryphal but true, of the north country trainer invited to one of the Colonel's Ascot lunch parties. Arriving early, the trainer and his wife were shown into the ante-room and given drinks, although Sir Piers was busy on racecourse duties and was not able to receive his guests in person.

Moments later, he arrived and immediately put them at their ease, saying 'Hello; I'm Bengough'. The bell rang for lunch, and the afternoon went its sweet racing way. Taking their leave after tea, the trainer approached his host and said 'Goodbye Ben, and give our regards to Mrs Gough.'

WINNER'S ENCLOSURE, 1973.

# AYR

IN the year 1503 Princess Margaret, eldest daughter of Henry VII, was married to King James IV of Scotland and put to an end an era which Charles Dickens described in his *History of England* with amiable understatement as 'a long period of disturbance'. During this time of diplomatic calm various peers were created from the ranks of the Scottish gentry. One such was the Earl of Eglinton and Winton, ennobled in 1507. The Anglo-Scottish truce was not to last for long, and in 1513 Henry VIII's troops killed James IV and destroyed his army at the battle of Flodden as a reprisal for taking the Gallic side in Henry's war with France.

The Earl of Eglinton and his successors retired to their magnificent castle at Irvine on the west coast of Scotland. Here in 1636 they established a race meeting on Irvine Moor later known as Bogside, although racing had taken place in the surrounding district for many years; these events were known as the Irvine Marymass Races, and celebrated the Feast of the Annunciation, or Lady Day, on 25 March.

The Marymass races were organised by the Provost of Irvine and other civic dignitaries, including local magistrates, and the official meeting, recognised in the Racing Calendar from 1808, was effectively sponsored by the occupants of Eglinton Castle. Unfortunately, as they won most of the races as well, the meeting foundered from sheer boredom and lack of competition by 1824.

However, this was flat racing, and in 1836 the Eglinton Park Racing Club was formed

to run races at Bogside with the hunting fraternity very much in mind. Professionally organised by J.D. Boswell, Clerk of the Course to the nearby Ayr Western Meeting, the races were on the flat and run in late April and early May, but the conditions were limited to hunters and the Atalanta Stakes was 'for horses that have been in the habit of carrying ladies, or are the bona-fide property of ladies; a quarter of a mile, to be ridden in bonnets'.

The following year, although there were two and three-year-old races, the emphasis was again on hunters and the Stewards, Lord Douglas and Sir Frederick Johnstone, stipulated that 'a horse which is merely shown the hounds for the purpose of qualification, will not be allowed to start'.

The revival was a great success, and the *Sporting Magazine* reported in 1838 that Bogside was 'the Goodwood of the North Countree', going on to eulogise; 'There on the last day of April commenced one of the best meetings ever known on the shores of the Clyde. There was a great gathering of the fairest of Caledonia's daughters and the elite of her sporting sons'.

No doubt a good time was had by both daughters and sons when they repaired after racing to enjoy the lavish hospitality on offer at Eglinton Castle, where the 13th Earl thought nothing of spending a quarter of a million pounds to mount an elaborate replica of a medieval jousting tournament to amuse his guests.

On 25 April 1839, Bogside started the first

steeplechase run in Scotland. Lord Eglinton owned two of the runners in a four mile sweepstake of fifteen sovereigns each, at level weights of 13st 7lb, and his Lordship had the honour of partnering Coventry to victory by seven lengths over his other entrant, Multum in Parvo, ridden by Mr Gilmour.

There were six runners from the original thirteen subscribers; eight turned out for the second event over the same four miles of country, and Pioneer won in the hands of his owner, Sir David Baird, from the only other finisher, Captain Spottiswoode on Sambo; a name which you would be hard pushed to register at Weatherby's today.

The meeting was staged again in 1840 and as steeplechasing gained in nationwide popularity largely thanks to the Liverpool 'Grand National' so the Bogside course became more formally arranged, with a preliminary hurdle to be jumped on the way to the start, and a mandatory brook as well as a wall and paling obstacle. The Stewards sensibly insisted that the last two should be tested by potential runners on the day before racing.

It is clear that the Stewards, Sir H. Campbell, M.P. and William Stirling-Crawford had in mind the safety of the amateur riders to whom all the races were limited, but events were to prove that they need not have concerned themselves unduly. By 1842 some top class Corinthians were around, including Mr Wentworth Hope Johnstone Sen, who rode ten winners over three days of the meeting.

The *Sporting Magazine* was able to inform us that 'Beauty, rank and fashion were never congregated at any place north of the Tweed in greater proportions than at this exclusive meeting'. This prosperity was to continue until after the racing in 1852, when the rich prizes were far beyond those offered for most English meetings at the time with the exception of Liverpool.

Lord Eglinton was now 40. His career on the Turf had encompassed three St Leger winners, including the great The Flying Dutchman, who also won the Derby in the Eglinton colours of 'Montgomerie tartan, yellow sleeves and cap'. It was The Flying Dutchman who vanquished Voltigeur at York in one of the most famous matches ever run, but he was not an immediate success at stud, despite covering fifty mares in his first season.

The Earl was reputed to be a man of great charm and sportsmanship, but not of high intellect. He was disappointed by the stud failure of The Flying Dutchman and it was characteristic that he should sell all his bloodstock interests for a paltry 2500 guineas and go into public service, accepting the Lord-Lieutenancy of Ireland, in which capacity he was popular for his geniality.

As a consequence Lord Eglinton closed the Castle and without his support, both financial and social, it became impossible to continue the race meetings at Bogside. It was fifteen years before racing resumed as the Eglinton Hunt Meeting, the 13th Earl having died of apoplexy at St Andrews, the

RED RUM

home of his close friend and sporting poet George Whyte Melville.

On 3 May 1867 Bogside staged a handicap chase over about three miles with £100 added money. It was called 'The West of Scotland Grand National' and was won by the Duke of Hamilton's The Elk, ridden by John Page and carrying 11st 9lb including a 10lb penalty for winning the Eglinton Hunt Handicap Chase over four miles the previous day. Page had succeeded in the Duke's colours on Cortolvin in the Liverpool Grand National about two months earlier. The son of a Warwickshire farmer, he won his first race at the age of ten and the Northumberland Plate of 1860 riding at 5st 8lb before increasing weight forced him into a career which included two Grand Nationals (Cortolvin, and Casse Tête in 1872) and two victories in the Grand Steeplechase de Paris.

The Elk, originally named Roulette, won the inaugural Conyngham Cup at Punchestown in 1865 as 'General Election', but it was as The Elk that he went down in Turf history as the first winner of what was later to become the Scottish Grand National, as the race was renamed officially in 1881.

The 1881 winnner was Bellman, the 6/4 favourite ridden by the intrepid Charlie Cunningham, who was to ride three more Scottish National winners. However, luck was not always on Cunningham's side; in 1883, he was 'carted' before the start on 4/1 chance Hughie Graham and took no part.

More literal carting was the order of the day of the 1900 winner, Dorothy Vane, as the mare pulled both plough and cart on a farm at Clongriffin in County Meath before winning the Tradesman's Cup at Punchestown in 1896 and going on to win the Scottish National, by now a handicap and open to professional riders. Dorothy Vane was ridden by Snowy Clarke, who trained her at Ayr.

By 1924, The Eglinton Estate was broken up as the landed gentry were forced to face the harsh economic facts of the 1920s. The fine Eglinton Castle, scene of so many aristocratic revels and romances, became dismantled and roofless. The Emperor's Plate, a superb work depicting the Labours of Hercules, was among many famous trophies which were sold, and Bogside racecourse was purchased by John Jackson, then chairman of Haydock Park, who formed a company to continue the promotion of race meetings.

The purchase included some nearby farmland, where Alec McHarg took up residence as manager and secretary to the course, immediately embarking on a programme of rebuilding both track and grandstands.

With the foreseeable future assured, racing at Bogside in the 30s produced some remarkable performances. One of the finest amateurs of the period, Captain Cecil Brownhill of the Irish Guards, rode his own horse Drintyre to victory in the Scottish National of 1930. Brownhill was killed in a car crash in South Africa shortly before the outbreak of the Second World War and in accordance with his wishes his ashes were brought to England and scattered on the course at Sandown.

In 1934 Southern Hero, ridden by Jack Fawcus, recorded the first of his three victories in the Scottish National. Southern Hero won again in 1936 and 1939 and was second in 1937 and 1938. He was fourteen when he gained his third win in the Bogside National and was still jumping faultlessly after a decade of high class steeplechasing.

Between 1940 and 1946, war activities precluded racing at Bogside, but in 1947 the meeting was revived, with Rowland Roy taking the honours in the capable hands of Mr Richard Black.

The main feature of the 1950s was the treble achieved by Queen's Taste, who emulated Southern Hero with Scottish National wins in 1953, '54 and '56. Unlike Southern Hero, Queen's Taste enjoyed the services of three different jockeys, Tommy Robson, George Slack and Dick Curran; but he was trained throughout his career by Herbert Clarkson at Bishop Thornton in Yorkshire.

The last really high class horse to win at Bogside was Merryman II, winner of the Scottish National in the year before his 1960 victory at Liverpool. He was the last winner to defeat the old-style upright Aintree fences, which caused such grief to lesser animals but were a gift to tough and clever equine athletes typified by Merryman II. He started his life in the hunting field and that was where he died, at the meet of the North Northumberland Hounds.

By the sixties the writing was on the wall for Bogside. The Horserace Betting Levy Board, which was formed in 1961 in the wake of the Betting and Gaming Act which made off-course cash betting legal and led to the establishment of betting shops, took over the major financing of racing in an era when it was plain that too many courses were uneconomic.

This factor, combined with the proximity of Nobel and Coy's explosives factory at Ardeer which conflicted with new safety standards for large crowds at sporting and other functions, forced Bogside to close in 1965. After Brasher, Jimmy Fitzgerald and Tommy Robson had won the Scottish National, Painted Warrior, ridden by Johnny Leech, brought down the curtain on three hundred and twenty-nine years of racing when they won the Bogside Farewell Handicap Steeplechase.

Alec McHarg's son Bill succeeded as Clerk of the Course at Bogside and was also joint Clerk at Ayr with Kit Patterson. National Hunt racing had taken place at the old Bellisle racecourse at Ayr and had continued, albeit with hunters' flat races only, when the Ayr Western Club opened the present course in 1907.

A new steeplechase track was laid down in 1948 and jump racing resumed at Ayr in 1950 when Mr Clive Straker rode Prince of Goldwell to victory in the Inauguration Cup on 10 October.

The course was flourishing with nine National Hunt fixtures in 1966 when the

Scottish National found a new home under the auspices of Messrs McHarg and Patterson and the Western Club. It was a day of mixed racing much in the tradition of the old Eglinton Hunt meetings when Johnny Leech rode African Patrol into the winner's enclosure after the Scottish National; also on the card were the National Hunt Centenary Scottish Champion Hurdle, won by Blue Venom from Spartan General, and four flat races including the delightfully named Snodgrass Stakes.

The distance of the race was now four miles and one hundred and twenty yards, and some famous names were to appear on the roll of honour. The Fossa, winner in 1967, took part in eighty chases without a fall; then came Arcturus and Pat Buckley, Playlord and Ron Barry, The Spaniard and the brilliant if wayward Barry Brogan, one of the finest riders over fences since the war; and Red Rum who completed a unique double in 1974 when he won the Liverpool and Scottish Nationals in the same year.

A bronze statue of Red Rum overlooks the parade ring at Ayr in permanent celebration of Noel le Mare's hero. Also remembered, by a plaque outside the weighing room, is the 1922 Scottish National winner Sergeant Murphy but here the memories are bitter-sweet. After winning at Bogside, Sergeant Murphy won the Liverpool Grand National in 1923 as a thirteen-year-old. It would be nice to think that he spent his declining years in happy retirement, but his young American owner thought otherwise, and Sergeant Murphy was killed in a minor event at Bogside at the age of sixteen.

From the farce of 1891, when neither competitor in the two-horse field could negotiate the second fence and the National had to be declared void after twenty-five minutes, to the tragedy of Sergeant Murphy and the glories of Red Rum and Sea Pigeon, winner of the Scottish Champion Hurdle in 1977 and '78, Bogside and Ayr have carved a strong and deep niche in the history of British steeplechasing. Perhaps the tartan silks of Pat Muldoon carried on Sea Pigeon by Jonjo O'Neill served to revive memories of those Montgomerie plaid colours worn for the house of Eglinton so many years ago.

J.J. O'NEILL AND SEA PIGEON.

# BANGOR-ON-DEE

THE charming city of Bangor in North Wales stands at the head of the Menai Strait below the Isle of Anglesey. There is a fine Victorian pier, the Cathedral of St Deiniol, probably the home of the oldest bishopric in Britain, and the University of North Wales. However the visitor will look in vain for a racecourse, as not a few geographically unversed jockeys, owners, trainers and horse-box drivers have discovered to their mutual chagrin in the past one hundred and thirty years.

The racing takes place at Bangor-on-Dee, about four miles south of Wrexham and for many years until quite recent times when Chepstow was formally recognised as part of the Principality, the only racecourse in Wales.

Fred Archer managed to find his way there at the age of twelve to ride the first winner of his career. The horse was a Galloway pony called Maid of Trent and Archer weighed out at 4st 11lb to win a steeplechase in the colours of Mrs 'Croppy' Willan, so called after her short haircuts and mannish garb.

The year was 1869 and races had been held since 1867 on an estate known as Bryn-y-Pys. This was once the name of a race at nearby Wrexham, which in the mid nineteenth century was one of several flourishing Welsh tracks including Brecknock, Aberystwyth, Cardiff, Swansea, Welshpool, Haverfordwest, Knighton and Holywell where they ran the delightfully named Hokee Pokee Stakes. This latter event at a

Hunt meeting was not surprisingly a seller, with the interesting condition that the owner of the last horse home should pay £5 over and above his original entry stake of £5 to the second.

This idea probably added more than a little to the hokee pokee, but sadly only a few of these charming little meetings survived with their quaintly named contests and weird stipulations.

Apart from Hunt fixtures only Cardiff and Bangor of that list saw the dawn of the twentieth century. Although merely a one day meeting, Bangor was convenient for Liverpool and both Gamecock and Cloister ran at the North Wales track in its heyday during the 1880s and 1890s.

Gamecock went on to win the National in 1887, and Cloister put up a record breaking performance at Liverpool in 1893, winning under 12st 7lb in 9 minutes 42 seconds by a distance of forty lengths.

The prize money was good for the standards of the time. The principal race was the Great Bangor Handicap Chase over three miles and a half, and worth £240 to the winner, while the three mile Bryn-y-Pys Chase paid £80. Equivalent events at Catterick carried prizes of only £38 and £33 respectively while Sandown averaged under £100.

During this period Frank Cotton became Clerk of the Course. A good amateur jockey who had ridden in one of the roughest Nationals on record, won by Old Joe in 1886 when not even Gamecock could get round, Cotton took charge at Bangor ten years

FRED ARCHER.

National and winner of the National Hunt Chase at Cheltenham in 1912 on The Rejected IV. Gilbert Cotton was to serve Bangor for fifty years, but perhaps more importantly served National Hunt racing generally for the same period as Inspector of Courses.

He did more than any other person to remove some of the cruel and unnecessary hazards of Aintree being responsible for filling in the ditch in front of the Canal Turn after Easter Hero became wedged in 1928. He also campaigned to remove the fence after Becher's as he considered that the runners had too little time to regain a proper balance after the drop, but in this he was unsuccessful.

If his wishes had been adopted the utter muddle of Foinavon's race in 1967 would never have occurred, but Cotton did succeed in having the fences sloped in the early sixties and thus making Liverpool more attractive to the class horse.

Today Bangor remembers Gilbert Cotton with a Hunter Chase named in his honour and there is also the Red Coat Novices' Hurdle, recalling the Red Coat Steeplechase which goes back to Bangor's earliest times. Finally, the Hokee Pokee days of Holywell are not forgotten with a seller, which is one of the worst races in the Calendar; but who would have it otherwise?

later, and maintained not only a good standard of racing but the social traditions as well. There have never been grandstands at Bangor and the gentry parked their carriages on the top of a steep grass bank on the south side of the course, where they place their shooting brakes today to picnic with friends and enjoy a good view of the sport.

In 1921 Frank Cotton handed control to his son Gilbert Cotton, a veteran of the 1913

# CARLISLE

By ANY standards Carlisle must rate as one of racing's great survivors. Sporting festivals, including horse racing, were organised by the invading Norsemen in the eighth century, doubtless as a relaxation after a hard day's rape and pillage, on the land now known as Kingsmoor.

Little more is known until 1559, during the reign of Queen Elizabeth I when Lady Dacre, wife of the Governor of the City, donated one of racing's oldest surviving trophies, the Carlisle Bell. Lady Dacre instructed the Gold Bell to be inscribed 'The Sweftes Horse This Bel to Tak For Mi Lade Daker Sake', and the contest took place on the Norsemen's old stamping ground at Kingsmoor.

Unhappily, racing was soon to languish as a victim of the thuggery which was the curse of all race meetings held on public ground. Doncaster, Newcastle and Epsom have all suffered over the centuries; Carlisle's problem was gang warfare, and William Armstrong, otherwise notorious as 'Kinmont Willie', used the race meeting as a chance to settle a few old scores.

CARLISLE CASTLE.

SPRINGKELL.

A revival in 1619 was extremely popular and the Mayor of Carlisle presented a bell to be raced for along with Lady Dacre's. Racing continued successfully under the auspices of the local authorities until the cheerless period of the Commonwealth – and although it may have been a part of the Cumberland sports such as hound trailing, hawking, bowling and archery held at Kingsmoor during the happy days following the restoration of the Merry Monarch Charles II, the next recorded meeting was a four day event in 1773.

The venue had been changed to the swifts, on land adjoining the River Eden owned by the Duke of Devonshire. The course was tight, and the sharp turn into the straight saw many wide-running horse giving his partner an early bath in the river much to the distraction of the Carlisle Otter Hounds.

However, the sport flourished, and huge crowds assembled on the Swifts to see Sir James Maxwell's Springkell win the Carlisle Gold Cup in 1825, '27 and '28. The attendance was well bolstered by Springkell's Scottish fan club who travelled with him from his home course at Dumfries to follow their favourite's fortunes on the English tracks. Perhaps the earliest example of the mass fever since inspired by equine heroes such as Brown Jack, Arkle and Golden Miller which is today epitomised by Desert Orchid, Springkell's devoted band of admirers at least proved that there is nothing new in this phenomenon, although it is doubtful if the contemporary sporting press dubbed it 'Springymania'.

In spite of victories by the Cumberland bred Lanercost, winner of the inaugural Cambridgeshire at Newmarket in 1839, but maybe in part because of an unsuccessful experiment with National Hunt racing in 1849, the course went into recession in the fifties and sixties. Not even the erection of a grandstand and the spread of the railways could halt the decline, and in 1904 the ninth Duke of Devonshire refused to renew the lease.

A fresh course was laid out at Blackwell on farmland south of the city. The newly formed Race Company had enthusiasm but lacked managerial skills, and within two years the local cattle seemed set to regain their grazing. Luckily Sir Loftus Bates was persuaded to take command, and much in the manner of John Hughes at Liverpool three-quarters of a century later, sorted out snags with brisk efficiency and put the new venture back on its feet.

To begin with National Hunt racing had to share the card with flat events and the sport was modest. Only two races were run in 1907, both hurdles worth £48, one of which was a seller. The well known northern riders George Gunter and Sid Menzies shared the spoils between them, with Gunter riding Yataghan to victory in the Blackhall Juvenile Hurdle and Menzies successful in the Durdar Selling Hurdle on the outsider of three.

By 1911, a full card had been established and run on Easter Monday. It was very much a Hunt meeting, with races for the United Cumbrian Hunts Challenge Cup, a chase over three miles, and the Border Counties Hunts Challenge Cup Hurdle supported by events open to professional riders such as the Londsdale Handicap Chase, named after 'The Yellow Earl' whose Cumbrian family claimed decent from the sporting Norsemen of ten centuries ago.

MAJOR C.D. PATTERSON.

Little had changed by the mid twenties, including the prize money, but the Easter fixture was spread over two days and Carlisle continued to thrive with the flat racing providing a subsidy for the jumpers. Sir Loftus Bates retired in 1946, his work well done, and handed over to C.D. ('Kit') Patterson, who guided the course successfully through the difficult post-war years.

Today the remains of Carlisle Castle, built by William Rufus before Sir Walter Tyrrel shot him in the chest with a well-aimed arrow while hunting deer in the New Forest in August 1100, remind the racegoer of the long history of the Lakeland city where the racing, albeit modest, has survived to serve what was the only course remaining in Cumbria before the boundary changes transplanted Cartmel from Lancashire.

The old names have also stood the test of time: the Durdar seller of 1907 is now the Durdar Handicap Chase, and the Corinthian riders still contend for the United Cumbrian Hunts Challenge Cup and the Border Counties Challenge Cup Hurdle.

# CARTMEL

THE late Major John Fairfax-Blakeborough, M.C., who must have been rated by any standards as one of the great racing historians of the twentieth century, was surprisingly forced to admit in the Steeplechasing volume of the *Lonsdale Library* in 1955 that he had never been to Cartmel. The gallant Major's excuse was that Cartmel was a one day holiday fixture which clashed with so many others. Fairfax-Blakeborough added the rider that there must be many with an equally wide experience of racing who had not had the opportunity of enjoying the rural pleasances of Cartmel for the same reason, and the author must confess that he is one of the latter.

The origins of racing at the lakeland track are lost in the mists of time, although monks from the nearby priory may well have organised mule races in medieval years to alleviate the boredom of endless trips across the sands to visit their Benedictine brothers in Lancaster.

Doubtless the prize to the winning monk was a nip of the famous liqueur which probably also went down well after the Inn-keepers Stakes of £15 in 1856. Despite the counter attractions of hound trailing and foot races, racing was slowly established in the mid-nineteenth century well supported by the local farm workers, 'who lay on their crowns and silver money and are generally chagrined if they lose'.

Show me a punter who was not. About a hundred years on, there were also some cha-grined bookmakers at Cartmel, as we shall see.

In 1888, the traditional Whitsun meeting had been recognised in the Calendar for thirteen years. Fields were small, to the extent that two horses, Game Chicken and Jim's Coat, shared the first two races between them. Game Chicken won the Hartington Plate, a two mile hurdle, by a length from Jim's Coat. Half an hour later, on identical terms, Jim's Coat reversed the form by a length in the Tradesmen's Plate over the same distance, with the other competitors well beaten off in both events.

However the punters were undeterred and such good crowds were to be found at the meeting in 1894 that one sharp operator made a little 'silver money' selling bogus racecards.

And so this tiny track, little more than a mile round, bisected by the finishing straight, and laid down adjacent to the village of Cartmel which is part of the Lancashire estates of the Dukes of Devonshire, entered the twentieth century as a reputable, if slightly raffish, Hunt meeting.

The prize money was good for this type of fixture, although it remained much the same for many years. Even so in 1925 Jack Anthony was happy enough to make the journey from Berkshire to land a short-priced double on Tangerine IV and Belgian Boy for the Malpas trainer Peter Barthropp.

While Jack gathered his breath between races, Billy Dutton popped in another Barthropp winner, L'Aiaglon, in the North Lonsdale Hunters' Chase, Dutton was a distinguished amateur rider who, like Lord Oaksey many years later, forsook the law for the racecourse with little regret. He was a superb rider over country, winning the Liverpool and Cheltenham Foxhunters-Chases, the 1926 National Hunt Chase on Cloringo and the 1928 Grand National on Tipperary Tim when they were the only partnership to complete the course without falling. The remounted Billy Barton was the only other to finish.

Little changed, as is the way of English country life which is unsurpassed at least to an Englishman, until 1969 when the Whitsun meeting, now a two day affair, was augmented by a fixture on August Bank Holiday Monday. The first race, a selling hurdle was won by Gaiety Moore, trained by Gordon Richards and ridden by Ron Barry, and the second, a novice chase, by Bee-Eater in the hands of future commentator Richard Pitman.

Hill House, perhaps best described as the innocent villain of the 1967 Schweppes Gold Trophy at Newbury, was a faller in the colours of bookmaker John Banks, and not even the talents of Michael Dickinson, then an amateur rider and claiming 3lb, could persuade Arctic Lad to complete the course. The scene was set for a racing coup that Edgar Wallace would have been proud to include in his racing novels which so enthralled the public in the twenties.

The plot was simple. Gay Future, a competent hurdler trained by Edward O'Grady in Ireland, was transferred at the last moment to the charge of Tony Collins, a little known Scottish permit-holder. The horse ran at Cartmel on August Bank Holiday, 1974, ridden by Irish amateur Timmy Jones, and won quite legitimately at 10/1.

Meanwhile off-course cash bets including Gay Future in trebles with two horses from Collins' stable which were subsequently declared as non-runners, were laid to lose a quarter of a million pounds. The non-runners meant that the bets were all up to win on Gay Future, and by the time the bookies smelled a rat, it was too late.

The planning of the coup by mastermind Tony Murphy had been done with the knowledge that there was no 'blower' (telephone service) between Cartmel and the off-course bookmakers on such a busy day.

It was impossible for the bookies to get the course in time to back the horse and force the starting price down. The biter was well and truly bit, and even recourse to the law brought purely nominal satisfaction, with Murphy and Collins fined only £1000 each and O'Grady exonerated, though Collins was later warned off for ten years by the Jockey Club. It would be a shame if Cartmel were to be remembered in history only for the exploits of Murphy and his merry men. But Cartmel survives to charm and attract the sporting crowds, some of whom may not appreciate the anecdote told by John Fairfax-Blakeborough in *Paddock Personalities*.

Old-time jockey Sid Menzies rode in a hurdle race at Cartmel. It was a bunch finish, and any one of three might have won. As they pulled up, they looked in the frame

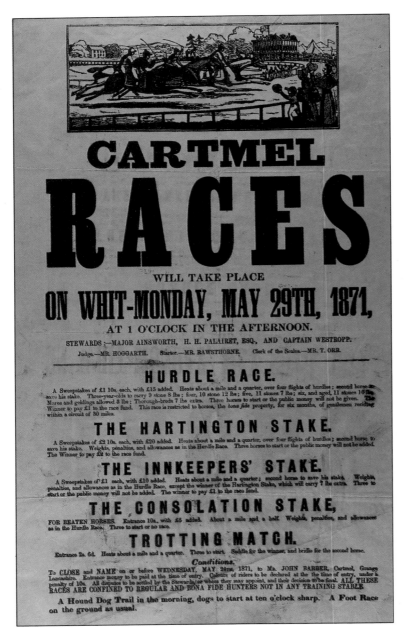

WHIT MONDAY RACING.

for the numbers, but none could be seen.

Trotting back, they spotted the judge leaning from his box waving. 'Which of you thinks he has won?' called the official. All three riders claimed to have done so, and the judge replied 'In that case I must give it to whom I think; but I wasn't sure about it.'

# CATTERICK

WOMEN'S liberation cannot be said, like Waterloo, to have been won on the playing fields of Eton; but it was won in the halls of *Akademia* by Emily Davies, the founder of Girton College, Cambridge in 1869.

It may seem a long reach from those repressive times and the early days of female emancipation to scarlet-faced girls crashing over fences to attempt to conquer the last bastion of male supremacy in sport but the thread is strong and true. As Noel Coward said, sex is here to stay, and vive la difference. The spirit of Emily Davies, to say nothing of the spirit of Florence Nagle and Norah Wilmot, lives to this day as women strive to find their place in racing.

The task is not an easy one, and the path has been hard and thorny since the Jockey Club first granted licences for women to ride under Rules over fences and hurdles in the wake of the Sex Discrimination Act of 1975, halfway through the National Hunt season. Those were heady days, and by the time the jumpers finally adjourned for their short summer break, 145 horses had been ridden by women over fences and hurdles, and ten of them were winners.

Of course, women had been riding successfully against men in point-to-points for many years, and it was no surprise that the champion lady rider in that sphere, Sue Horton, better known by her maiden name of Aston, was one of the first women to take advantage of the freshly acquired freedom and rode Le Toy in an amateur riders' handicap hurdle at Ascot in February 1976.

Three weeks' earlier, Muriel Naughton had the honour of being the first of her sex to take part in a steeplechase, at Ayr, but it was Diana Thorne (now Henderson) who provided the first 'National Velvet' happy ending when steering Ben Ruler home to win the Nimrod Hunters' Chase at Stratford on 7 February 1976.

The prospect of women riding over obstacles did not please everyone, including Lester Piggott, who was against girl jockeys in general on the grounds that 'their bottoms were the wrong shape', and many people in racing were concerned for the safety of women in the world's toughest equine sport.

Strictly speaking, the Jockey Club did not have to grant licences to women riders under National Hunt rules, as Clause 44 of the Sex Discrimination Act provided that sporting contests could be confined to one sex if 'the physical strength, stamina or physique of the average woman puts her at a disadvantage with the average man'.

Taking the view that the horse did 80% of the work during a race, and that therefore race-riding was not a straight man-against-woman contest (as would be the case in a boxing match, to take an extreme example), the Club proceeded. Sadly, the prognostications on the grounds of safety have both been realised; the impact of women jockeys, with the exception of a few highlights, has been minimal and on 8 November 1986 Jayne Thompson fell at the first flight in a novice hurdle at Catterick and sustained injuries from which she died six days later.

Jayne was the first girl jockey to be killed on a British racetrack. Thankfully, she is also the only one, although there was a poignant postscript to her death. Kindred, a selling plater trained by Jayne's father, Ron Thompson, at Stainforth, pined for her; she had ridden Kindred to nine victories and looked after the horse at home. Kindred rapidly lost weight and died just two months after Jayne.

Their deaths provide yet another example of the price paid by those who entertain us, as we chase around Britain in pursuit of pleasure from the superlatives of Cheltenham to the commonalty of Catterick.

Catterick Bridge takes its name from the bridge over the River Swale which flows past the northern extremity of the course. On the bridge their once stood a chapel and nearby the George and Dragon Inn and posting house, presided over by Tom Ferguson.

Ferguson was the owner of the 1819 St Leger winner, Antonio, a moderate horse who won the northern classic at long odds after two of the fancied animals had been left at the post in a shambles of a start. A re-run which Antonio did not contest, staged to appease a rowdy Doncaster crowd, was later declared void by the stewards of the Jockey Club, and Ferguson, who primarily dealt in coaching horses, was hardly able to believe his luck.

It is an old racing adage that you make your own luck and if a spirit of enterprise can be said to make a contribution, then Ferguson deserved all the good fortune that came his way. His technique for clearing a snowbound course where flat racing had taken place since 1873 was to drive a flock of sheep on endless circuits of the track until the snow could no longer 'ball' in the horses' hooves.

Racing over fences came to Catterick Bridge in 1867, but hunters' flat races were run as early as 1813, when the then Mr Tatton Sykes's Sunley won the Pipe of Port Wine for gentlemen riders by a length at 4/1. The meeting was attended by the Duke of Leeds, Lord Queensberry and the famous gambler and north country sportsman, Edward Petre. Although optimistically described by one local commentator as potentially 'the best meeting north of the Trent', this expectation was never realised.

However, in the mid nineteenth century Catterick was a popular and well patronised sporting fixture, given the limited catchment area. Prize money compared well with other local meetings, which was all the more remarkable as there was no gate money until 1888 when Lord Zetland, Sir John Lawson and a few other sportsmen who officiated on the race committee decided that cheerful improvisation was no longer enough.

Having underwritten a deficit of £1400, to which one should add a couple of noughts to equate to today's terms, the committee charged the public for admission for the first time on Thursday 5 April and they were not disappointed.

Fireway, trotted up for Charlie Cunningham in the Bedale Open Hunters' Chase at 2/1 on and George Lambton won the North Riding Hunters' Plate on the 2/1 joint favourite Bellringer, but not before the ten lengths 'first past the post' Ducal had been disqualified for missing the last fence, easily done in the heat of battle on the days when the final obstacle was aligned with the water jump, with a hurdle to follow.

Even so, the punters might have jibbed at paying for Catterick's limited facilities. The 'grandstand' was primitive and built over two cottages occupied by the employees of Teasdale Hutchinson, who lived at the manor house in Brough Park where the racing was staged. Perhaps the cramped conditions contributed to the general discontent when John Fairfax-Blakeborough, then in the early stages of his career as a National Hunt jockey, won a steeplechase on a mare called Lady Pauline.

It was the second day of Catterick's April meeting early in the nineties. On the first day, Fairfax-Blakeborough was well clear of his solitary opponent, Murray Thriepland on Frontier, but Lady Pauline refused at the hurdle, leaving Frontier to win as he liked. On the second day, Lady Pauline won in a canter from a field of eight, well covered up by Fairfax-Blakeborough until the hurdle was safely negotiated. The stewards naturally understood the reason for these contrasting displays, but the aggrieved punters who had backed Lady Pauline on the first occasion but ignored here on the second, preferring

the odds-on Nimrod, were incensed. The jockey needed a police escort to the weighing room and thence from the course, while Lady Pauline's owner, Captain John Rogerson, a useful boxer in his day, saw off the thugs with a brisk bout of fisticuffs and later collected Lady Pauline who was running loose in the paddock, terrified by the shenanigan.

In Edwardian times, Catterick enjoyed two fixtures in April and October but, as before, shared the card with flat racing. The course was now in the charge of Sir Harry Lawson, who inherited the title from his father Sir John in 1910, having persuaded the old baronet to put up a proper grandstand in 1906.

Sir Harry's elegant style survived well into the twenties, although he leased the course to the Catterick Race Company in 1923. The scion of an old Catholic family, Sir Harry married into the family of the Duke of Norfolk and maintained a beautiful chapel at Brough Hall where the chaplain, Father Curry, was no stranger to the paddock at Catterick and was said to enjoy 'a good flutter'; whether the source of the Reverend Father's information was spiritual or temporal is not recorded.

Doubtless Father Curry was a popular guest at Sir Harry Lawson's luncheons at the Bridge Hotel on racedays, but meanwhile the racing at Catterick had slumped into mediocrity and it was not until 1946, when Major Leslie Petch, M.F.H. took command, that the course emerged from the doldrums.

While Petch sorted out the financial difficulties and improved facilities for the patrons both human and equine, C.D. 'Kit' Patterson acted as Clerk of the Course for the National Hunt meetings, adding to the straight and realigning the fences. The course always attracted plenty of runners for modest prizes, and in 1953 a group of local enthusiasts put up the stake for a £1000 Grand National Trial Chase over three and a half miles, with a piece of plate worth £100 for the winning owner, and a gold mounted whip for the successful jockey.

The event has survived and Catterick now provides twelve days' National Hunt racing. It is practical rather than picturesque and today Father Curry would find the scream of the NATO jet fighters on exercise a little distracting if he looked heavenwards for inspiration; but since he had just endured the 'great war for civilisation' he may have taken comfort from their presence.

# CHELTENHAM

*'I remember the lowering wintry morn*
*And the mists on the Cotswold Hills*
*Where I once heard the blast of the huntsman's*
*   horn*
*Not far from the seven rills.'*

Adam Lindsay Gordon

GORDON was a man after the author's own heart. He was of similar background, the son of a soldier and of a mother who suffered from acute depression, a man who appreciated the cool elegance of winter and loathed the sultry heat of summer. Unhappily Gordon had to endure the heat in Australia whither he was consigned by an angry family after falling in love 'out of his class'.

Gordon, who was educated at Cheltenham, epitomised the chasing world of mid-nineteenth century England in his poetry and his life, and it is satisfying to know that this student of Greek and Latin literature not only succeeded in irritating the Antipodeans who scorned such heights of *Akademeia*, but also beat them at their own game and rode the winner of the Adelaide Grand Steeplechase.

In Gordon's time, Cheltenham was a spa town of some 22,000 inhabitants. Taking its name from the river Chilt, a tributary of the Severn, the town gained fame from the mineral springs, which were discovered in 1716. In 1738, an enterprising Captain Skillicorn erected a brick pavilion over the original well, built a pump room and laid out gardens and walks to accommodate those seeking to cleanse the liver in relaxed surroundings.

There was little accommodation for visitors, however. In 1780, the town boasted only thirty lodging houses, but following George III's decision to flush the royal system at the then popular spa in 1788, Cheltenham became a notable resort and by 1840 15,000 visitors annually were enjoying the elegance of the buildings and the Montpelier and Imperial Pump Rooms as well as the pleasures of the theatre and the concert hall.

At that time, the only permanent fixture at Cheltenham was a two day flat race meeting run in early July over the Improved Old Course on Cleeve Hill, where racing had been established in 1819, although not to everyone's satisfaction. The vicar of Cheltenham Parish Church, the Reverend F. Close, warned his flock from the pulpit on the 17 June 1827: 'I verily believe that, in the day of judgement, thousands of that vast multitude who have served the world, the flesh and the devil, will trace up all the guilt and misery which has fallen on them either to the race course or the theatre.'

The reverend gentleman then went on to assert that 'The Heathen festivals of Venus and Bacchus are exceeded on a Christian raceground'; which inadvertent advertising was doubtless excellent for the takings in the beer tents and the income of the 'ladies of the town.'

# Cheltenham

Although some claim the year as 1831, the most reliable records indicate that steeplechasing was first properly established in 1834, when Fugleman won the inaugural Grand Annual Steeplechase in the Vale of Prestbury. Thereafter, racing took place at a variety of venues, including Andoversford, Knoverton, Kayte Farm or round the back of the cemetery. But wherever the races were run they were the centrepiece of a week of festivities lead by such luminaries of the sporting fraternity as the Holman family, William Archer, Tom Olliver, Adam Lindsay Gordon and George Stevens.

Stevens won five Grand Nationals, a riding record which may never be equalled, let alone beaten, and each victory (in 1856, 1863, 1864, 1869 and 1870) was celebrated by a bonfire on Cleeve Hill. He weighed less than nine stone and won only seventy-six chases in twenty-two seasons, but he accepted few rides and enjoyed a winning percentage which would be the envy of many a modern cavalier.

Flat racing came to an end in 1855 after Hothorpe and Duet had dead-heated for the Consolation Scramble Handicap over four furlongs, with Hothorpe winning the run-off by half a length at 6/5 on. Steeplechasing continued to flourish, and by 1875 Master Mowbray was winning the second of his three Grand Annuals in the capable hands of George Holman at the Prestbury Park Spring Meeting on 1 and 2 April.

Holman was a leading member of a famous Cheltenham family headed by his father William, who trained three Grand National winners and won the Grand Annual five times as a jockey. His six sons included Alfred, manager of Cheltenham racecourse, and Frederick, a keen amateur rider. Frederick's grand-daughter married 'Frenchie' Nicholson and the dynasty continues with 'Frenchie's' son David, a successful trainer today after a fine career in the saddle.

Cheltenham, although much in the shadow of Liverpool in the latter half of the nineteenth century, was 'a place of sport', as the contemporary form books called them, in a much more literal sense. It was the adopted home of 'Black Tom' Olliver, whose fluctuating fortunes made him such an expert in the art of litigation that he was moved to describe the law as 'being like a country dance. You get led up and down by a coquettish partner, your attorney, till you were tired but never satisfied.'

Olliver was the 'Frenchie' Nicholson of his day, a superb tutor of jockeys including William Holman and William Archer in the professional ranks and Adam Lindsay Gordon amongst the Corinthians.

Later, Gordon wrote of his riding-master:

*He cares not for the bubbles of fortune's fickle tide*
*Who like Bendigo can battle and like Olliver can ride.*

William Archer was originally a flat race jockey and returned in 1845 from a stint riding for Tsar Nicholas I of Russia at Tsarkoe

Zeloe to take up steeplechasing and went on to win the 1858 National on Little Charley. On retirement he played host to the Cheltenham sporting crowd at the King's Arms in Prestbury. The most famous member of the family was William's son Fred, perhaps the greatest flat race jockey who ever graced the weighing room.

Since steeplechasing has always been regarded as the poor relation of flat racing, at least in financial terms, it is interesting to compare the rewards available in the 1870s. A six race card at the Epsom Spring Meeting, where the feature race was the Great Metropolitan Handicap, offered £2068. At the Cheltenham Spring Meeting, with the Grand Annual, also a handicap, as the star attraction, the prize money for six events totalled £790. Even a minor flat race meeting at Windsor paid £785 for half a dozen races but the Grand Annual has survived to this day and was worth nearly £16,000 to the winner in 1989 compared to the £520 collected by Master Mowbray in 1875.

Not that any of these considerations would have disturbed Dr Fothergill Rowlands. The game was the thing; a game, in the words of Will Ogilvy, 'for brave men's playing' and if you needed money it could be made with a few shrewd tilts at the ring. 'Fogo' Rowlands was the son of a Monmouthshire doctor and practised medicine until the lure of the Turf became too strong and he became a leading amateur, principally in the colours of Lord

CLARA WALTERS (SKITTLES).

Strathmore, grandfather of Her Majesty Queen Elizabeth, the Queen Mother, whose runners carry the same 'blue and buff stripes, blue sleeves' today.

Rowlands did much to revive the fortunes of steeplechasing in the late fifties and early sixties, when the sport was at its lowest ebb, and fancied himself as a master of the epigram. As such, he was hardly in the Oscar Wilde class, his best effort being 'Experience is worth nothing unless you pay for it, but the less you pay for it the better'. He later became a successful trainer, initially at Cheltenham and subsequently at Epsom. Among his patrons were the Prince of Wales, the Duke of Hamilton and Sir John (The Mate) Astley, but his lasting memorial is the National Hunt Steeplechase.

Founded by Rowlands at Market Harborough in 1859 as a race for farmers and other hunting men, the event got off to a poor start with only two hunts subscribing; the Vale of the White Horse and the Old Berkeley. In 1860 things improved and twelve major hunts provided thirty-one runners for a four mile chase for maidens at starting, a sweepstake of £10 each with £500 added, the amateur riders to carry twelve stone. The course was stiff and more than one stirrup cup was needed before the Corinthians faced up to the formidable obstacles, but in the end all was well as Bridegroom proved the twenty lengths winner ridden by the former Oxford rowing Blue E.C. Burton.

The post-race festivities were enlivened by the spectacle of the delectable Caroline Walters, better known as 'Skittles', clearing the massive brook in her own fearless style. 'Skittles' earned her nickname from her original job of setting up the pins in a skittle alley in her native back streets of Liverpool, but her unconcealed attractions soon led her to become one of the most celebrated of the Victorian 'Bedroom Beauties'. Mistress of Lord Fitzwilliam, a gentleman who, as Douglas Sutherland neatly observes in *The Yellow Earl*, 'allowed her unusual latitude in the matter of meeting his friends', 'Skittles' was socially ineligible to grace the hunting house-parties, but from her headquarters at the Haycock Hotel at Wansford she would ride out, impeccably mounted, on her lover's superb horses. Such was her reputation at the art of what the bloods called 'mattress polo' that many wives with no interest in the chase would insist on keeping their husbands company during the hunting season.

There was a muddle over the venue in 1861 which resulted in two races, one at Cheltenham and the other at Market Harborough. The Freshman, runner up to Bridegroom in 1860 won the Cheltenham version, ridden by George Ede, and Queensferry, the property of Bridegroom's owner B.J. 'Cherry' Angell triumphed at Market Harborough. Angell was to be a founder member of the National Hunt Committee in 1863.

For the next forty-eight years the National Hunt Steeplechase shuttled around courses as varied as Crewkerne, Newmarket, Abergavenny and Irvine, Sandown, Leicester and Warwick and twenty-five tracks staged the race before it finally came to rest at Cheltenham in 1911. It was by now the third richest race in the Calendar and did much to enhance the prestige of the March meeting, which had been established at the present course at Prestbury Park in 1902.

The Kaiser's war forced Cheltenham out of business in April, 1915, but peacetime racing in the early twenties found the Prestbury course presenting four meetings; the National Hunt Meeting in March, a two-day affair dominated by the National Hunt Steeplechase worth £1415; a two-day May Meeting featuring the three mile Cheltenham Steeplechase; two days in November and a single fixture in late December. There was little to distinguish Cheltenham from a host of other courses from Aldershot to Wye, excepting Liverpool, which reigned supreme. However, Liverpool's ace was the Grand National and even if worth a massive £7075 to the winner it was only a handicap. No race in which the poorest entrant is theoretically given as good a chance as the best can be considered a proper test, even if it may be spectacular and produces a strong betting market and Aintree's principal condition race, the Champion Steeplechase, rarely attracted a top class competitive field, despite a prize of around £1200.

Such was the position in 1922. The Cheltenham executive under the chairmanship of F.H. Cathcart took the view that the preponderance of handicaps did nothing to improve the long term prospects of a sport which was very much run for the benefit of the participants at all levels. The classic tale of the period concerns a horse blatantly 'stopped' at a country meeting. 'What are you going to do about that?' inquired a young steward of his senior colleague. 'Do?' said the old boy. 'Do? Back it next time out of course.'

Cathcart and his committee decided to frame a race where the best could meet the best on level terms, with five-year-olds allowed 9lb. Thus the weights were 11st 5lb and 12st; the distance was three miles and two furlongs. They decided to call the race the Cheltenham Gold Cup, in honour of the original Gold Cup, a flat race over three miles at weight for age dating back to the old days on Cleeve Hill in the 1820s, when the Reverend F. Close was still breathing fire and brimstone from the pulpit.

The course started behind the stands and in its early stages followed the National Hunt Steeplechase four mile circuit before branching off after the water to take an open ditch followed by two plain fences 'on the collar', followed by a turn and another open ditch. As the ground fell away, two more plain fences led to the turn for home and uphill to a plain fence. The field then turned in front of the stands and went round again, jumping the water and the open ditches twice.

In 1924 there were still decades to go before the introduction of overnight declarations of runners, blinkers and, in flat racing, the draw. Newspapers could publish only the intended runners, with likely riders, which were described as 'probables' and printed accordingly; the remaining entrants were listed at the foot of the race under the heading 'also engaged'.

Those 'also engaged' were shown on the racecard at the meeting along with the 'probables' and all were entitled to run. Even the racegoer did not know the definite runners until about twenty minutes before the race when they appeared in the number board. The off-course punter, betting on credit by telephone (legally) or with half-a-crown wrapped in the paper containing his instructions and passed surreptitiously to the pub barmaid or local garage hand (illegally) had little chance of knowing the real intentions of owners and trainers.

It followed that there were many instances of 'surprise' winners from the ranks of those 'also engaged' and I remember that my late father had a system on horses 'also engaged' when a good jockey with stable connections was at the meeting but did not have a ride amongst the 'probables' for a particular race.

On the day before the inaugural running of the Cheltenham Gold Cup on Wednesday 12 March 1924 the 'probables' included Alcazar trained by George Poole who retained the champion jockey Dick Rees. The horse had an outstanding record over park courses and the press made him odds-on to beat Conjuror II, third in the 1923 National, and other Liverpool contenders Old Tay Bridge, Gerald L, and Forewarned, the favourite but a faller in the 1923 National. Little was made of the prospects of the only five-year-old in the field, Red Splash, although he was a fresh horse and had beaten Old Tay Bridge over three miles at Hawthorn Hill even though he was receiving two stone.

Had the Gold Cup been a handicap Red Splash would have received a similar amount from Alcazar, but at weight for age the difference was only 9lb. Red Splash's trainer, Fred Withington, one of the few men elected to the Jockey Club without ever having had a flat race runner, considered that his young horse, a May foal not yet five in real terms, was at a distinct disadvantage, the more so since Withington had been unable to secure the services of a suitable jockey;

Dick Rees, who had ridden Red Splash at Hawthorn Hill, was claimed for Alcazar.

When Fred Withington left the course on Tuesday Red Splash was amongst those 'also engaged'. As he arrived at the course the following morning the trainer was delighted to learn that Alcazar was to be kept for the Champion Chase at Liverpool in seventeen days' time, which the horse duly won. Withington promptly snapped up Dick Rees, declared Red Splash to run, and the rest is history.

Red Splash started at 5/1 after strong market support and Rees made the running. Six furlongs from home Red Splash seemed to tire but he was shaken up and held a fractional lead at the last from Conjuror II and Gerald L.

In a driving finish, Red Splash held on by a head from Conjuror II, ridden by Harry Brown, with Gerald L a neck away in third. The 3/1 favourite Forewarned could finish only seventh for former champion jockey Jack Anthony. Conjuror II and Gerald L had won the National Hunt Chase and the National Hunt Handicap Chase respectively, and the form looked good, but unhappily Red Splash proved to be unsound and never won again. He was by all accounts a fine looking horse, and was one of only three five-year-olds to triumph in the history of the Gold Cup; the others were Patron Saint in 1928 and Golden Miller when he recorded the first of his five victories in 1932.

By the early thirties the Gold Cup was firmly established as a top class event in its own right and no longer simply a stepping-stone on the route to glory and riches in the Grand National. A companion event, the Champion Hurdle Challenge Cup, was inaugurated in 1927 and won by Blaris, ridden by that king of hurdle race riders, George Duller, by eight lengths from Billy Speck and Boddam, with Dick Rees on Harpist back in third.

Blaris was equally able over fences and won eleven chases. He was trained by former champion jockey Bill Payne and owned by the formidable Mrs Hollins, who chased Captain 'Tuppy' Bennet round the Aintree paddock with her umbrella after the gallant Captain had remounted Mrs Hollins's Turkey Buzzard no fewer than four times in the 1921 Grand National. After that experience 'Tuppy' might have reflected that the old adage 'there are fools, bloody fools and people who remount in a steeplechase' should carry the amendment 'and ride for irascible lady owners'.

Similar thoughts could well have occupied the minds of those cavaliers and captains of the heath who served the Hon. Dorothy Paget between the wars. Jockeys and trainers came and went swiftly into and out of the life of the eccentric daughter of Lord Queenborough but recriminations were in future when Eton- and Cambridge-educated Basil Briscoe answered the telephone at the training establishment which he had set up at his family home, Longstowe, near Cambridge, a city which had been represented in Parliament by Almeric Paget,

Dorothy's father, before his elevation to the peerage.

The call was from the Paget lair at Hermit's Wood near Chalfont St Giles. Tersely she enquired as to the availability for purchase of any good horses. Never lacking in confidence, Briscoe replied 'I have the best chaser in the world, Golden Miller, and the best hurdler in England, Insurance'. Miss Paget bought them both for £12,000, a huge sum for National Hunt animals in 1931 but in the event one of the great bloodstock bargains of all time. Within fifteen months Golden Miller and Insurance had won two Gold Cups and two Champion Hurdles in the blue and yellow hooped Paget colours.

Although Golden Miller had run in only four chases, winning three and narrowly beaten in the other (he was subsequently disqualified from one on technical grounds after it was discovered that Briscoe, never a man for pettifogging detail, had misread the conditions) he showed the superiority which was to be the hallmark of his career in no uncertain manner when he made his debut at Prestbury Park on 1 March 1932.

The obstacles at Cheltenham that year were exceptionally severe, so much so that the Inspector of Courses insisted that six inches were cut off the top of each fence. Although the height was less awe-inspiring, the remaining birch offered all the resilience of a brick wall, and fifty-six horses fell during the three days of the meeting. Ridden by Ted Leader, Golden Miller was easy to back at 13/2, with the 1931 Grand

GOLDEN MILLER, 1935.

GOLDEN MILLER (NEAREST CAMERA) AND THOMOND II, 1935.

START OF THE NATIONAL HUNT HANDICAP CHASE, 1936.

National winner Grakle a firm favourite at 11/10 on. The race was decided at the fence after the water, where Aruntius made a bad error and unsighted the impetuous Kingsford, who fell with fatal consequences. Grakle swerved sharply to avoid the prostrate Kingsford and his rider Jack Fawcus was unseated, leaving Golden Miller to win as he liked from Inverse and Aruntius. Later in the afternoon Insurance completed a handsome double in the Champion Hurdle and gave Ted Leader the rare distinction of riding the winners of the Grand National (Sprig, 1927), the Gold Cup and the Champion Hurdle.

Golden Miller dominated Cheltenham in the thirties as Cottage Rake was to command the post-war years and Arkle to bestride the sixties. A thinking horse in the best sense, Golden Miller loved Cheltenham and loathed Liverpool. He lost only once at Prestbury Park when he was beaten two lengths by Morse Code in his final race for the Gold Cup at the age of eleven in 1938, and it must be long odds against any horse beating his record five consecutive wins in the race which he did so much to establish as the Blue Riband of steeplechasing.

As the cream of English county and rural life relished the Miller's exploits at the

# Cheltenham

National Hunt Festival which had now become the social centre-piece of the chasing season, Adolf Hitler had risen to power in Germany and Mr Chamberlain had returned from Munich proclaiming 'Peace in our time'. It is now claimed that he never actually said those words, and the whole thing is a celebrated misquote. The first wartime Gold Cup was in 1940. The winner was Roman Hackle, owned by Dorothy Paget, and the race was run six days later than planned. The original meeting was scheduled for only two days to conform with wartime restrictions, and the National Hunt Steeplechase course was under plough as the nation started to 'Dig for Victory'. Accordingly, this race and the hunter chases were abandoned, and snow fell on the second day, making racing impossible. This turned out to be a blessing in disguise for Roman Hackle, who enjoyed a pipe-opener over two miles at Windsor before winning the postponed Gold Cup to complete a treble at the Festival for Dorothy Paget and her trainer Owen Anthony, already winners of the Champion Hurdle with Solford and the National Hunt Handicap Chase with Kilstar.

In 1941 a proposal to run a substitute Grand National at Cheltenham was quashed by the Home Office but the course was one of the few National Hunt venues to be granted fixtures. The Gold Cup, reduced in distance to three miles by the agricultural activity as it had been in 1940 and was to remain so for 'the duration', was won by Poet Prince. Seneca was ridden to victory in the

MRS 'PHIL' CRIPPS AND MR JAMES BAIRD –
SOCIETY AT CHELTENHAM, 1935.

Champion Hurdle by Ron Smyth, now a popular Epsom trainer, and champion jockey in 1941–2 with twelve winners; the lowest championship total recorded this century, in a severely restricted season.

By 1942, public opinion was hardening against the continuation of the sport, despite an assertion by Lord Rosebery that every member of the War Cabinet, doubtless under the guidance of Prime Minister Winston Churchill, was in favour of racing. In the event, there were only eighteen days' jumping in 1942, as the weather closed in and the population froze in their siren suits from the middle of January to 14 March, when Cheltenham staged the Grand Annual Steeplechase, won by Red Rower. In order to maximise the war effort in munitions factories and other industrial plants, the meeting was run on consecutive Saturdays. A week after the Grand Annual, Medoc II and

FULKE WALWYN AT THE UNVEILING OF THE
GOLDEN MILLER STATUE, 1989.

'Frenchie' Nicholson won the last war-time Gold Cup from Red Rower, who was badly baulked at the last open ditch.

There was to be no more steeplechasing in Britain until 6 January 1945, when Cheltenham resumed nearly two and a half years after the Government had refused to sanction the winter sport for the 1942–3 season. A 'Dad's Army' of elderly geldings, some well into their 'teens, contested the opening meeting. Victory in Europe was still five months ahead, and only four courses were usable – Cheltenham, Windsor, Wetherby and Catterick. Nonetheless, and in spite of peace-time restrictions which many

found to be more onerous than the war-time versions, especially those who had returned from the battle areas with hopes of happier times, the meetings were packed for the early post-war seasons.

Two widely differing elements were now to play major roles in the development of British steeplechasing. Wartime agricultural policy designed to grow cheap food for a beleaguered home population was funded by subsidies to the farming community which produced a newly rich yeoman land-owner whose prosperity was greatly increased when the war-time provisions were much enhanced in the Agricultural Act of

1947, and the era of the frequently scorned 'feather bed' farmer was born.

Running a horse of two 'on the farm' in both the literal and financial sense became a popular hobby, and for all the rich sportsmen attracted to National Hunt racing since the war, the farming permit-holder remains the backbone of the game.

But if times were good during the 1939–45 conflict for Britain's farmers, things were not so hot for the Irish rural community, who were as isolated by neutrality as the French were by the German occupation. However, the result for racing under both codes was the same; as French breeding flourished at the cost of all those English classic prizes which found their way across the Channel in the forties and fifties so the Irish steeplechasers, whose growth and preparation had been undisturbed by Dorniers or Doodle-bugs, were ready to take Britain by storm. The advance party came in the form of Prince Regent, a fine bay gelding foaled in 1935 by My Prince, the sire of Easter Hero and Gregalach. This was an impeccable jumping pedigree, as Easter Hero had won two Gold Cups and Gregalach the 1929 National. Red Rower had finally found the compensation he so richly deserved when he took the Gold Cup in 1945 and it was a revived Cheltenham which Prince Regent faced in March 1946.

The plough had gone and the race had been restored to its original distance. Prince Regent had raced once before in England, when winning the Bradford Chase at Wetherby in December 1945 at odds of 10/1 on. The Irish trainers by now had a definite advantage over their English counterparts, who not only had to grapple with a largely untrained labour force, petrol rationing, ancient equipment and shortage of building materials, but a Labour Government who regarded steeplechasing as an outdated amusement for 'the idle rich'.

Of the seventy-nine courses licensed by the National Hunt Committee in 1939, only forty-six remained at the end of the 1946–7 season. Times were lean, and it was a poor field which took on Prince Regent in the Gold Cup. The winner of twelve races in Ireland, including the Irish Grand National under 12st 7lb, Prince Regent strolled away from the others and won as he liked. Only his closest connections, jockey Tim Hyde and trainer Tom Dreaper, knew that at eleven he was past his best, robbed of a brilliant career by the cruel chance of war. Proof was soon to come in the Grand National at Aintree, where he started 3/1 favourite and carried the crushing burden of 12st 5lb into a commanding lead over the fences of the toughest steeplechase course in the world. But by the line poor Prince Regent was out on his feet, and could only finish third to Lovely Cottage and Jack Finlay.

The second wave of the Irish invasion came in the form of Hatton's Grace, Cottage Rake, Aubrey Brabazon and Vincent O'Brien.

Mr Leonard Abelson's National Spirit won the Champion Hurdle in 1947 and 1948. He won fourteen flat races and nineteen over hurdles though his victory over Le Paillon in 1947 was considered to be lucky as the latter's rider, Alec Head, was unfamiliar with the course. Le Paillon went on to win the Prix de l'Arc de Triomphe in October. But not even National Spirit was a match for Hatton's Grace, the triple winner of the Champion Hurdle in 1949, 1950 and 1951. He could finish only fourth in 1949 and 1950, and fell at the last in 1951 when in the lead from the Irish horse who was then ridden by Tim Molony.

Meanwhile, Cottage Rake had won the 1948 Gold Cup and went on to complete the treble in 1949 and 1950. He was a brown gelding by Cottage, the dominant sire of chasers in the forties and fifties. Cottage got three Grand National winners and two Gold Cup winners; in 1939 and 1948 he was the sire of the winners of the National and the Gold Cup.

Cottage Rake started his career on the flat as a five-year-old at Thurles. Vincent O'Brien, then training on his late father's farm at Churchtown, County Cork won a hurdle race with him at Limerick and a bumpers' (amateur riders) race at Leopardstown. This latter victory, under the noses of the leading Irish horse-copers, attracted a good deal of interest, including an offer of £3500 from Major 'Cuddie' Stirling-Stewart, the owner of Cool Customer, of whom more later.

Apparently unhappily for Dr 'Otto' Vaughan, Cottage Rake's owner and breeder, the horse was 'spun' by the veterinary surgeon, Maxie Cosgrave who was later to become famous as medical attendant to Arkle. Cosgrave suspected a wind infirmity, and Cottage Rake returned to Churchtown for a summer break. He was to fail the vet on two more occasions, but O'Brien persuaded his first owner, Frank Vickerman, to buy the horse for £3500. Vickerman was under the impression that he had paid only £1000 deposit against the vet's report, which was unfavourable but, as in the case of Dorothy Paget's purchase of Golden Miller and Insurance, it was to prove a shrewd deal.

After two 'quiet' runs on the flat in Vickerman's colours, Cottage Rake landed a nice touch in the Naas November Handicap, winning comfortably in the hands of one J. Tyrrel. At this stage, Aubrey Brabazon came into his life.

Champion jockey in Ireland in 1945 and as skilled on the flat (he won the Irish 2,000 Guineas and Oaks) as over jumps he was a superb stylist in a country not renowned for elegant riding. Brabazon joined forces with O'Brien and Cottage Rake in the gelding's next race, the high class Carrickmines Novices' Chase at the Leopardstown Christmas meeting.

Cottage Rake won at 4/7 on by twenty lengths which could have been fifty in the opinion of his rider, and a partnership was born, immortalised in the doggerel rhyme which was shortly to ring out of the throats of thousands of Irishmen from Prestbury Park to Cleeve Hill beyond.

> *Aubrey's up, the money's down*
> *The frightened bookies quake*
> *Come on my lads and give a cheer*
> *Begod, 'tis Cottage Rake.*

Hatton's Grace and Cottage Rake lit the torch which was to illuminate Vincent O'Brien's path from the humble farm at Churchtown to the heights of Ballydoyle. Between 1948 and 1955, he trained the winners of four Gold Cups, three Champion Hurdles and three successive Grand Nationals, before turning his attention to flat racing with equally devastating results.

Cottage Rake's victory in the 1949 Gold Cup was perhaps his finest hour; certainly the race was to highlight two of those delicious ironies of chance so typical of horseracing.

Cottage Rake's principal opponent in a six horse contest was Cool Customer, owned by Major Stirling-Stuart, who had been advised to reject the Rake three years before. Cool Customer had fallen at the first when 7/2 favourite in 1948, but he was a high class chaser whose string of wins in Ireland and England included ten in the hands of none other than Aubrey Brabazon.

While his owner contemplated these quirks of fate from the grandstand, Cool Customer lived up to his name as he made his way to post under Pat Murphy in the all-scarlet colours made famous by the Duchess of Montrose in Newmarket's late Victorian heyday. The race took place on 11 April, having been postponed from the frozen-off final day of the March meeting. It became a two horse affair from the top of the hill on the second circuit, and Cottage Rake and Cool Customer battled it out as they cleared the last open ditch.

It was soon clear that the champion was in trouble as Brabazon went for his whip with Cool Customer a length and a half up and travelling well as they turned into the straight. Cottage Rake was on the wrong end of a punishing ride as Cool Customer cleared the last with only the Cheltenham Hill between him and glory.

It was not to be. The Rake summoned all those reserves of strength and courage which distinguish a great horse, and eighty yards from the post he struggled clear to win by two lengths.

The 1950 Gold Cup was a formality but from then on Cottage Rake declined quickly and he failed to win in his last four seasons.

In the early fifties, as Britain slowly shook off the miseries of post-war austerity, the cost of racing still included the pernicious Entertainment Tax. Admission to Tattersall's at the Festival Meeting was 32/6d which included 15/10d tax; in modern currency, £1.62 and 79p. The Silver Ring patron paid 10/6d and you could watch Sir Ken win the first of his three successive Champion Hurdles for 4/6d from the infield.

The Irish influence fell away, at least in

# Cheltenham

MARTIN MOLONY AND SILVER FAME, 1949.

Cheltenham's major events, in the fifties which were enlivened by the exploits of Lord Bicester's Silver Fame, winner of the 1951 Gold Cup, Four Ten, winner in 1954, and Linwell in 1957. Silver Fame was a Cheltenham specialist. He won twenty-eight of his forty-seven races, eight of them at Cheltenham, and his owner was the doyen of the National Hunt scene. Lord Bicester's private stable of strong, bold chasers typified by Roimond were trained by George Beeby and his jockeys were Dick Francis and Martin Molony.

It was Molony who rode Silver Fame in 1951, in a field which included Manicou, owned in partnership by the Queen and the then Princess Elizabeth, Freebooter, winner of the 1950 Grand National, and Greenogue, the outsider at 100/8.

Freebooter was the master of Aintree but hated Cheltenham and rarely completed the course. True to form, he blundered three from home and left Greenogue and Silver Fame to fight it out to the line. It was a controversial finish. Many thought Greenogue had won and in those pre photofinish days, as many thought that a dead heat would have been fair. Perhaps so, but Silver Fame was given the nod, and that was that. It was Martin Molony's swansong at Cheltenham and the winner and runner-up were owned by two of steeplechasing's staunchest supporters in Lord Bicester and J.V. (Jimmy) Rank, owner of Prince Regent.

Four Ten was the first product of the point-to-point field to win a Gold Cup. Bred just below the rolling slopes of Gunville Down adjoining Cranbourne Chase in North Dorset, Four Ten revelled in the heavy ground in 1954 and came home by four lengths from Mariners Log. He was ridden by Tommy Cusack and trained by John Roberts at Prestbury, hard by the course.

Limber Hill also graduated from between the flags to win the 1956 Gold Cup and in 1957 Ivor Herbert, the distinguished journalist and writer of definitive books on racing sent out Linwell to score a length victory over Kerstin.

Linwell was bought by Herbert for £750 on behalf of Sir David Brown. He was not a great success in point-to-points, but it was a different matter under rules, where he won nineteen races from forty-four starts, and was only seven times unplaced. Herbert did not receive any formal credit for Linwell's success, as the National Hunt Committee considered that his journalistic activities precluded him from holding a licence. Thus the honour went to his head lad, Charlie Mallon, as Linwell gave Michael Scudamore his only winning ride in the Gold Cup.

Irish fortune was back with a vengeance when Arkle, trainer Tom Dreaper and jockey Pat Taaffe dominated not only Cheltenham, but the whole world of National Hunt racing in the mid-sixties. The potentially titanic struggle between the giant Mill House, Gold Cup winner in 1963, and Anne, Duchess of Westminster's superb bay racing machine

PART OF THE OLD COURSE, NO LONGER USED, IN 1963.

A YOUNG FRED WINTER.

FRED WINTER.

has been well chronicled elsewhere, as indeed has the story of the mighty Arkle and his three Gold Cups.

At the meeting on 11 April 1964, the steeplechasing world witnessed the last day of riding for Fred Winter. He had won Gold Cups on Saffron Tartan (1961) and Mandarin (1962); he had seen three Champion Hurdlers safely into the winner's enclosure (Clair Soleil in 1955, Fare Time in 1959 and Eborneezer in 1961) and he had been champion jockey on four occasions, including 121 wins in 1952–3, a record at the time. Winter had ridden two Grand National winners, Sundew in 1957 and Kilmore five years later, and was destined to train two more in Jay Trump and Anglo, but he was not destined to ride a winner at Cheltenham on that April afternoon.

It really did not matter. With the affectionate cheers of his racegoing supporters ringing in his ears, Fred Winter left Cheltenham to commence a brilliant career as a trainer tragically cut short by a fall at his home at Uplands in Lambourn in 1987.

Today, with flat racing in real danger of being swallowed up, at least on the top level, by a money-inspired Middle Eastern monopoly, and Irish racing fortunes at their lowest ebb for many years, Cheltenham stands out as the home of the game which may become the standard bearer for sporting achievement on the Turf. Although sophisticated modern methods of training have produced the level of excellence which enabled Michael Dickinson to train the first five home in the Gold Cup of 1983 and Dawn Run to complete the unique Champion Hurdle-Gold Cup double in the mid-eighties, there remains in National Hunt racing more than a whiff of Adam Lindsay Gordon's lowering wintry mornings and misty Cotswold hills; his spirit is there, too.

# CHEPSTOW

URING the 'boom' 1980s corporate entertainment became the name of racing's commercial game. Many courses naturally succumbed to the easy income to be made from packaged visitors in tented villages, who paid little attention to the racing but were thrilled to meet the wife of the managing director of United Poppet Valves in agreeable social circumstances.

So far, so good, but in due course the managements of the tracks began not only to build special accommodation for the guests but also to take parts of the existing racecourse facilities, usually those with the best vantage points and hitherto the territory of the enthusiastic paying punter, and convert them into boxes for the dispensing of corporate hospitality.

The inevitable forerunner was Goodwood. It was the first course to have boxes in the grandstand facing away from the racetrack, and has subsequently erected the Charlton Stand with the benefit of a Levy Board loan which is not a stand at all, but a restaurant complex with a balcony specifically designed for the entertainment of companies, sponsors and their guests.

Many courses are now following suit, including Chepstow where a prime viewing area has recently been removed from the reach of the true racegoer. It is the intention of the author to write a history and not to prognosticate, but even the most casual glance at the social and economic past of Britain will reveal severe times of financial recession. Chepstow was built during one

such, in 1926, and a return to even mild stagnation would certainly curtail company expenditure on expensive hospitality. Those people so entertained at present are unlikely to forge an enthusiasm for the sport and are even more unlikely to return to support racing. Meanwhile, the genuine racegoer may have been disaffected by the loss of his favourite bar or position in the stand.

In which case chromium plated restaurant suites may soon have all the attraction of a White Elephant stall at a vicarage fete. Only time will tell, but Chepstow has survived more than one financial crisis since Lord Glanely, popularly known to 1920s' racegoers as 'Old Guts and Gaiters' and a founding father of Chepstow, directed the traffic as the crowds dispersed from the jammed car parks after the inaugural meeting on 6 August 1926.

That was flat racing, but a tradition of National Hunt sport had existed in the locality for many years, probably originating with an Easter Monday steeplechase at Cophill Farm in 1839. It was, of course, a hunt meeting and drew a huge crowd. An annual fixture was established, with a different venue from year to year, which finally came to rest at Oakgrove, in the beautiful surroundings of Piercefield Park, a large estate to the north of the pleasant market town in the shadow of the Norman Chepstow Castle.

Oakgrove House and the land on which the old hunt meetings had been run was originally a part of the Piercefield Park estate, and had been presented as a wedding gift to Henry Hastings Clay and his bride Mabel Williams in 1891. The donor was the bridegroom's father, Henry Clay, who inherited Piercefield House and the estate on the death of his father, also called Henry in the classic way of nouveau riche Victorian dynasties. Henry senior had acquired the Piercefield lands of 1300 acres on retirement from the smoke-filled skies of Burton-on-Trent at the height of the Industrial Revolution in 1861.

In truth the wedding present was something of a pig in a poke, as Oakgrove House was the residence of a sitting tenant, Mr Herbert Crocker. To pass the time, or perhaps to persuade Mr Crocker to leave, Hastings Clay and his bride, who were quartered somewhat less comfortably at The Woodlands, St Arvans, laid out a National Hunt course encircling Oakgrove House.

Clay's partner in the venture was Walter Smedley, a St Arvans lawyer and racing buff who controlled racing at such now long-departed venues as Bromyard, Monmouth, Abergavenny, Tenby and Usk. The first two-day meeting at St Arvans was in March 1892 and established racing on a proper basis as distinct from the old hunt meetings at Oakgrove.

Although it attracted little local interest, the meeting was well recorded in metropolitan papers, and by 1895 was able to support the Chepstow Grand Annual Steeplechase, a £400 event over two miles and three furlongs, and the two mile Western Hurdle, worth £200. In 1899, the Grand Annual was worth £1,000, a huge prize for the period and the third richest race in Britain. Mr Crocker vacated Oakgrove House in the same year to the satisfaction of his unwilling landlord.

Walter Smedley died in 1899, but for a while racing continued on a similar scale as before and some legendary names appeared in the number board, including the luxuriantly-moustached 'Tosher' Walsh, who rode Duke of Wellington to win the Grand Annual in 1900, and Captain Darby Rogers, mounted on the superb match-racer Bosphorus. The white blazed Bosphorus went to war in 1914 as a cavalry remount and was killed in the Dardanelles.

The Anthony brothers and Dick and Bilby Rees were happy enough to cut their early teeth in the saddle at St Arvans, and in 1911 Jack and Ivor fought out the finish of the Tintern Handicap Chase, but the writing was on the wall. Since the death of Walter Smedley standards had declined and the Tintern was worth only £46 to the connections of Apex and Jack Anthony. Even Bosphorus, also ridden by Jack, was competing in a £36 handicap chase on the same day and finished third, under top weight of 12st 2lb after starting 7/4 favourite.

Hastings Clay had taken over the running of the course himself but he was ill-suited to the task of administration, being happier with his pack of otterhounds and his domestic life with Mabel and their four offspring, to say nothing of his public duties as Justice of the Peace and Deputy Lieutenant of

Monmouthshire. The spring meeting at St Arvans in 1914 was the last of its era and it was to be twelve years before racing resumed at Piercefield Park.

Unable to finance the revival from his own comparatively slender means, Hastings Clay formed a consortium of local men of substance, including Dorothy Paget's father Lord Queenborough, Lord Glanely and Lord Tredegar, a man grown rich on the proceeds of a stretch of railway line which ran across Tredegar Park, from which his lordship derived an income of a penny per ton of coal which passed through this 'Golden Mile'.

Glanely was born William James Tatem and after a brief career at sea became a shipping clerk in Cardiff. By 1909 he was running his own company and rose to control a vast merchant fleet. He was prepared to spend huge sums in the sale ring to acquire top class bloodstock, and his presence at Tattersalls would have much the same effect as a representative of the Maktoums does today. So much so that his absence from the salesring would provoke considerable jitters on the part of vendors with quality lots to sell, and also from the auctioneers. Racing and cricket were Glanely's joint passions and on one occasion he arrived at the Newmarket Sales immaculate in white ducks and buckskin shoes, a garb more suited to Lord's than the 'tweeds and breeches' sartorial tradition of Headquarters. As he settled down over a bottle of champagne in the bar to peruse the catalogue, Glanely seemed likely to miss the choice lot of the day, but with timing as elegant as his attire he appeared just in time to bid. A relieved auctioneer jocularly posed the question 'At which end will you open the bowling from, my Lord?' and Glanely went on to pay a high price for an animal which turned out to be useless, as did so many of his purchases.

Nonetheless Glanely owned six classic winners, including the 1919 Derby hero Grand Parade, and together with Hwfa Williams, who had masterminded the huge success of Sandown Park, was the driving force behind the new course. It was a force desperately needed to launch Chepstow in the teeth of a General Strike and deep economic depression; but those who genuinely love racing are not fair-weather friends, and despite cash crises which were to continue for more than a decade the Piercefield Park venture was a public success. Sadly, Hwfa Williams died before the 1926 opening and it was William Lysaght, the owner of Bosphorus, who took his place prior to the inaugural National Hunt meeting on 2 March 1927. Henry Hyde, Clerk of the Course at Kempton, assumed the same role at Chepstow and the new fences were designed on the Kempton pattern.

The weather was extremely wet but attendance was good, despite a clash of fixtures with, unbelievably, Kempton and a major colliery disaster with high loss of life on the previous day. The opening Hughes Morgan Steeplechase was worth £200 and won by

Phibisher, ridden by Arthur Waudby. The selling hurdle went to Mr Speaker in the elegant hands of Bilby Rees, and the Monmouth Moderate Handicap Hurdle prize was won by Ben Warner's Rum and Coffee, ridden by Tommy Duggan and trained by Owen Anthony.

The appalling conditions made the steeplechase course unsafe for the Lysaght Amateur Chase which was lost, and a miserable day's proceedings came to an end with the victory of Berkeley Bridge in the Penarth Hurdle. After a further inspection of the course, it did not take co-founder Sir David Hughes Morgan and his fellow stewards long to decide that the second day would have to be abandoned.

In spite of this inauspicious start, Chepstow meandered happily enough into the 1930s rather like an amiable old mistress, usually short of cash but always willing for a bit of fun. As with the flat racing side of the venture, the course soon established a reputation as a track providing opportunities for horses of moderate ability, albeit piloted by some of the star riders of the period, including Gerry Wilson, Billy Stott and his great rival Billy Speck, Jack Moloney, Tim Hamey, Tommy Cullinan and, as ever, the ubiquitous Dick and Bilby Rees.

So things might have continued after Chepstow had survived the inevitable military occupation of World War II, when troops took over the stands and the stables, with the officers quartered in the now decaying mansion of Piercefield. Flat racing

resumed in 1947 and National Hunt sport the following year, with new men in charge; Hastings Clay had died during the war, along with Sir David Hughes Morgan and William Lysaght, but not surprisingly it took Hitler to see off 'Old Guts and Gaiters' who was killed by one of the few bombs to fall on Weston-super-Mare.

The Ely racecourse at Cardiff, home of the Welsh Grand National since Deerstalker won in the colours of Tom Cannon and ridden by George Mawson in 1895, closed in

# Chepstow

THE NEW COURSE, 1926.

1939 never to reopen; houses now stand where once 'Tich' Mason, Keith Piggott, Herbert Smyth, Gerry Wilson, Jack Fawcus and Bruce Hobbs rode the winners of Wales's premier chase. Save for the bitter winter of 1946–47, Cardiff would have re-emerged, but racing had to be abandoned and the National was staged for the only time at Caerleon, Newport in 1948. Caerleon became bankrupt not long after Bora's Cottage had scored for Captain Ryan Price and jockey Eddie Reavey, thus handing the Welsh Grand National to Chepstow.

It was the turning point for which Chepstow had been searching since the twenties. Not all that inspiring as a flat race track, the undulations of Piercefield made top class chasing country, not easy but able to bring out the best in the best.

And the best were not long to emerge. The first winner of a Chepstow Welsh National was Fighting Line, ridden by Dick

PERSIAN WAR, 1969.

Francis, a young jockey of promise who was gaining compensation for defeat in the Liverpool National on Roimond, who was second to Russian Hero in the same year.

Francis was to gain reparation once more in the Welsh National on Crudwell in 1956, following the bitter disappointment of Devon Loch's inexplicable fall within yards of victory at Liverpool, and it was to be Dick's last major victory in the saddle. Greater rewards were awaiting Francis from millions of avid readers of his thrillers around the world.

The Welsh National put Chepstow on the steeplechasing map, but the supporting events were nothing special. In the early days of sponsorship in 1959, Rhymney Breweries founded a three mile chase to be run in early December as a reasonably well endowed prep race for horses likely to contest the King George VI Chase at Kempton or the Liverpool Grand National, and TWW, the television company which then held the franchise for Wales, put up the cash for a two and a half miles novice chase at at the February meeting in 1962.

The Rhymney Breweries Chase and the TWW Champion Novice Chase were immediate successes, with Pas Seul, Happy Spring and What A Myth winners of the Rhymney, and Buona Notte, one of the most exciting chasers of the 1960s until he broke his neck in the Great Yorkshire Chase, won the TWW in 1964.

By 1969 neither race was in existence, as TWW lost their broadcasting licence in the TV franchise round of 1968 and the Rhymney became briefly the Whitbread Wales Trophy, before losing its character as the Quarry Handicap Chase. Prize money for both events had been more than twice the average for the time, thanks to sponsorship and television coverage, and the prospects were not encouraging.

However two heroes, one equine, the other human, were about to transform National Hunt racing at Chepstow as the Welsh National had in the immediate post-war period.

In 1962, Oakgrove House, the old home of Hastings Clay, was purchased by the leading amateur rider Colin Davies who set up a training establishment. In October 1967 Davies agreed to train a rather undernourished hurdler called Persian War for Mr Henry Alper. The horse had won the Triumph Hurdle at Cheltenham and had recently returned from France.

Persian War won the 1968 Schweppes Gold Trophy at Newbury under 11st 13lb

START OF THE CORAL WELSH NATIONAL HANDICAP CHASE, 1986.

and went on to victory in three Champion Hurdles, a feat which put him in the company of Hatton's Grace and Sir Ken. He was trained by Davies during the height of his career, although a volatile style of ownership placed one of the finest hurdlers of the century with three subsequent handlers.

Basking in reflected glory, Chepstow repaid their locally trained hero with a bar named in his honour, and Persian War gracefully performed the opening ceremony in December 1970.

In the year that Persian War was beating all comers at Newbury and Cheltenham, John Hughes became Clerk of the Course, replacing Captain Bobby Vivian, the distinguished former Life Guards officer and amateur rider who had guided Chepstow since 1962. Hughes, a man famous for his optimistic going forecasts, was the finest racecourse manager which the sport has known since the war. Ideas spilled from him with all the effervescence of a Welsh mountain stream, and reorganisation came swiftly and effectively.

Fresh funds were obtained from the Levy Board to upgrade the course, increase the prize for the Welsh National and found a new race for the Welsh Champion Hurdle. Reasoning that the traditional Easter date of the National was too close to Aintree and the Scottish National at Ayr to attract either failures or aspirants, Hughes moved the race to February, and the new Champion Hurdle was planned for Easter.

The weather let down Hughes in

JOHN HUGHES.

February 1969 and the National had to be abandoned, but Persian War was on hand at the Easter meeting to clinch the inaugural Welsh Champion Hurdle in the hands of Jimmy Uttley, who rode the Champion hurdler to most of his eighteen victories over timber.

Bula, Canasta Lad, Comedy of Errors, Lanzarote and Night Nurse were soon added to the Champion Hurdle roll of honour, but after Rag Trade had become the first Welsh National winner to go on to complete the double at Liverpool in 1976, the cruel February weather played a vicious hand. The race was abandoned for three successive years, and in 1979 Peter Scot won the first National run in December.

Now part of the National Hunt feast of

THE MEMBERS' ENTRANCE, WHERE LORD GLANELY DIRECTED THE TRAFFIC.

Christmas racing, the Welsh National is worth £30,000, nearly double the prize in Peter Scot's year and a far cry from the 460 sovereigns won by Herbert Smyth on Mark Back in 1920 over the old Cardiff course.

John Hughes' death in September, 1988 robbed racing of one of its most original and innovative minds. A February fixture features the £15,000 John Hughes Grand National Trial in his memory and the whole course underwent a £2.5 million redevelopment scheme in 1989-90.

Needless to say, hospitality suites are high on the list of priorities. It all seems a long way from 1926 and Old Guts and Gaiters directing the traffic on the Monmouth Road.

# DEVON AND EXETER

IN 1839 James Christie Whyte, racing historian and social observer, found Exeter to be 'A large city and capital of the country . . . Exeter contains a magnificent cathedral, and its see gives name to a bishopric, which includes nearly the whole of Devon and Cornwall. The salubrity of the air, with the cheapness of provisions, especially fish and poultry, attract to this city numerous families with limited incomes.'

Limited incomes or not, the punters still managed to find their way to the racecourse at Haldon where early meetings had taken place in 1738. At one fixture around this time Squire Fulford, a member of the local gentry, brought his jester with the remainder of his retinue to the races. Garbed in his motley, the jester managed to obstruct the view of an aggrieved punter, presumably with his money down and unable to pick out his horse. 'Whose fool are you?' he demanded. 'I'm Squire Fulford's fool' replied the clown, 'whose clown are you?' However, the jester was doubtless adept at flattering his employer, which was the main purpose of his ancient calling, and to take your own fool to the races does smack of a certain style.

During the early part of the nineteenth century the main features of the so-called agricultural revolution were the Enclosure Acts, a rationalisation of land away from the smallholder and into the corporation of large estates. These Enclosures often included common land such as Haldon, and in

1823 the course passed into the ownership of Sir Lawrence Palk, later Lord Haldon.

The dashing Sir Lawrence lost no time in broadening the scope of the card, and three years later the City of Exeter put up a £100 prize and there was a Ladies' Purse of £80, contributed by the gallant baronet himself, considered to be a neat horseman when at the reins of his four-in-hand. All this was in addition to the established Silver Tureen and the Devonshire Stakes, both won by Lord Palmerston, who loved a day at the races away from his Parliamentary duties.

A stand was erected in 1829 and by the time James Whyte was commenting on the inexpensive fish and poultry obtainable locally another feature race had been added, the Home Stakes, which incorporated the County Members' Plate. The race, run in two mile heats, was confined to local animals and carried the quaint back-handed compliment of a condition: 'to be ridden by gentlemen, or by persons residing in Devon and Cornwall.'

Haldon became a steeplechase course in 1898. Although credited with the status of a Hunt meeting, the regular two day fixture in August was from its inception very much a professional affair, and even Bill Dollery found it worth his while in 1900 to travel down from Bishop's Sutton in Hampshire to partner Sweet Marion to win the two mile Exeter Steeplechase at odds of 5/1, thus foiling a local gamble about 11/10 favourite

UP AND OVER.

Tavora. Sweet Marion came out again on the second day and was astonishingly allowed to start at 5/4 for the two mile Haldon Hurdle, which she won by twenty lengths.

Slowly, Devon and Exeter developed into the course we know today, with extreme undulations set against the dramatic backdrop of Dartmoor. The two mile circuit is demanding for horse and rider, with a hunting seat more serviceable than the professional crouch, but the course which can claim to be the largest in Britain in terms of acreage is a favourite with trainers who can rely upon Haldon to reveal a fair measure of their animals' ability.

Well To Do won his first and his last race at Devon and has a race named after him, while other famous names who have made at least some of their reputations on the track include Diamond Edge, Master Smudge, Ben Nevis (who fell at the last when challenging for the lead) and . . . yes, you've guessed it, Desert Orchid, who won his first steeplechase here on 1 November 1985.

# DONCASTER

NATIONAL Hunt racing has failed at Newmarket. At Epsom it would be impossible if not lethal; so Doncaster is the only one of England's three classic flat courses where jumping takes place.

Even so, as John Fairfax-Blakeborough commented in his *Northern Turf History*, one does not naturally associate Town Moor with steeplechasing, although hunt racing for members of the local packs such as the Sandbeck and the Badsworth took place on the flat from 1825 onwards.

The idea was to provide some easy end of season sport for the members and to repay the hospitality of the farmers over whose land they hunted. Thus the March 1825 fixture, described as the 'Doncaster Hunt Meeting', featured a Silver Cup donated by G.S. Foljambe Esq, Master of the Sandbeck, for a two mile race 'for horses not thoroughbred to be ridden by and be *bona-fide* the property of farmers residing with in the Sandbeck country; three-year-olds 9st 10lb, four-year-olds 10st 9lb, five-year-olds 11st 4lbs, six and aged 12st.'

The inscription on the handsome trophy handed to the winning rider, Mr Dyson, made the point; '. . . not as a bribe for the preservation of foxes, but to encourage the sports of the field, and above all others, the chase.'

Of course; why ever should a hunt wish to preserve foxes? No doubt this lovely piece of tongue-in-cheek cynicism which illustrates so well the social distinctions of the days before the concept of the gentleman farmer was received in the spirit in which it was intended.

There were three more races on the card, including the Sandbeck Hunters Stakes run in three heats over the St Leger course, and a consolation race for beaten horses over two miles.

To round off this sporting occasion, the Earl of Scarborough's Foxhounds met at Park Lane, Doncaster on Wednesday 30 March and according to *The Sporting Magazine* 'afforded an opportunity for the visitors as well as a number of inhabitants to join in the pleasures of the chase, consequently there was a numerous field.'

Similar meetings were held until 1829, when the hunts switched their attention to the Knavesmire at York, an ill-conceived venture given the nature of the terrain. Nonetheless, a Union Hunt Club was formed in 1835 for hunters' flat races, and bona-fide jump meetings took place at York from April 1867 to April 1885, when a lack of web-footed quadrupeds made it impossible to continue on a track better suited in winter and spring to snipe shooting.

Meanwhile, steeplechasing and racing over hurdles had resumed at Doncaster on 19 March 1847. The meeting was over the old Cantley Common course, and was distinguished by the last ride in public of Captain Martin Becher, one of the most famous names in steeplechasing history, but sadly the gallant Captain sustained a fall.

The meeting was promoted the following year under the rather grandiloquent title of

# Doncaster

TELEGRAMS
UNCLAIMED! 1875.

The Doncaster Grand National Steeple-chases and Hurdle Races. At the Spring Meeting on 14 March 1850 the first race on the card was a handicap hurdle, £5 stakes with £30 added, over two miles and six flights of hurdles; this was a decent prize for the period.

Nonetheless, the grandiose titles awarded to the races well outstripped the quality of the fields. A Grand National Steeplechase and a Northern Steeplechase featured in 1852 and continued for some years, but by 1862 the principal event was the Great North of England Steeplechase.

Nothing daunted, Doncaster came up with a Grand National Steeplechase in 1866, but rather ruined the effect by making the selling hurdle on the same card the next most valuable race. In the 1870s the fixture

reverted to the old Doncaster Hunt event and was run in February. There were five hunters' flat races on the programme and one hurdle race, the Skelbrooke Park Plate of £30, which although described as a plate was in fact a sweepstake in common with the other contests.

The Corinthian riders included Maunsell Richardson, who was in the Harrow cricket team that beat Eton by an innings and 67 runs and rode the winner of the Scottish Grand National in 1871 on Keystone and the National proper on Disturbance and Reugny in 1873 and '74. Also taking part were Rippon Brockton and Tom Spence, other leading amateurs of the time.

The meeting prospered and by 1883 was a two day fixture, with races for professional riders mixed in with the Doncaster Hunt events and no more flat races. As far as the amateurs were concerned Tom Spence and Rippon Brockton had things quite nicely sewn up, winning five of the ten races between them, including hunt and open contests. The most successful professional was Tom Skelton, who rode a double on the second day.

Messrs Spence and Brockton were going strong two years later, although Brockton could manage only third in a revived hunters' flat race. Spence rode a double on two odds-on shots, but more formidable names were starting to appear in the number board; George Lambton, Charlie Cunningham and E.P. (Ted) Wilson, to say nothing of George 'Abington' Baird.

At this time the Hon George Lambton, fifth son of the Second Earl of Durham, was at the height of his fame in the saddle. As a younger son he had an income of rather less than £800 a year and this would hardly have met his tailor's bill, so he had to depend on betting and the quality of his mounts, and although his talents over country ensured many good rides, he was frequently forced to seek the services of the egregious Cork Street moneylender Sam Lewis.

Lambton's wins included the Grand Steeplechase de Paris in 1888 and the National Hunt Chase at Cheltenham in the same year. He never had much luck in the Grand National and his mount Savoyard toppled over two from home in 1888 with the race at his mercy. Lambton, in his definitive work on racing *Men and Horses I Have Known*, blamed himself for not driving his horse hard at the second last fence, the conventional tactic at the end of a long chase; on the other hand, Savoyard had a twisted foreleg and many observers thought that the animal just tripped himself up.

Lambton was to gain compensation as the finest trainer of his day, first under both Rules but later only on the flat, sending out the winner of thirteen classics.

Charlie Cunningham, who rode Highgrove, winner of the Stapleton Park Steeplechase at Doncaster in 1885, was leading amateur in 1882 and 1883 and rode four Scottish Grand National winners.

Ted Wilson was another top class Corinthian rider who partnered two Grand National winners, Voluptuary in 1884 and Roquefort in 1885, but George Baird, who rode a winner at the 1889 Doncaster meeting under his usual nom-de-course of 'Mr Abington' was something else. Baird inherited a fortune from his father, a Scottish ironfounder, and a substantial amount from an uncle who had previously donated £200,000 to the Church of Scotland, an action sometimes described as the greatest fire insurance policy ever taken out.

An education at Eton and Cambridge knocked few corners off Baird's inborn rough and loutish personality. A close friend of Lily Langtry, Baird used his vast wealth to indulge his passion for race riding in an era when amateurs were allowed to meet professional jockeys on equal terms in flat and National Hunt races. He maintained horses in training all over the country, and would rather have ridden a winner at Winchester than own the winner of the Derby; which he did when Merry Hampton took the premier classic in 1887.

With such patronage, it is perhaps surprising that by the early years of the twentieth century, Doncaster was in decline. The Stapleton Park Steeplechase won by the professional jockey Frank Morgan on March Flower in 1907 was worth only £6 more than the £37 collected by Charlie Cunningham and Highgrove twenty-two years earlier.

Significantly, races were now being sponsored by the local Corporation, which had run Doncaster since Elizabethan times. The place which was known to the Romans as the Danum of Antoninus and had been the residence of the Kings of Northumbria when the Saxons called it Dona Ceastre, was by now a mining town hollowed and hewed from the soot and grime of the Industrial Revolution. It was no longer a centre for country sports and the Doncaster Hunt meeting had gone, remembered only in the names of a few races.

With Town Moor one of the most famous flat race tracks in the land and the home of the world's oldest classic race, the St Leger, steeplechasing at Doncaster slipped quietly into oblivion in 1911. The two day meeting on 20 and 21 February failed to cover its costs and the prudent corporation burghers called it a day after Bill Smith, later to win the 1914 Grand National on Sunloch, had taken Conte d'Hoffman into the winner's

enclosure following the two mile Try Again Chase.

It was to be thirty-five years before Doncaster tried again, and as the disgruntled punters (there had been only one winning favourite and one market leader, Upjohn (5/4) had fallen in the last) streamed slowly away into the dusk of Bennethorpe, it seemed as though the final curtain had descended on the winter sport at Town Moor.

Perhaps the course was responsible, as much as any other cause, for the closure. As can be seen from F.H. Bayles's map of 1903, the course was on the inside of the flat race track, as it is today. However, this was long before the Sandal Mile was straightened and the sharp turn of fifty degrees after jumping the brook must have been an unacceptable hazard, even if Bayles could describe the fences as 'simple' and the country as 'improvised', which it certainly was.

However in 1949, Colonel H.A. Cape, D.S.O., the Northern Inspector of National Hunt courses was able to report:

'The first steeplechase meeting was held on 6th and 7th December 1946 since which time the course has been gradually improved to the effect that it is now one of the best, if not the best, in the North of England, and some jockeys say, anywhere. Every suggestion had been acted upon and fences are excellent and there is room for large fields at each. The going had improved beyond all recognition, and no part of this extensive course is other than very good indeed. The meetings have, of course, the advantage of the amenities of the flat, so nothing more need be said.'

Perhaps not; but the 'amenities of the flat' consisted of John Carr's old grandstand, built in 1777. It was intended to replace those elegant old buildings just before the second World War in 1939, but post-war building restrictions based on the scarcity of materials left little leeway for such inessentials as racecourse grandstands, and it was 1969 before John Carr's building which had stood the test of time for nearly two hundred years was finally demolished in favour of a stand more practical than stylish.

Hopes ran high in the early years after the war, and the Great Yorkshire Chase, which rapidly became an important Grand National and Cheltenham Gold Cup trial, was inaugurated along with races named after the then Princess Elizabeth, now Her Majesty the Queen, Princess Margaret and the Princess Royal, otherwise Princess Mary, daughter of King George V.

The Great Yorkshire Chase, over three miles and forty yards and first run in 1948, soon became known as 'The Jewel in January' in Northern chasing circles. The distance was increased to three miles and a hundred and five yards in 1960 and between 1967 and 1987 the length of the race was three miles and two furlongs, although the race was lost to the weather seven times during that period.

Cool Customer, a horse unlucky enough to be foaled in the same year as Cottage Rake, won the inaugural Great Yorkshire. Cool Customer carried 12st 7lb around Doncaster but Freebooter, the National winner in 1950, carried 11st 11lb to victory before bearing the same weight to glory at Aintree.

Knock Hard was the winner in 1953. A good horse on the flat and the winner of the Irish Lincoln, Knock Hard did just that to his fences for all the schooling of master trainer Vincent O'Brien but still won the Great Yorkshire by five lengths from the 1952 National victor Teal who was conceding 2lb and running for the first time that season. Despite his inaccurate jumping, Knock Hard went on to win the Cheltenham Gold Cup, ridden by Tim Molony, and to emphasise the importance of the Great Yorkshire.

The 1957 race was won by a previous National winner E.S.B. who snatched the Aintree marathon in 1956 when Devon Loch fell on the run-in with the contest in the bag. Although those sensational events inevitably overshadowed E.S.B.'s career, he was a good horse in his own right and in the ownership of Mrs Leonard Carver, a fine horsewoman who trained him for a time.

However, E.S.B. was handled by Fred Rimell at the height of his success and ridden by Dave Dick, one of the tallest riders to grace the professional ranks over fences and the holder of a unique record as the only jockey to have won both the Lincolnshire Handicap (on Gloaming in 1941) and the Grand National.

HAPPY HOME LEADING COTTAGE RAKE AT NATIONAL HUNT MEETING, CHELTENHAM 1948.

The 1962 Great Yorkshire went to another former National winner, the grey Nicolaus Silver. Also trained by Fred Rimell at Kinnersley, Nicolaus Silver was ridden by Bobby Beasley and never fell in a chasing career which included three Grand Nationals.

Only a handful of horses have progressed from the ranks of the hunting field and point-to-pointing to become top class chasers; Linwell, Halloween, The Dikler and Grittar come to mind along with Reg Tweedie's Freddie. Trained in the Buccleuch border country by his owner, Freddie finished second to Jay Trump at Aintree in 1965. The next year he won the Great Yorkshire en route for another crack at the National, but again was second at Liverpool, beaten twenty lengths by Anglo.

Freddie ran again in the Great Yorkshire in 1967, but could finish only fifth in a good field, with Spear Fir winning from Dormant and Mill House.In 1969 Playlord won when ridden by Ron Barry, who is now Jockey Club Inspector of Northern courses, and continued his winning ways in the Scottish Grand National after finishing third to What a Myth in one of the worst Cheltenham Gold Cups.

Sponsorship by John Smith's Brewery in

1970 failed to halt a steady decline in Doncaster's fortunes as a jumping track, although they flickered briefly into life in 1973 when Charlie Potheen won before a sparkling victory in the Whitbread Gold Cup.

The bookmaking firm of William Hill took over sponsorship in 1978, and were rewarded with a vintage field as the lightly-weighted Autumn Rain outpointed subsequent Grand National winner Lucius, Uncle Bing, April Seventh and Royal Marshall II. Those last two won Hennessy Gold Cups and a Whitbread Gold Cup between them.

The inferior Jer became a false fancy for the National after beating the 1979 Aintree winner Rubstic into fourth place in 1980 and the last good horse to win was Bregawn in 1982, albeit in controversial circumstances. His rider, John Francome, elected to run up the inside of the field a mile from home and in so doing knocked over a marker post. Tony Charlton, who rode runner-up Megan's Boy, objected, but after an inquiry lasting two hours, Bregawn was confirmed the winner for 'Born Lucky' Francome.

After the undistinguished Get Out Of Me Way won luckily in 1983, after Raemac had fallen three out with the race at his mercy, the weather closed in for four successive years. The whole purpose of the Great Yorkshire had long since been lost, and although the race was reincarnated as the William Hill Golden Spurs Handicap Steeplechase in 1988 the names of the winners, Bob Tisdall, Proverity (1989) and Man O'Magic (1990) did not make the heart sing.

Doncaster now provides only modest fare for modest horses with the £11,647 prize for the William Hill Spurs the best on offer over six days racing and four meetings. Considering that the Spurs in the guise of the Great Yorkshire was worth £4724 in 1978 this is pretty modest and the Doncaster Corporation must have thought so too when they offered the National Hunt track as an all-weather circuit.

They were unable to reach agreement with the Horserace Betting Levy Board as to financing. The all-weather project was aborted and National Hunt racing continues at Doncaster. The world's oldest classic casts a long shadow on what used to be important events.

# FAKENHAM

*He calls' hunted fairly' a horse that has barely*
*Been stripped for a trot within sight of the*
*hounds,*
*A horse that at Warwick beat Birdlime and*
*Yorick,*
*And gave Abd-El-Kader at Aintree nine pounds.*

Adam Lindsay Gordon.

STEEPLECHASES were run at Fakenham in 1839, the year that Lottery won the Grand National, and despite its lowly status as a country meeting, the course can claim to have been established at the birth of National Hunt racing as it is known today.

As the sport evolved from the heady early days, through the decline and corruption of the fifties and sixties, to emerge on the plateau of contented Victorian values in the eighties, so what were known under the rules of the Grant National Hunt Committee as bona fide Point-to-Point meetings proliferated. Many were under the auspices of the local hunt, and such events, often for hunters on the flat, were strictly speaking already under the jurisdiction of the Committee.

The races were all steeplechases or hunters' flat races and some of the Rules make rather bizarre reading now. For instance, Rule 158 concerning remounting stipulated that if the horse was caught and brought back to the point where the part-nership was severed, but the jockey found to be disabled 'his horse may be ridden home by any person of sufficient weight, provided he be qualified according to the conditions of the race. No penalty shall be exacted for carrying overweight in this instance.'

Unhappily shadows fell over these innocent Corinthian capers. Their very simplicity made them vulnerable to the unscrupulous type of owner described by Arthur Coventry and Alfred Watson in the *Badminton Library* volume on *Racing and Steeplechasing*: 'If a man have a racehorse, a local meeting is not his proper hunting ground . . . a thoroughbred horse that is not quite good enough to win on a popular racecourse will often have a great chance of carrying all before him at the annual gathering of a Hunt, the more so as the horse of this character which would be likely to make the attempt usually belongs to owners who are to say the least, sharp practitioners.'

Coventry and Watson go on to mention 'one well-known nobleman who takes a hearty interest in steeplechasing' who was so cynical about hunt meetings that he always specified that his subscription should be a prize for the third horse in certain stakes, explaining 'Sometimes he (the third) may be a bona-fide hunter; the first two never are'.

Going on to mention a 'so-called gentleman rider' who regularly took a small farm in different districts in turn, all hunted by several packs in order that he might call himself a farmer and take part in races confined to bucolic yeomen of limited skill in the saddle (to say nothing of considerable overweight), the authors concluded that 'several local (hunt) meetings have sunk into disrepute because men would make every effort ingenuity and cunning could suggest to win races with anything except the class of animal for which the race was intended'.

Of course many did succumb, but Fakenham was not among them, if only because of the patronage emanating from the royal house-parties on the nearby Sandringham estate, presided over by H.R.H. The Prince of Wales himself. Then as now racing took place at East Winch, headquarters of the West Norfolk Hunt Club, and on one Easter Monday in the eighties the Prince and his brother, Prince Albert Victor, had runners in the County Stakes of two sovereigns each, with 25 sovereigns added, for hunters and run over three miles of Fakenham's almost square track.

Hohenlinden represented the heir to the throne and Paddy ran for Prince Albert. The field of four was completed by Merrylegs and the appropriately named Monarch.

Hohenlinden, already the winner of two hunters' races at military meetings that season, won by six lengths at 6/4 on, with Monarch second and Paddy third. Merrylegs' pins were not so happy as his name might suggest and he fell.

Another feature of the meeting was the neat double completed by Mr W. Goodwyn's Curaçao, winner of both the Local Hunt Light Weight Steeplechase and the Farmers' Chase, ridden by his owner.

By the time the Prince of Wales was mid-way through his nine year reign, stakes had risen to an average of £40. Admission prices were £1 for the Club, open to members of the West Norfolk Hunt, carriages with four wheels were charged 10/-, and those with less than four wheels 5/-. For a shilling, the punters who had walked the three-quarters of a mile from the Great Eastern Line station at East Winch could enter the course.

They would have to walk considerably further today, as the nearest station is now at King's Lynn, twenty-two miles away, but one cannot suppose that Dr Beeching was much concerned with minor racecourses when he swung his infamous axe in the early 1960s, a course of action much regretted in the oil-starved seventies.

Fakenham continued happily in its pleasant time-warp for the next few decades, outlasting two World Wars and the presence in East Anglia during the latter conflict of American troops who were sometimes unkindly, if perhaps accurately, described by the indigenous population as 'over-paid, over-sexed and over here.'

In 1964 Pat Firth became Clerk of the Course and lost no time in directing major improvements. The parade ring was moved to the front of the stands and Tote buildings were acquired from the recently defunct Lincoln and from Ascot. Plans were drawn for a range of improvements which were

# Fakenham

KNIGHTING A JOCKEY –
WHATEVER NEXT.
CARTOON OF
EDWARD VII, 1885.

implemented three years later and in 1975 a new stable lads' hostel was opened at a cost of £20,000

At the same time an eight-year-old chaser called Honey End was winning at both the August and September meetings, trained by Earl Jones at Hednesford and ridden by Jimmy FitzGerald. Eighteen months later Honey End joined the big and brave band of unlucky losers of the Grand National. In 1967, by then trained by Captain Ryan Price and ridden by Josh Gifford, he was second to Foinavon after being embroiled in the melee at the twenty-third fence.

Fakenham now sports six modest fixtures between October and May. The age of commercial sponsorship has inevitably drawn a more professional involvement, and things are no longer dominated by amateur riders as they were until as recently as 1975, but the West Norfolk Hunt still have their point-to-point in May and the traditional day of the old Hunt meeting on Easter Monday has remained in the Calendar; the feature races are the Prince of Wales's Cup, given by the future George V in 1904, and the Queen's Cup, donated by Her Majesty, Queen Elizabeth II, both hunter chases.

# FOLKESTONE

IN the mid nineteenth century racing flourished in Kent: Lee, then described as a small village near Eltham; Tunbridge Wells 'a fashionable watering place . . . chiefly frequented by the rich'; Rochester and Chatham, where the races were rather unusually sponsored by members of Parliament as well as officers of the garrison; Ashford, Canterbury, which offered 'balls and other gaieties'; and Dover all gave the Kentish Man or the Man of Kent a catholic choice.

National Hunt racing was staged at Dover in 1855, albeit in the form of hurdling then under Newmarket rules. On Thursday 13 September the Hurdle Stakes of £19 was won by Alfred the Great, ridden by Mr Sait, after two heats of 'about a mile and a distance'.

By 1875, now under Grand National Committee rules, the race was known as the Tradesmen's Cup and over two miles, eight flights and worth £30. However, by the 1890s Dover had vanished along with all the other venues, although National Hunt racing had been started at Wye and Westenhanger Park, eight miles from Folkestone.

F.H. Bayles, that Hazlitt of the Turf, had no doubts as to the root cause of the decline. 'Most Kentish Men, or Men of Kent, are not endowed with very much enthusiasm for racing . . . they are probably wiser in their endeavour to transfer the produce of their productive pastures into that enviable commodity; the coin of the realm'. While the fruit farmers were still reeling from that fine piece of invective, Bayles put the other boot in. Speaking of Wye, he averred: 'It has is own clientele, who welcome the chance of winning a small race, with a very moderate animal, and to that class of owners who advocate the reduction of steeplechase jockeys' fees.'

It seems extraordinary today, but this was a favourite owners' bleat at the time, reasoning that the prize money at courses such as Wye and Folkestone rarely exceeded added money of £36, a sum invariably swallowed up in the cost of winning the race, including jockeys' fees which were then £10 for a winning ride, £5 for a losing ride, plus expenses of £1 a day.

Bayles, rightly, would have none of it, arguing that anyone who took up horse racing as a hobby was well aware of the costs and the risks, adding 'I shall always veto with the firmness of a Cromwell any attempt to reduce the old scale of our steeplechase jockeys' fees, because I submit it leaves a loophole for the exercise of such practices as would otherwise not arise.'

Wye finally capitulated in 1974, leaving Folkestone to soldier on as the last racecourse in Kent. It was lucky to do so as the opening meeting on 30 March, 1898 was such a shambles that the original Racecourse Company chaired by Lord Hardinge of Penshurst was hastily dissolved and Messrs Pratt and Company, the well known 'course doctors' were brought in to exercise their customary skills.

Although the enthusiastic reporter of the

THE QUEEN MOTHER.

# Folkestone

*Folkestone Herald* had optimistically taken the view that, as the course was the nearest one to France, 'large numbers of the French aristocracy will be attracted to the various meetings, especially those of international appeal . . . Folkestone will then be rendered a household word' the going, in every sense, was sticky for some years to come and not even Horatio Nelson could have potted a Frenchman in the grandstand; the Parisians naturally preferred the easier delights of Longchamp to the brisk chills of a Channel crossing.

Pratt's task was not made any simpler by the tenacious nature of the ground, which provided reasonable going for the flat racing in the summer, but was considered to be 'simply wicked' in the wet, with horses literally sinking to their fetlock joints. In the early 1900s a new-fangled motor car, crossing to the Club enclosure much patronised by the county gentry and the officers of the Shorncliffe garrison, became stuck fast for several days.

At another meeting twenty-two runners started for three chases but only five managed to pass the post, and four of these had been remounted. In 1905 a chase was declared void as five of the six runners fell and the other repeatedly refused as the adhesion of the loamy soil left the poor beast with no strength to jump the fences. On the same day an aggregate of nineteen contestants in three races produced only eight finishers, and at a subsequent meeting so many animals fell that the stewards ordered all the fences to be trimmed down

in the pious hope that things would be easier for the runners on the second day.

To be fair, the course was easy to negotiate in fair weather, and Pratt & Co. persevered in their attempts to attract a public. A private station at Westenhanger was built for the first class passengers, with a fare of 10/- from Charing Cross. Lesser mortals paid 5/- and alighted at a halt. For an annual membership of five guineas you could take two ladies into the Club, and free parking was provided for your carriage. A daily badge cost 30/- with an extra 10/- for your lady and 5/- to park.

The 'reserved enclosure' (which we would now call Tatt's) was 12/6d for a gentleman and 5/- for a lady, the public stand cost 5/- and you could watch the proceedings from the infield for half a crown.

However the bargain buy in Edwardian times was the 20/- first class return from London which included admission to the reserved enclosure. There was stabling on the course for 120 animals, lads' quarters, veterinary and farriers' services, and the by now all important motor attendant provided free of charge.

With catering in the hands of Letheby and Christopher, it was hard to see how the management could do more, and slowly the policies paid off. For nearly ninety years, Folkestone has provided modest sport in pleasant surroundings for south coast holidaymaker and urban racegoer alike. In the twenties, and thirties the course was a happy hunting ground for Sussex and Epsom train-

GAY RECORD (RIGHT) MR JOHN LAWRENCE (LORD OAKSEY) UP.

ers in particular, and the Rees, Woottons, Specks and Dullers to say nothing of Staff Ingham, were happy enough to compete for the prizes which rarely topped £100.

Postwar the dominant figure was Peter Cazalet who sent out streams of winners from his stable at Fairlawne, near Tonbridge and only thirty miles from Westenhanger. Dick Francis, who became first jockey to Cazalet in 1953, rode many of his winners at Folkestone, as did Bill Rees and David Mould; and not a few of those were in the blue and buff colours of Her Majesty Queen Elizabeth the Queen Mother. In the mid sixties, Cazalet was leading trainer with twenty-four winners in six seasons, his nearest rival, the Epsom trainer John Sutcliffe, trailing nineteen behind.

Gay Record gave Her Majesty her hundredth winner on this course, and a race is named in his honour, but the royal connection is not over. In February, 1990, Dudley and Admiral's Leap completed a double for the Queen Mother bringing the total since she entered ownership in 1949 to three hundred and seventy-eight.

# FONTWELL

ONE of the greatest pleasures of racing in the south of England is the opportunity to enjoy the beauty of the Sussex downs. It is not many years since it was the agreeable custom to put up at some convenient and hospitable watering hole, such as the Norfolk Hotel in Bognor, and spend what was known as the Sussex Fortnight on the equine playgrounds of Goodwood, Brighton and Lewes.

Modern methods of transport have outdated such a leisurely approach and Lewes closed in 1964, but for the National Hunt enthusiast there are compensations to be found in late summer racing at Plumpton and Fontwell Park.

Fontwell was laid down in 1924 in the attractive parkland which had been the training ground of Alfred Day. Day was a member of the famous Danebury family, and his career had included many winners at his local track at Goodwood, taking the Cup with Barmecide in 1893, the Stakes with Ignition in 1911 and Romsey won the Stewards' Cup in 1910.

Apart from Windsor, Alfred Day's design of a figure-of-eight steeplechase course is the only one of its kind in British racing, but unlike Windsor where the elliptical track makes it difficult to follow the running, Fontwell's hour-glass layout ensures perfect viewing from any vantage point.

Alfred Day's old friends from his happy hunting ground at Goodwood were well on hand when the course opened on 21 May, 1924. The Duke of Richmond was President,

FONTWELL, 1986.

his heir Lord March officiated as Senior Steward and the Duke of Norfolk came from nearby Arundel Castle to honour the venture as Patron.

The first race of the two-day fixture was the Walburton Chase over three miles and victory went to the 'jolly' 5/4 favourite Gem, ridden by champion jockey Dick Rees and trained at Epsom by Gil Bennett. Epsom stables won four of the six races, including a treble for Bennett, but Harry Escott took

H.R.H. PRINCESS ELIZABETH TALKING TO JOCKEY TONY GRANTHAM, TRAINER PETER CAZALET AND LORD MILDMAY, 1949.

the selling hurdle with his Lewes-trained Tuscan, albeit ridden by Epsom jockey Frank Wootton.

The little course was an immediate success, and at the end of the second two-day fixture in October could boast a membership of three hundred. An extra one-day card on 1 June made up a five day calendar for 1925, but the pressure of the General Strike forced Fontwell back to four days the following year.

The Sussex track remained a fragrant backwater of the National Hunt scene yet popular with the aficionados as it is today. The programme was extended in 1939, and ten years later, on 10 October 1949, the Fontwell crowd cheered home the first winner to carry the colours of Her Majesty The Queen, then Princess Elizabeth.

The horse was Monaveen, trained by Peter Cazalet and ridden by Tony Grantham, and the race was the Chichester Handicap Chase. A few months later, Monaveen finished fifth to Freebooter in the Grand National, and though he was killed at Hurst Park in December 1950 his place in Turf history is assured and one of Monaveen's racing plates still hangs in the weighing room at Fontwell.

Fontwell is far removed from the rugged significance of Liverpool, Cheltenham, and Newbury; rather it is a rendezvous for racing's socialites, chatting easily in the elegant surroundings. The fixture list now offers fifteen days' racing between August and May during the season and although commercial

MONAVEEN
FONTWELL, 1949.

NATIONAL SPIRIT,
'FRENCHIE'
NICHOLSON UP.

sponsorship plays its inevitable part, the names of Fontwell's races also remember old friends, including Salmon Spray and the superb National Spirit.

Dual winner of the Champion Hurdle in 1947 and 1948 and almost unbeatable at his best, National Spirit was defeated only twice over hurdles between the spring of 1946 and the autumn of 1949 and also won fourteen flat races for his owner-breeder Leonard Abelson and Epsom trainer Vic Smyth. Many of these flat victories were in the silken hands of Teddy Underdown, a gentleman rider in every sense who perhaps would epitomise the sporting spirit of Fontwell, a course born into the golden age of racing.

# HAYDOCK

THE word 'spiv', a slang term defined in Collins Dictionary as 'one who manages to get a living by other means than lawful work' may derive from the Regency term 'spiff', meaning smart and dandy. From there may stem the fictional characters made famous on the stage, screen and television by Arthur English and George Cole.

The term has also been applied to police informers and bookies' runners, and in Edwardian times was used to describe unemployed stable lads who would hang around the horse-docks at railway stations in the hope of picking up a runner to 'do' and lead round in the paddock.

For centuries horses had to be walked to the races as the jockeys hacked to the meetings with their saddles tied behind their backs. In 1836, the horse box drawn by post-horses designed by Lord George Bentinck was a revolutionary innovation which widely expanded the system of horse transport, but meanwhile George Stephenson had produced the first practical steam locomotive at Killingworth Colliery, near what was then Newcastle racecourse.

The opening of the Liverpool to Manchester Railway by the Duke of Wellington, then Prime Minister, in 1830 spawned a huge rail network and by the turn of the century nowhere was better provided for than the County Palatine of Lancashire. One beneficiary of this prime example of Victorian technology was the newly opened Haydock Park racecourse which was served by no fewer than three lines.

LORD GEORGE BENTINCK.

# Haydock

The Great Northern and the Midland Railways connected to the station at Ashton-in-Makerfield which was within 350 yards of the stables and the Great Central platform was adjacent to the paddock. Here the 'spivveys' would cluster round the horses as they were unloaded and offer their casual services.

The king-pin among the spivveys was known as Malton George, so called because he was originally butler to Sir George Renwick at Auburn Hill, Malton. Accordingly, he resented being addressed as 'spiv' and always insisted on being referred to as a 'paddock assistant'.

Together with his confederates Spider, Scottie and Lucky Durham, Malton George travelled the railways between courses without ever descending to such a mundane practice as that of buying a ticket. A collection of 'found' pieces of pasteboard kept in an old tobacco tin usually saw them through to destinations such as Manchester, Haydock and Nottingham, but Ayr was a different matter.

However, the confrères knew the lines well and also where and when the tickets would be examined. There were no travelling inspectors in those trusting days, and at the stop before the station where the check was due, Lucky Durham donned a 'found' porter's cap and crying 'All tickets please!' made his own collection for the benefit of the gang who suavely presented them when the real collector appeared.

Haydock's first meeting in 1899 was pre-ceeded by a hundred and forty-seven years of racing in the area, first recorded on 16 June 1752 at Golborne Heath when 'horses the property of subscribers to the Newton Hunt. . . . not in the Sweats (training) before March' competed for a £50 cup.

In the early nineteenth century the sport was concentrated on Newton-le-Willows and the Newton Gold Cup was founded in 1807 with conditions identical to those of the inaugural running of the Ascot Gold Cup in the same year. Both events were to stand the test of time, but what is now known as the Old Newton Cup and Ascot's centrepiece are very different races today.

Racing flourished but eventually outgrew the course at Newton Common where National Hunt racing had been introduced in 1883. The first meeting was on 28 April and the champion amateur Charlie Cunningham made the punters happy when cantering up by twenty lengths in the opening Haydock Open Hunters' Steeplechase on Delaware, returned at 6/4 on. Un-happily, it was downhill all the way after that for Mr Cunningham and his many followers.

Little Pink 'Un, 5/4 favourite for the South Lancashire Hunters' Chase, was a faller. The mudstained Cunningham took a breather while Compton Lad won the Newton Selling Chase, but could then only finish third on Laddie, the 6/4 market choice for the next, another seller. Finally, Delaware was taken to post again to cover his second three miles at racing pace in one afternoon, but it was too much and the even money favourite for the United Hunters' Chase came to grief.

In 1896 the Clerk of the Course was Cecil Frail, a fine racecourse administrator who realised that it was essential to find new ground to expand the quality of racing. At first the Jockey Club were not impressed with Frail's application to stage the sport in a 127 acre park leased from the first Baron Newton, a descendant of the Legh family who had donated the £50 cup in 1752.

A justifiably exasperated Frail informed Weatherbys, the Jockey Club secretariat responsible for licensing; 'This case can scarcely be considered as an application for a new racecourse as it will be merely a change from one place to another. . . . We have little hesitation in saying it will be one of the best courses in England.'

To be fair to the authorities, it was then generally considered that there were too many fixtures cashing in on the prosperity of late Victorian England under the benign Conservative Premiership of Lord Salisbury.

A few years later even the great John Porter was unable to launch Newbury without a personal appeal to the King, but eventually all was well at Haydock and the new course opened on 10 February 1899. The first event was a Maiden Hurdle over two miles for a prize of £38 which went to the four-year-old Snarley-Yow. The top prize on the card was the £136 Warrington Handicap Hurdle, won by Imbroglio, trained by J.G. Elsey of the well-known Lincolnshire dynasty.

Two months later at the traditional April fixture Tom Coulthwaite enjoyed the first of the many Haydock victories which led to the foundation of a race in honour of the man who trained three Grand National winners. For many years a good National trial, the three mile Tom Coulthwaite Handicap Chase has been renamed as part of the sometimes regrettable but necessary progress of commercial sponsorship and is now the Peter Marsh Chase.

During the reign of 'King Teddy' Haydock continued to provide good class racing with prize money above the average. George Gunter, Frank Lyall and Sid Menzies dominated in the saddle, along with Alf Newey, who won the 1907 Grand National on Eremon. Trained by Tom Coulthwaite, Eremon warmed up for the National with a ten length victory in the Lyme Park Chase over three miles at Haydock in March.

In the year of Eremon's National Arthur Reader, a Yorkshireman who later became a successful trainer at Doncaster, was making his mark as a jockey. Between 1907 and 1911, Reader struck up a rare understanding with a horse called True as Steel and the partnership became a standing dish at Haydock.

True as Steel was one of those horses who could not settle in a strange stable without the companionship of another animal; in this case, a cat. The cat would travel in a basket, and as the horses detrained at the horse-dock, the spivveys would enquire of Reader, who always travelled with the horse, 'Na lad, has tha fetched t'cat?' knowing full well that it would be pointless to back True as Steel the next day if he was pining.

In the twenties Haydock maintained its position as one of the best courses in England, as forecast by Cecil Frail. The top southern jockeys including Frank Wootton, George Duller and the Anthony and Rees brothers were happy to take on the local contingent headed by the now veteran Bob Chadwick, and Haydock's stiff fences have always provided an admirable proving ground for Grand National aspirants.

A number of National winners have followed in Eremon's hoofprints, including Sheila's Cottage who won a three and a half mile chase on 28 November, 1947. Her outspoken trainer, Neville Crump, immediately announced to anyone who would listen that the mare would win the National 'going on when all the others have started to cough!'

Few paid heed, to their regret when Sheila's Cottage and Arthur Thompson ran home at 50/1 from forty-two rivals at Aintree the following March. Thompson was to ride another National winner for Crump on Teal in 1952, but he never forgot Sheila's Cottage who was buried at the bottom of his garden.

Today Haydock remains a premier track and the stands which had survived since 1899 have been replaced by a development at a cost of two million pounds. Now officially in Merseyside, the course attracts noisy enthusiasts rather than the languid racegoer to first class racing all the year round. As Martin Trew reported in his *Times Racecourse Guide* (1989), 'trousers and shirts are required in the members~', which sounds like a classic case of the apparel proclaiming the man.

# HEREFORD

ONCE the capital of Saxon West Mercia, Hereford stands on the Welsh borders in the centre of a rich agricultural district especially noted for the production of cider. The twelfth century cathedral is the home of the celebrated Mappa Mundi, King Stephen's eight hundred years old chair, the best library of chained books in the country and many fine tombs.

With the possible exception of the fermented apple-juice, little of this would have interested Harry (Charlie Peppercorn) Brown, champion jockey, wit, raconteur, racing mentor to the Prince of Wales, first-class shot and equally skilful with rod and line. Having arrived at Hereford to ride Dudley, whom he also trained, for Lord Londesborough, Brown found time on his hands and accordingly backed himself to catch the biggest salmon of the season on the nearby Wye and then to ride a winner within an hour.

HEREFORD CATHEDRAL, 1805.

FISHERMAN, 1858.

A forty-four pound salmon was swiftly landed and duly recorded but Dudley made one of his rare jumping errors and fell at the last when ten lengths ahead of his nearest rival. The horse soon made amends, winning fifteen consecutive races for Brown in 1924–5 and forty-four in all, setting a record bettered only by Crudwell more than thirty years later. No doubt the salmon tasted good, as well.

Racing had taken place at Hereford since 1771. At a meeting on Tuesday 27 August Mr Foley's bay horse beat Mr Dilly's brown horse at level weights after three two mile heats for a prize of £50. Three days later a similar event over four miles went to Lord Chedworth's bay horse Weazel who 'won easy' from Mr Hunt's Dormouse.

Hurdle racing was introduced in 1840 with a sweepstake of five sovereigns each and twenty-five sovereigns added. This event, a four mile contest with 'four leaps' on each circuit, was run at the end of the usual two day meeting in late August. Steeplechasing came in 1842 and by the early fifties crack riders including Tom Olliver and William Archer were competing in the Hereford Grand Annual.

Meanwhile, flat racing continued and on 28 August 1857 the record-breaking Fisherman won the Queen's Plate, albeit by only a neck from Cotswold. Fisherman started at 7/2 on and could be forgiven for feeling a little jaded; during the 1857 season he ran 35 times, winning 22 races, and his career total was 70 wins from 121 starts, including 26 Queen's Plates and the Ascot Gold Cups of 1858 and 1859.

Fisherman went to stud in Australia and became one of the great foundation sires of the Antipodes although he died within five years.

Flat racing degenerated into a dreary collection of sellers, plates and poorly endowed handicaps and ceased in 1883, but steeplechasing flourished although on a modest level until the outbreak of the Kaiser's war.

One meeting was held in 1915 and on resumption in 1920 the fields were strong and the riders included Peter Roberts, Ivor Anthony and Bilby Rees. Prize money was good for the standards of the time with the Coronation Steeplechase worth £400, and so this happy sporting fixture paddled pleasant-ly in the backwaters of National Hunt racing until interrupted by World War Two.

The course was orginally public land and was still controlled by the local council in 1946, when a company was formed which took over the track and faced up to post-war Britain with three meetings. Since then the programme has gradually increased to the fourteen cards on offer today. As usual there are holiday fixtures, and it was on May Day 1975 that Hereford put itself into the record books along with Fisherman when forced to stage fourteen races featuring 219 runners. What should have been an evening meeting commenced at 1.30pm, and the official reason why this marathon was not split into a two day event was that it would have been inconvenient for the caterers. Let's hope the gin didn't run out.

# HEXHAM

At three o'clock in the morning of 24 March 1603, Queen Elizabeth I died in the forty-fifth year of her reign. As the Queen's Messenger galloped north to inform King James VI of Scotland that he was now the King of England, James I was proclaimed in the streets of London.

A few days later the new monarch set out from Edinburgh with his mixed retinue of homosexual favourites and rugged Scots noblemen to claim his throne. It was to take him a month to reach the capital, and in the course of the royal progress he created two hundred knights, ennobled sixty-two peers, and hanged a pickpocket without trial at Hexham.

His regal authority thus established beyond doubt, James declared the attractive town on the River Tyne within a Roman spear's throw of Hadrian's Wall to be 'The Heart of all England'. Whether this was due to an excess of flattery in a desire to please his new subjects or a flimsy knowledge of geography is uncertain. However, we can be sure that the citizens were delighted, and the royal utterance is remembered today at Hexham races by the Heart of All England Hunter Chase, run at the April meeting.

The inaugural event was won by Redscar in the hands of Mr C. Pawson on 2 May 1907. Redscar trotted up by thirty lengths to collect the £145 prize, thus completing a sequence of four victories since starting the season with a facile win in the Bank Top Handicap Chase at Shincliffe under Bob Chadwick, Tom Coulthwaite's retained jockey who was des-

tined to win the 1910 National on Jenkinstown.

Racing first came to Hexham in 1721 when the sport was staged on Tyne Green, the traditional town fairground. In 1738 entries were accepted at the Black Bull for horses, mares or geldings to take part in a three heat contest, the distance being three times round Tyne Green, with half an hour allowed for rubbing down between heats.

All seemed happy enough, even if the local populace were more concerned with gambling on cock-fighting than horse racing, but in June 1740 the government led by Sir Robert Walpole on behalf of King George II legislated severely against the Turf with a view to preventing cheating on the track and ruffianism off it.

Perhaps those who cavil about Parliamentary action to prevent the thuggery now endemic in association football should take a glance at the face of history and a powerful precedent which caused the demise of many minor courses. Even local authorities were affronted and in 1744 the Grand Jury of Northumberland decided that the morale of the working man was depleted as a result of too much sport, resulting in 'loss of work' (absenteeism) and 'extravagance at cock-fights and illegal race meetings' which led to 'vice, profanities and immorality'.

However racing was recorded again in the Calendar of 1775, and seems to have continued intermittently until 1809. A meeting controlled by the Hexham Hunt was contested during the mid-nineteenth century over

JAMES I.

country at Yarridge Heights, which is roughly the site of racing today, but was defunct by 1880. Meanwhile, some enthusiasts had attempted to stage a meeting on an island in the middle of the River Tyne in 1840, only for the river to flood and seriously curtail the sport.

A local poet was inspired to compose a long poem, of which one stanza will suffice:

*"Oh dear ! pray, what's been the matter,*
*Betwixt the people and the water?*
*The people wished to have a race*
*And fixed upon a certain place,*
*The Tyne its awful power did show,*
*And for a while, it was 'no go.'"*

Ten years after the demise of the old Hexham Hunt Meeting, Charles Henderson decided to lay down a steeplechase course on his property at Yarridge Hill, incorporating much of the former hunt course. Henderson roped in a few of his distinguished racing friends to help him with the project, including the former champion amateur rider Charlie Cunningham, Colonel Johnnie

McKie, who was another leading Corinthian, and the ubiquitous and formidable Captain, later Brigadier-General, Sir Loftus Bates.

Tom Coulthwaite, who was to train three Grand National winners and may be best described as the Martin Pipe of his day, built and placed the fences for the opening meeting on St George's Day 1890.

It was a largely amateur affair, with only three professional jockeys present, although they included George Williamson who was to win the 1899 Grand National on the great Manifesto and the Bohemian Grand Steeplechase four times on the intriguingly named Handy Andy. Colonel McKie took the principal honours with a treble and among the others to share the total stake money of £225 were Capt. J.E. Rogerson and, needless to say, Charlie Cunningham.

Mr Fred Straker, a member of the new committee, also 'went round' and thus established a connection with Hexham which this well known Border racing family has enjoyed for many years.

All in all the venture was voted a great success, with, in the words of John Fairfax-Blakeborough 'plenty of runners and no end of fun'.

Much of the fun was to be had in the company of Charles Henderson who held open house at his home The Riding and provided a champagne lunch for anyone who rode, trained or owned a runner at the meetings. What effect this had on the results is impossible to calculate, but Henderson himself usually had a winner, trained by Tom

Coulthwaite and ridden by a jockey with the delightful name of Conkie.

In May 1910, just before the death of King Edward VII brought a brilliant social era to a close, Hexham was graced by the presence of the black boxer Jack Johnson and his wife. Henderson welcomed them with his usual charm and hospitality, but when they later appeared in the club enclosure Loftus Bates, now Clerk of the Course, had the couple removed.

It was probably the only ungracious act of which Bates was guilty in a career of race-course administration which spanned fifty-four years. It was also fortunate for the then Colonel that Johnson, who was the reigning heavyweight champion of the world, did not take exception to his treatment, or the gallant officer might have found himself halfway to Newcastle before he knew what had hit him.

Hexham continued as a sporting fixture for knowledgeable racegoers, more used to judging confirmation than form and more concerned with racing than betting. As such the meeting ambled happily into the nineteen-twenties to find Henderson's son, Captain Tommy Henderson, taking over after his father had died in 1914.

Leaving his mother to occupy The Riding, Captain Henderson continued the family's hospitable traditions at Target House nearby, so called because it had been built as a shooting range by Henderson Sen.

As ever champagne was on offer but the speciality of the house in the decade of the cocktail was a particularly palatable dry martini, mixed by the host who fancied his chances as a barman and flavoured the vermouth overnight with the peel of an orange.

The connection is not as obscure as it may seem. When a Frenchman in Betsy's Bar in downtown Yorktown cried 'Vive le cocktail' at the height of the American War of Independence, he probably had in mind the half-bred horses with docked tails which raced in Paris and indeed the rest of Europe, the 'cock-tail' distinguishing them from the thoroughbreds.

Such equine anomalies were ironed out by the 'Jersey Act' of 1913 which made rigorous stipulations for entry in the General Stud Book, but who can doubt that the dry martini, a drink of mixed parentage named after a horse of similar descendance, and christened by a Frenchman will live for ever?

Modern Hexham owes much to Kit Patterson, Clerk of the Course for many years and now Managing Director, while the Henderson connection is sustained by the present Clerk Charles Enderby, the great-grandson of Charles Henderson who now lives at The Riding.

Those who speak of 'Glorious Goodwood' have not been to Hexham where the sporting spirit of rural England lives high above the spectacular scenery of Northumberland, and where Bobby Renton, trainer of the 1950 Grand National hero Freebooter and host of other steeplechase winners built on big-boned, old fashioned lines, rode his final race at the age of sevent-five. Perhaps King James was not so wrong, after all.

# HUNTINGDON

'A brewer may be as bold as Hector
When he has drunk his cup of nectar
And as a brewer may be a Lord Protector
As nobody can deny'.

Anon.

OLIVER CROMWELL, self styled Lord Protector of the Commonwealth from 1653 until his death in 1658, caused the death of a king in the name of democracy only to institute a Parliament incorporating the totalitarian exclusion of Catholics and Royalists. Much has been written about this sturdy man of the people, but little publicity has been accorded to his lineal descent from a publican; indeed he was a brewer himself in his early days, as enemies were not slow to point out in doggerel rhyme. Such intelligence would not have gone down well with the Protector's puritanical friends, but in 1572 his grandfather, Sir Henry Cromwell, was the owner of the George Inn at Huntingdon, the country town later to be well known as the birthplace of 'Old Noll', and where he was educated at the local Grammar School.

By the mid nineteenth century, coaching inns such as the George were being driven out of business by the new-fangled iron horses of the Great Northern Railway. The hotel was then in the tenancy of John Jenkins, who in turn passed the lease to his daughter Elizabeth and her husband, John Goodliff.

Goodliff was a popular local sportsman,

and while Mrs Goodliff kept the home fires burning and ran the business, Goodliff hunted with his friends the Duke of Manchester and Lord Sandwich, together with the rich Cambridge students who stabled their horses at the George.

The 1870s and 1880s were years when steeplechasing was developing strongly after the slough of '60s and John Goodliff was a keen paticipant. Wearying of long journeys to ride in races, he considered the idea of opening a track at Huntingdon. So, at one of those dinners which seem to have decided the future of every race from the Epsom Derby to the Thirsk Hunt Cup, Goodliff and six of his like-minded companions in the hunting field assembled at the George to plan a track on Waterloo meadows, the property of Lord Sandwich.

Like all water meadows they were subject to flooding, a problem which was to persist until the early 1970s. The meadows, four in all, were separated by hedgerows which were swiftly adapted as obstacles and at Easter 1886 the inaugural race, a three mile chase, was won by Catherine the Great.

Racing had taken place in the area as early as 1603, when 'Mr Oliver Cromwell's horse won the syluer (silver) bell and Mr Cromwell had the glory of the day. Mr Hynd came behind.' The Cromwell referred to was the future Protector's uncle who lived in some style with an income of £5000 a year. A visitor to the grand Cromwell residence at Hinchinbrooke House, a regular haunt of King James I, recorded the intriguing diary

THE GEORGE INN.

note 'Mr Oliver with his owne and all his ladyes is the greatest esquire living in these parts.'

More formal racing was recorded on the flat in the Calendar of 1773 at Portholme about a quarter of a mile from the town and yet another part of Huntingdon's luxuriant spread of water meadows, much praised by William Cobbett in his 'Rural Rides'. For many years around the turn of the eighteenth and nineteenth centuries Portholme races were 'farmed' by the legendary Frank Buckle, who lived at Peterborough and rode the winners of twenty-seven classics.

At the two day meeting on 1 and 2 September 1885 Charlie Wood rode a couple of hot favourites and duly landed the odds for owner Sir George Chetwynd and trainer Robert Sherrard, and completed a treble with Ripon in the five furlong seller at odds of 25/1. That must have caused a little con-

sternation all round, since Wood was not in the habit of entertaining an angel unawares. All three men were later the subjects of the most famous Gimcrack speech ever made.

Soon afterwards the Portholme meeting started sliding gently into oblivion, and finally succumbed in 1896. Occasional attempts at revival failed and left John Goodliff's old track at Waterloo Meadows to fly the racing flag, albeit with the lowly status of a hunt fixture.

The Goodliff family connection continued for many years. In 1907, it was decided to allocate money for the placed horses at both the spring and autumn meetings, which must have consoled Percy Whitaker, then a crack Corinthian and later a distinguished trainer. Having taken the opening race on 1 April, the Brampton Maiden Hurdle of £29 on 3/1 chance Master at Arms, Whitaker could only finish second in

THE EARL OF SANDWICH.

a two horse race for the Fitzwilliam Hunt Chase on Park Hack, made 2/1 on on the strength of a good second in a selling chase at the Oakley Hunt meeting at nearby Kimbolton.

In the 20s and 30s, Huntingdon settled down as a casually run holiday fixture, with popular meetings at Easter and Whitsun. Facilities were poor, and so were the finances since much depended on the income from a hay crop mowed from the meadows, which could be lean after a wet summer.

After the hiatus of the Second World War, Huntingdon reopened in 1946. It was as popular as ever and even a little more profitable as returning servicemen enjoyed the financial luxury of their gratuities, but the now ageing directors of the course were in

for a rude shock when they applied for a third fixture.

As it was a Bank Holiday meeting, Huntingdon had escaped any kind of official inspection by the Jockey Club, as there were far too many fixtures on holiday dates for the stewards to cover. This would be impossible today as the Club have a list of reserve stewards drafted in for the purpose, but in 1948 the old system still applied, in spite of the rule that a Jockey Club steward should attend every meeting.

The new date was in early summer, and

THE STEWARDS.

the man from Headquarters was not impressed with the roofless stands, the lean-to weighing room and the Victorian sanitary arrangements.

As a result a younger board of directors was appointed and Bob Lenton, a thirty-eight-year-old local farmer, was made Clerk of the Course. He remained in charge for twenty-five years and took Huntingdon from the status of a hick track to the attractive country meeting which it is today.

In the early forties the brothers Josh and Macer Gifford were born in a farmhouse which overlooks the track. Their father, Tom Gifford, was a fine point-to-point rider and by the '60s the brothers were leading jockeys, Josh becoming champion jockey four times and both winning the Whitbread Gold Cup on Michael Marsh's superb steeplechaser Larbawn.

Josh Gifford is now a leading trainer and in 1989 was awarded the M.B.E. for his services to racing. Macer died in 1985, and is remembered by the Macer Gifford Handicap Chase over two and a half miles and run in November. Needless to say, Josh always supports the race and trained the winner in 1985 and 1988.

By a nice touch or irony 'Old Noll' Cromwell is also commemorated, but with less affection, by the Lord Protector Handicap Hurdle at the April Meeting. He would definitely not have approved as he was no friend of the Turf or amusements of any kind, and the paradoxical puzzle remains; how did the fun-loving Cromwell family produce such a harsh and unyielding puritan?

BOB LENTON, TALKING TO HIS PREDECESSOR GEORGE FRANCIS.

# KELSO

"October 21st, 1786. Day charming but too clear for sport. Sir Alexander Don, with a politeness peculiar to himself, offered me all his hunters to see the harriers out, and every other mark of genuine civility; but I rather preferred attending his Grace of Buccleuch and Lord Haddington to see Fleurs, the seat of the Duke of Roxburghe. . . . The approach to the house is not finished; when complete it will be very handsome. . . . the rooms are numerous, but in general, rather small. There is neatness to a degree, free from gaudiness and show, which is very pleasing. The offices, with the kitchen etc, are not to be excelled for comfort probably on the whole island. The view to the south (commands) the town of Kelso."

So wrote Colonel Thornton, the distinguished Yorkshire sportsman, in his diary of a tour of Scotland. Today Floors Castle, as it is now known, is the largest inhabited house in Britain, the seat of the Duke of Roxburghe. It is not surprising that the gallant Colonel found a great number of rooms, as there are 365 windows in this mansion modernised in the Colonel's time from a building designed by Sir John Vanbrugh in 1718 and built one mile to the north-west of the birthplace of Sir Walter Scott.

Kelso is steeped in the history of the Border country, and it is not surprising that Thornton found himself amongst friends in an area long known for racing, breeding,

hunting and salmon fishing. A ladies' man himself and protector (some say husband) of the beautiful Alicia, darling of York's Knavesmire for her skill in the saddle, he doubtless found Lady Harriet Don even more charming than her husband, Sir Alexander, Lady Harriet being described by no less an authority than Robert Burns as 'a devine lady'. This was recorded in the poet's journal on a visit to Kelso, which all goes to show that the Border town was as much a social vortex as a home of sport.

Sir Alexander Don was one of the twelve founding members of the Caledonian Hunt, and in 1760 he established racing at Averton Edge, five miles from Kelso, under the auspices of a group of sporting gentlemen known as the Bowmen of the Borders.

Flat racing had taken place at Claverton on an irregular basis since around 1734, and the Hunt had given a fifty guinea plate for a meeting in 1751. The Caledonians were the principal racehorse owners in Scotland, and it was their habit to forgather at a different venue each year. These gatherings lasted nearly a fortnight, and in 1765 they happily joined up with the Bowmen of the Borders to witness Sir Alexander Don's grey Cheviot vanquish 'a horse of Sir John Paterson's'. Local records go on to say 'The match was for a considerable sum, and owing to the speed and bottom of Cheviot and the skill of his jockey (Tommy Hudson), he won easily.'

In those days 'bottom' referred to courage and not a part of the anatomy; and while the Caledonians lacked neither courage nor the social graces they were sometimes a little too boisterous for the sensitive Robert Burns. In 1772, Thomas Pennant in his *Tour of Scotland* reported 'These (Kelso Races) are founded not on the sordid principles of gaming, or dissipation, or fraud but the beautiful basis of benevolence . . .' Pennant detracts a little from these kind words when he has to admit that he actually missed the races by turning up a week late, but doubtless the Caledonians were still in evidence at the Cross Keys Hotel and told him all about it.

The following year, only Edinburgh and Kelso were considered worthy from the Scottish meetings to be included in Mr Weatherby's inaugural Racing Calendar. Kelso sported a three day meeting commencing on Tuesday 17 August. It was the period when hunters' flat races were much in vogue, and on the first day there was an event worth £50 for 'hunters of last season that had not been in the sweats since the first of January and 1st April 1773, carrying 12st and running two heats each of four miles'. If a horse was 'in the sweats' it was in training, and this race was for bona fide hunters.

The winner was Charon, owned by the Hon. Captain Keith Stewart. Charon turned out again the next day for another hunters' flat race, and trotted up from the Duke of Buccleugh's Cockspur, who was conceding 18lb. Charon's activities in the hunting field must have kept him pretty fit.

The remainder of the card was devoted to flat racing, and continued intermittently until racing under Jockey Club rules at Kelso finally ceased in 1888. The frequency of the fixtures depended very much on the itinerary of the Caledonian Hunt Club, who held a meeting at Kelso every year in October from 1779 to 1785, returning in 1787. Thereafter, the Club patronised Dumfries, Stirling, Hamilton, Ayr, Edinburgh, Perth and Kelso by rotation.

The Cross Keys Hotel was the place to stay, and also where you had to enter your runners before noon on the day prior to the race. The 1782 meeting was postponed to 21 October on account of a late harvest and not until all was safely gathered in were horses with such splendid names as Capt. Tart, Little-thought-of, Sober Johnny, Stay-till-I-Come and Young-Harry's-the-lad able to take the field.

The rather more elegantly, if less amusingly, named Sandy-o'er-the-Lee was a nailing good horse who won not only a clutch of hunters' races but sweepstakes under rules as well for her owner, Mr Baird. Indeed Sandy-o'er-the-Lee was well nigh invincible at Kelso between 1783 and 1785; it was all the more disgraceful, therefore, that this good servant should end her days pulling a diligence (stage-coach) between Glasgow and Edinburgh in 1798.

*'While the harness sore galls,*
*And the spur her sides goad,*
*The high mettled racer's*
*A hack on the road'.*

# Kelso

Kelso races were at their height when Colonel Thornton made his visit in 1786 and life at the Cross Keys certainly was not dull. Although not sponsoring the meeting, the gentlemen of the Caledonian Hunt gave a ball, and when the ladies retired at four o'clock in the morning the Caledonians stayed up to drink their healths. Ringing for breakfast at eight and gaining no response from 'stupid waiters', Thornton bumbled downstairs to find the Hunt still happily knocking back the claret and intending to continue until the hounds went out. To cap it all, the Colonel found himself with a bill for two guineas a night for his room, 'the most expensive ever heard of', and returned grumpily to Yorkshire.

Soon the old vice of Scottish racing in the eighteenth century began to exert its influence, and the events involved only a few aristocrats with good animals, and sportsmen of lesser means both financial and equine were unable to compete. Although there was the accolade of a King's Plate in 1793, accompanied by a week of revels, the fly in the ointment was that the King's Plate of 100 guineas and known as the 'King's Guineas' was awarded to the Caledonian Hunt, and they took the prize around with them to the fixture they supported. The matter became farcical in 1803, when a card of four days attracted only three horses, and every 'event' was a walk over.

Things had improved somewhat by 16 September 1813 with the endowment of a Gold Cup. The prize money was trivial to the rich landowners competing, but there was much cachet in trophies at this time and a Gold Cup looked handsome on the sideboard. It was to little avail, and Agnes Sorrel's victory carrying the pink jacket and black cap of Mr Alexander Don was the highlight of a one day meeting. Later, as the new baronet following the death of his father, Sir Alexander frightened off most of the opposition at Kelso, his Fitz-Orville walking over for the Gold Cup in 1817.

A change of venue from Caverton Edge to Blakelaw failed to stop the rot but in 1822 the hour produced the man. The Blakelaw meeting had become a travesty, with wrestling matches and bizarre pedestrian events but at this stage the fifth Duke of Roxburghe intervened from his seat at Floors Castle where Colonel Thornton had found the plumbing so efficient.

The Duke had done his best to help the course at Caverton Edge by building a grandstand and stabling for the runners, only for the buildings to be vandalised by gypsies specialising in sheep stealing. Blakelaw was a failure and so the Duke, still spry at the age of 87 having fathered a son only six years earlier, laid down a course at Berrymoss, where racing takes place today.

On 12 July 1822, the Duke laid the foundation stone for 'an elegant stand of polished stone'. Modelled on the Yorkshire architect John Carr's design of the stands at Doncaster, there were two tiers of galleries for the spectators and 'Beneath, an excellent dwelling for the person who keeps it'.

# Kelso

This building, which is now the Members' stand after a hundred and sixty years of service, was erected to the west of a mile and a quarter circuit which is still in use and provides one of the sharpest hurdle tracks in Britain. Before racing could get under way extensive drainage work had to be carried out on what became known as 'the Duke's Course'.

Unhappily, the Duke did not live to see the fruits of his benevolence and enthusiasm, departing this life shortly before the inaugural meeting at Berrymoss on 16 April 1823. The Clerk of the Course was Mr Robert Bruce, the crowds were 'immense', and the first hunters' flat race went to Sir Thomas, ridden by Captain Campbell and winning by 'half a head'.

For a time all was well, and the Caledonians took over the course for a week of racing and revels in October, 1824, but in an age when patronage was important socially and financially, the deaths of the old Duke and Sir Alexander Don weakened Kelso's position. Attempts to broaden the appeal of both the April and October fixtures by the introduction of races for farmers and 'members of any Yeomanry Corps' were successful in boosting the fields, if not the quality of jockeyship, in the late 1830s and early 40s. Also, the enterprising efforts of a new Clerk of the Course, James Hunter, brought good horses to Kelso to race under Jockey Club Rules, notably Lanercost, known to Scottish enthusiasts as 'Lazy' Lanercost and winner of the Ayr Gold Cup in 1839 before going south to Newmarket with jockey William Noble to collect the inaugural race for the Cambridgeshire under top weight.

Prize money too was boosted and the October 1840 fixture, attended by the Caledonians, was described by John Fairfax-Blakeborough in his *History of Horse Racing in Scotland* as 'the most ambitious yet arranged for Kelso'.

'The Ladies of the North' presented a plate worth 100 guineas, the Roxburghe Gold Cup was valued at 200 guineas, and Lord Eglinton's Dr Caius won the Caledonian St Leger. No doubt the rafters of the Cross Keys Hotel rang with merriment late into the night when the Caledonians met up with 'The Ladies of the North'.

After all, as one of racing's finest administrators, the late Geoffrey Freer, was fond of saying 'racing is meant to be fun', and anyone who does not believe that should stay well away from the racecourse. But for the Caledonians, their ladies and for Kelso, the fun was to be short lived. By 1847, very few horses were fulfilling their engagements and racing was discontinued in 1849.

However, the Caledonian Hunt held their own meeting at Kelso in 1853, and joined with the seventh Duke of Roxburghe in forming the Border Racing Club 'for the purpose of giving increased encouragement and support to racing in the eastern part of Scotland and northern parts of England'.

This move restored the sport on a fairly regular basis, but Kelso's chequered flat racing career finally petered out after the only surviving one day card under Rules was run for total prize money of £610 on 28 September 1888. Meanwhile, the future for Kelso had been assured when the United Border Hunt Steeplechases had been transferred from Stodrig five years earlier.

The 1883 programme of six events included the Open Hunt Steeplechase of £60, and the United Border Hunt Steeplechase of £30 for local packs, plus the usual hunters' flat races. The move from Stodrig had been motivated by a difference of opinion between Mr John Usher, on whose land the racing took place, and the Committee of the Border Racing Club over the construction of the open ditches.

The Club did not think a guard-rail was necessary on the take-off side of the ditch; Mr Usher demurred, and insisted that a rail was imperative in the interests of safety. The Club huffily moved to the declining Berrymoss, but were sporting enough to appoint Usher as the judge for the first meeting.

Within two years, Usher was vindicated and all ditches were protected by a guard-rail, as they are on every course today, and thus John Usher found his niche in history and steeplechasing came to Kelso.

However, it soon became evident that the original circuit was too small for chasing, and with the co-operation of the tenant farmer, Mr Dames, three fields which were part of the adjoining Hendersyde Park estate owned by Sir Richard Waldie Griffith were made available to extend the track and

three jumps built on them. Until 1925, at least one field was always under plough, but this was not unusual on steeplechase courses and this terrain and the three obstacles constitute the back straight at Kelso today.

Sir Richard was a leading owner of the period and was third in the owners' list in 1899. His fortune was based not so much on his Scottish land as a collection of coal mines in Bohemia, and this income ceased on the outbreak of war in 1914. Having served in France at the age of 64, he died in 1933, still attempting to claim £5,000,000 from the Government of what had become Czechoslovakia, but in the meantime Sir Richard's estate at Hendersyde had been broken up and the eighth Duke of Roxburghe stepped in in 1926 to purchase the three fields of the back straight and ensured the continuity of racing.

Meanwhile, no less a figure than Sir Loftus Bates had become Clerk of the Course in 1897. Sir Loftus, Brigadier-General, D.S.O., former trainer and variously Clerk at Hamilton, Carlisle, Hexham, Perth, Thirsk, Pontefract and Catterick, was one of the great racing impresarios of the time. In 1928 a company was formed under the name of the United Border Hunt Steeplechase Ltd to lease the land from the Roxburghe estate and secure the continuity of racing. Sir Loftus eventually handed over control to his son, Captain Giles Bates, but served as Managing Director at Kelso almost up to his death in 1951.

The Second World War brought 'devastation and ruin' in the words of John Fairfax-Blakeborough; the damage not caused by enemy action, but, as at Newbury, by the military occupation. Alec McHarg took over as clerk when racing resumed, to be succeeded in turn by his son Bill and grandson David.

As I write, Peter Scudamore has just ridden his 1,139th winner from 5,823 rides to become the most successful National Hunt jockey. His winning percentage is 19.56, his total was gained in his twelfth season, and doubtless there are more winners to come. Comparisons between generations in racing are a futile as they are fascinating, but it is interesting to reflect on Scudamore's

achievement in the light of Charlie Cunningham's nineteenth century record. Cunningham was born at Morebattle Tofts, about ten miles from Kelso. An intended military career was thwarted by the premature death of his father, but the army's loss was racing's gain when he settled down to the life of a country squire on his Border estates. Six feet two inches in height and going to scale at little less then twelve stone, most of his victories were inevitably in hunters' races, but he also won the Scottish Grand National four times within eight years, a record which still stands, and was second in the 1889 Liverpool National on Why Not. Cunningham had to sweat down to 11st 5lb to do the weight on Why Not, only to be beaten a length by Frigate, who was receiving 1lb. Two years later he was nearly killed when Why Not fell at the last at Aintree when well in contention.

Charlie Cunningham took part in 952 races, rode 417 winners, was placed on 305 occasions, being out of the money in only 230 of his contests, and his winning percentage was 43.8. The nineteenth century world which Cunningham inhabited was light years away from modern high speed travel and I do not suppose there were too many mild winters in the rugged Border country.

Cunningham was paid the handsome compliment of being barred, at least unofficially, from riding at Whitehaven as no other jockey would take the field against him. An amateur in the true sense at a time when

CHARLIE CUNNINGHAM.

quite a number of 'gentleman' riders were wearing the Bond Street pavements thin as they collected their Asprey's cigarette case (the usual present to a winning amateur jockey) in cash, Cunningham was the kind of sportsman par excellence who formed the backbone of National Hunt racing in the central years of the game's development. As Will Ogilvie wrote, doubtless with men like Charlie Cunningham in mind:

*So they forge through wind and weather*
*To the creak of straining leather,*
*Lashing at the leaps together,*
*With the fluttering flags to guide them,*
*Taking what the fates provide them.*
*'Tis a game beyond gainsaying,*
*Made by Gods for brave men's playing.*

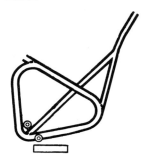

# KEMPTON

'Kempton is like a sirloin of beef cut the wrong way.' – Fred Archer.

THAT is a comment from a man who should have known, although he was discussing flat racing and his acquaintance with National Hunt sport was limited to a win in a Galloway (pony) steeplechase at Bangor in 1869, the first winner for the future champion. Given the difficulties he experienced with his weight, Archer's knowledge of beef sirloins could not have been very extensive, either.

However Archer was not alone in his criticism of Kempton when the course opened in 1878. Sir George Chetwynd, a Steward of the Jockey Club, complained that the jockeys never could obey orders, as sharp the turn into the short straight equally negated instructions to ride a waiting race or to make the running.

Sir George later had to quit the Turf when the inconsistent form of his horses became an open scandal, and may well have been talking through an inadequately lined pocket while again his comments applied principally to the flat. Nonetheless there was plenty of carping about the steeplechase track as well. In 1903 F.H. Bayles reckoned that the water jump came too soon after the turn beyond the stands, although this plea fell on deaf ears; the water is still in its original position and perhaps not the hazard Bayles imagined it to be.

However it was not until George Boon became Clerk of the Course in 1972 that fences were re-sited to give Kempton the status of a top class National Hunt track which it now enjoys.

The story began in 1872 when Mr S.H. Hyde came to London for Derby week. A descendant of the Lancashire cotton kings who so happily combined the slave trade with the textile business, Hyde was a frustrated Tory agent in a Bristol constituency. Presumably he could not get his candidate elected, but this cannot have been easy at a time of fluctuating parliamentary fortunes when not even the brilliance of Disraeli could command a Tory majority in the Commons.

Accordingly Hyde studied racecourse management under John Frail, a member of the distinguished family of Turf administrators, and decided to open his own track. Taking a day away from the dust of Epsom following Cremorne's victory, Hyde and his wife embarked on a steamer trip up the Thames followed by a drive in the country.

As the horses clip-clopped through leafy Middlesex, Hyde spotted a sign advertising the Manor of Kempton together with a park of four hundred acres. Wandering in the glade of chestnut trees where the future Queen Elizabeth I was courted by Prince Philip of Spain, Hyde realised that he had found a home for his family and his racecourse.

The land had a sporting heritage dating from the days when Henry III built a hunting lodge and stocked the park with deer. Hyde thus felt that the portents were in his favour and lost no time in leasing the property and putting work in hand to open a 'drawing room' course modelled on the successful style which Sandown pioneered.

Kempton soon became a haunt of the Marlborough House set led by the Prince of Wales whose interest in racing had been stimulated while relaxing from the diplomatic longeurs of a tour of India in 1876. Fairplay won the appropriately named Royal Handicap Steeplechase in the Prince's colours on 29 April 1882, but the most famous steeplechaser to sport royal silks was Ambush II.

Trained and ridden by Henry Linde's pupil at the Curragh, Algy Anthony, Ambush II came from Ireland to win the Grand National in 1900 for the future King Edward VII. Having been off the course throughout the year of Royal mourning for the death of Queen Victoria in 1901, Ambush II reappeared at Kempton in February 1902 and won the Stand Steeplechase.

Although he won eight chases for the King, Ambush could not be called a lucky horse. Apart from his enforced rest in 1901, he split a pastern before the 1902 National and did not run again before the Stewards' Steeplechase at Kempton on 30 January 1903.

Here in the words of the reporter from the *Illustrated London News*, 'the animal unfortunately had a mishap at the water jump and came in a bad fourth.' Ambush

almost certainly needed the race, but worse was to follow when he fell at Aintree's last fence with the National at his mercy. A fall at the third a year later finished the career of the only National winner in royal ownership.

As the German Zeppelins floated through the skies of Europe in 1915 Kempton became a transit depot for military vehicles soon after Ernie Piggott had won the Bushey Park Handicap Hurdle by four lengths on Toiler at the final meeting on 22 February. It was 1919 before Kempton could reopen, unscathed by enemy action but with £43,844 compensation due for damage caused by a destructive combination of moles on the course and the British army on the stands.

In the 1920s Kempton introduced an optional selling chase over three miles. An optional seller was a race in which an owner may enter a horse to be sold or claimed in the usual way, but might opt for the choice of running inviolate of those conditions. If he opted for the latter the horse was burdened with considerably more weight than those runners who could change hands. Thus, for example, the 1921 Grand National winner Shaun Spadah carried 12st 7lb in the Manor Optional Selling Chase at Kempton on 22 February 1924, and finished fourth to Greenogue, partnered by Anthony Escott.

Greenogue was sold for 270 guineas; Shaun Spadah was no back number at the age of thirteen and had already won the Brook Chase at Gatwick in January. Ridden as always by his beloved Dick Rees, he lived to fight another day and was still winning

THE KING INSPECTS AMBUSH II AS ALGY ANTHONY PREPARES TO MOUNT, KEMPTON 1903.

races at Sandown in 1924, when he beat the 1922 National winner Music Hall in a match by 10 lengths at 13/8 on.

Having survived the fire of 1932 which put Kempton out of action for five months, the Manor Optional Selling Chase was still in the Calendar for the late February meeting of 1937, but events beyond the trivialities of racing were playing their part. Edward VIII had become king in January 1936 on the death of George V, but a matrimonial and constitutional crisis forced his abdication in December of the same year.

The Kempton Park executive planned a tribute to the new King, only to find themselves with a problem similar to a manufacturer of Coronation mugs with Edward VIII already embossed on the side. Using commendable presence of mind, they turned the Manor Optional Selling Chase into the King George VI Steeplechase, worth £500 to the winner, plus a piece of plate worth £50 to the successful trainer.

On the face of it this was not an attractive prize for a three mile chase even by standards of the time, but all the top horses entered, including Golden Miller, the dual Grand National winner Reynoldstown, and the up and coming Royal Mail. The latter pair were sons of My Prince who also sired Gregalach, Easter Hero, and Prince Regent.

In the event Reynoldstown did not run and Golden Miller also defected, declining a re-match with Royal Mail who had beaten him in the Becher Chase at Liverpool in November. Perhaps ironically the Miller's

connections went for the Optional Selling Chase at Birmingham on the Monday before the King George, and picked up a prize of £127.

Nonetheless the quartet who finally faced the starter at Kempton on Friday, 26 February 26 1937 did not lack quality. Royal Mail was the 7/1 ante-post favourite for the Grand National, Southern Hero was at the time a dual Scottish Grand National winner, and Brienz had finished third to Trigo in the 1929 Derby as well as being a course winner in the Coventry Chase and a good fourth in the Gold Cup behind Golden Miller, beating Southern Hero.

The rains came down and a sodden crowd watched Southern Hero plough through the mud to beat Royal Mail by four lengths with Brienz two lengths back in third. The following month Royal Mail won the National and in 1939 Southern Hero won his third Scottish National. The King George Chase had arrived, only to depart as the shadows of war lengthened after Airgead Sios had won in 1938 for Epsom trainer Victor Tabor.

Once again Kempton had to suffer the indignities common to so many racecourses in time of war and become a depot or a dump; on this occasion Kempton played reluctant host to prisoners of war until the last was repatriated by September, 1946.

Racing resumed in 1947 and the King George was moved from the February meeting to Boxing Day. The advantage was that the race would no longer be a severe test too close to Cheltenham and Liverpool; the dis-

ROYAL MAIL RIDDEN BY HIS OWNER HUW LLOYD THOMAS.

advantage was the harsh mid-winter weather and the post-Christmas sloth of a nation happy before blazing fires with hairs of the dog in their hands.

The gamble paid off and Rowland Roy won from Klaxton and Fortune Founded in perfect sharp winter weather. The field reads like a Who's Who of the sport; Rowland Roy was trained by Fulke Walwyn, who had been leading amateur three times and won the National on Reynoldstown; he was already champion trainer. Rowland Roy's jockey Bryan Marshall had survived a bullet in the neck during the Normandy landings and was en route to becoming champion jockey; Klaxton's rider Ron Smyth rode three

Champion Hurdlers to victory: and Fortina's partner Dickie Black had ridden him to take the Gold Cup.

The punters came too, and soon an afternoon in the brisk fresh air to blow away the cobwebs of festive excess became as traditional a Londoners' day out as Derby Day had been for generations. The King George was back to stay, and the roll of honour abounds with equine heroes. Cottage Rake won in 1948, Her Majesty Queen Elizabeth won with Manicou in 1950 and Mandarin triumphed in '57 and '59. Another dual winner was Halloween, and Statecraft and Lochroe carried the Mildmay colours to victory in 1954 and 1958.

HALLOWEEN AND FRED WINTER.

The giants of the sixties, Mill House and Arkle, won in 1963 and 1965 respectively, but the next year Arkle broke a pedal bone and limped home behind Dormant in what was to be the champion's last race. Kempton Park itself came under threat from that menace of the pendulum years, the property developer. Hurst Park had already gone in 1962 to become a housing estate, and Sandown survived a similar fate only after a government enquiry at ministerial level in 1963. Kempton came under pressure in the first instance because of the valuable gravel deposits on the now three hundred acre estate, but few could doubt that if the park fell into unsympathetic hands, development would follow and racing be extinguished.

A sale was averted but as the gravel was extracted under licence, Kempton declined in both the standard of sport and facilities for the racegoer.

The engineering firm of Taylor Woodrow tried to buy the property in 1969 but were outbid by the millionaire racing buff and philanthropist, Mr (later Sir) David Robinson.

Sir David was a self-made man who had the misfortune to be ahead of his time. His plans for a giant leisure complex on American lines incorporating a race track and a park to be used on non-racing days were frustrated by the planning mandarins, but with typical generosity he sold Kempton at cost price to the Levy Board and the course passed to the Board's subsidiary United Racecourses which was in charge at Epsom and Sandown.

George Boon took over as clerk of the course in 1972 and revamped the tired image of a course which had acquired the reputation of being the poor relation of suburban racing. A key improvement was the re-siting of the stable block adjacent to the paddock from the original building hard by the open ditch. This fence was a difficult enough hazard at the best of times and it did not help a horse's concentration when he spotted a nice warm stable, greatly preferable to being kicked and goaded over another mile or so of birch fences. In the words of Tim Fitzgeorge-Parker, 'the horse's ears went backwards and forwards. . . . it was a nasty feeling for the rider.'

Crisis on all fronts having been averted, Kempton marched firmly into the future with the King George still attracting the best of the best, with The Dikler, dual winners

DESERT ORCHID AND
RICHARD DUNWOODY, 1989.

Pendil, Captain Christy and Silver Buck, while Wayward Lad was successful in 1982, '83 and '85.

And so to 'Dessiemania', a fever inspired in the followers of Desert Orchid, winner of the King George in 1986, '88 and '89. It is impossible to calculate the pleasure which this modestly-bred grey horse has given to millions of people, many of whom do not go racing and know nothing of racing life.

As always in the bitter-sweet brew of National Hunt sport, such pleasure is not cheaply bought. The day after 'Dessie's' third King George triumph had left his supporters grappling with each other to get to the unsaddling spot with all the fervour of Vietnamese boat people catching the last junk to freedom, the hopelessly over-matched novice chaser Manton Mark was killed in a fall at the second fence and Methano collapsed and died after finishing third in a novice hurdle race.

The joy on the face of Desert Orchid's girl attendant was in bitter contrast to the tears in the eyes of Methano's lad as the corpse of his horse was heaved into the knacker's van. There will be no 'Methiemania'.

KEMPTON, FEBRUARY, 1988.

# LEICESTER

*Now for the fences and now for the flags on 'em;*
*Now for the half breds in mud to the hocks;*
*Now for the riders with jolly red rags on 'em*
*Out of respect to old Reynard the Fox.*

Will H. Ogilvie

**S**O wrote Ogilvie in his evocative poem Point to Point. Racing between the flags has always signalled the days of celebration for the fox hunting fraternity and in no other county of Britain do they pursue the fox with greater enthusiasm than in Leicestershire. The most fashionable hunt is probably the Quorn, favoured by His Royal Highness the Prince of Wales, which enjoyed its heyday when Hugh Lowther, fifth Earl of Lonsdale, was Master in the 'Naughty Nineties'.

Known as 'the Yellow Earl', Lonsdale was a superb exponent of the art of fox hunting with a fine eye for a line of country. Little missed his attention; every movement of stock and every sudden turning of a flock of birds registered swiftly in the sharp brain of a born hunting man. He was also a stern disciplinarian in the field and dealt severely with the 'hooray hooligans' and thrusters. Even Lord 'Hoppy' Manners, a former Master and winner of the Grand National on Seaman did not escape the accusation of over-riding the hounds. Manners was, though, entirely innocent; the pack had run in a circle and he was simply being lapped.

The house parties hosted by the hunting set provided plenty of opportunity for fun of

LORD LONSDALE.

a different kind in the evenings, after be-slippered ladies and gentlemen had consumed a hearty tea before a blazing fire followed by a lengthy dinner. Grace, Lady Lonsdale, recorded in her diary on one occasion 'Jolly fun after dinner. . . . a game of hide-and-seek with Lord B. and I as searchers. We couldn't find many people, so after a time we gave up and I went to bed.' On another occasion, long after lights had ben extinguished, Lord Lonsdale set out along winding corridors in the darkness to see if his fellow guest, Mrs Edward Langtry, was in a receptive mood. As he was feeling his way with caution his outstretched hand encountered the elegant shape of the beard sported by the Prince of Wales coming from the opposite direction.

An encounter of a different kind at a hunting house party was to change the history of England. At Melton Mowbray in 1931 the then Prince of Wales met Mrs Wallis Simpson. They discussed central heating, an unlikely topic to spark a romance which caused a major constitutional crisis and led to the abdication of a monarch.

Since hunting is the foundation stone of the National Hunt sport it is surprising that no major course has survived in the Midlands which is the heartland of the hunting community. It is a case of quantity rather than great quality, and Leicester is one of those minor tracks known in the jargon as 'a trainers' course'. Stiff and severe, it is ideally located for most training centres and provides plenty of opportunities for novices and moderate horses.

One such novice, at least at the time, was Golden Miller, whose victory in the Gopsall Maiden Hurdle on 20 January, 1931 was the first in the career of a champion; Leicester was good at finding human champions, too, as the local visitors had seen Gordon Richards ride the first of 4870 winners ten years earlier.

Racing at Oadby started in 1884 when Tom Cannon laid out a track to replace the one at Victoria Park, considered by the Jockey Club to be unsuitable for racing which had been held at Leicester since 23 March 1603, the penultimate day of the reign of Queen Elizabeth I. The sport was under the patronage of the Earl of Rutland who provided five shillings and eightpence worth of sack, plus a pound of sugar for 'the gentlemen at the horse running'.

The sugar is an intriguing item and later in the year the Earl kindly disbursed 9/4d to pay for a gallon of sack and two gallons of claret for some thirsty chaps, Sir Thomas Griffin, Sir William Faunt and 'other gentlemen', based at the Angel for the races.

It must have been quite a party. The races were run at Abbey Meadow, and were successful enough to warrant a transfer to St Mary's Field in 1741 when a local entrepreneur by the name of Langton found it profitable to hire the Town Hall to accommodate visitors to the meetings.

There were two principal events, the Burgesses' Purse and the Gentlemen's Plate run off in the usual heats; one race could last all day which is more than the contestants Gamester, Duster and Marcus did in 1783. The heats were so closely run that the punters started fighting over the steward's (judge's) decisions and the poor animals were almost literally knackered.

The customary non-conformist moralists put their spoke in around the turn of the century and following the enclosure of the fields the meeting moved to Victoria Park. A certain Major Morris donated the proceeds of a handsome win by his Two-Shoes to erect a grandstand and racing got under way at the new venue in 1806.

By now the Earldom of Rutland had been translated to a Dukedom (in 1703) and His Grace was on hand from Belvoir Castle to add twenty guineas to the prize money for the Belvoir Stakes, the opening race on the card.

Victoria Park prospered and at the time of the closure enforced by the Jockey Club in the teeth of a petition signed by eleven thousand punters was presenting a series of two day meetings with mixed cards in spring and autumn.

The protests were of no avail, and racing at the Park ended on Friday 7 September 1883. John Osborne rode the winner of the final flat race, Her Majesty's Plate of £210, on Ishmael, and George Lambton partnered Julius to win the opener, the Selling Hunters' Hurdle. The horse was bought out of the race for one hundred guineas by a Mr Taylor, and Lambton proceeded to take the final event on the card and at Victoria Park by steering Julius to victory in the Harborough Hurdle, sporting the new owner's colours.

Oadby was not an immediate success, especially from the social point of view, and although the meetings were well supported by trainers, and many top class riders competed, the steeplechase track came in for a good deal of criticism. An attempt to maintain a natural line resulted in a twisting course with a hideous drop fence, and two mile races finished over a brook opposite the stand, with a plain fence to be taken at the end of the three miles alongside it. This arrangement gave rise to a certain amount of controversy in March 1902 when only two runners went to post for a three mile chase.

Mr Brockton rode the 7/2 on Hillmorton while his opponent Gossip had the services of a professional jockey H. Hewitt.

Described as being 'three fields in front' as he approached what he though was the last obstacle, Hewitt and Gossip jumped the brook, thus taking the wrong course, and by the time the jockey had realised his error and pulled up to turn around, Mr Brockton and the favourite had strolled home alone. In the words of the contemporary reporter 'To reiterate the benedictions bestowed (in the 'bookies' vernacular) on the anatomy of Mr Brockton would not elevate the pages to a turf classic, I am afraid.'

The matter was soon rectified with the brook removed to the far side and a single fence for all races built in its place. The whole National Hunt track was then realigned on the inside of Tom Cannon's flat course.

And so matters have much remained. Leicester never really recovered the social cachet of Victoria Park, as signified by a recent decision to abolish the annual membership, and nowadays, would be considered townie rather than horsey, though Golden Miller is remembered by a hurdle race in his honour at the third January meeting.

# LINGFIELD

'A CHARMING little fixture, halfway between London and Brighton, with a station closely adjacent to the course. It was established in the year 1890 as a steeplechase and hurdle race fixture, but in the year 1894, a petition was presented to the Stewards of the Jockey Club asking for Lingfield to be recognised under flat-racing rules. This being granted, its energetic committee, with the brightest of hopes for a good future, set to work to make their new undertaking a success which it now undoubtedly is. Much labour, of course, was entailed, and possibly some anxious moments were passed in securing this good result, for it is no easy matter now-a-days to embark upon and carry out to a happy issue a racing enterprise against the numerous and (in this case at any rate) neighbouring oppositions which already exist. But the

THE ALL WEATHER TRACK

Lingfield executive piloted their ship without mishap through all the shoals and quicksands which beset them, and it is now, with skilful management and under Royal favour, safely anchored in the harbour of success. I believe I am correct in stating that the initial outlay was £75,000. This money has been most judiciously expended . . . (and) that all-essential feature, the cultivation of the ground, has received it's due share of careful attention.'

So F. H. Bayles reported on the course at Lingfield in his *Race Courses Atlas* of 1903. Bayles added the rider that the course would 'always be very deep in bad weather.'

In this he was not mistaken and many Lingfield meetings were to be lost due to waterlogging in future years. It was not until the mid 1980s that extensive drainage work remedied the problem and it was no surprise that Lingfield was the first course to stage racing on an all-weather surface on 30 October 1989.

Although the construction of the all-weather track inevitably spoiled some of the charm which entranced Bayles at the course known for years as 'Lovely Lingfield', the atmosphere remains much as the great geologist found it.

The first race at the inaugural meeting in November 1890 was the Selling Hunters' Flat Race of £98 over two miles and the winner, Mr Harvey Spiller's Old Tatt ridden by Mr W. E. Drury gave first blood to the punters as Old Tatt started at 4/1 on.

Bill Dollery, who was to win the 1893 Grand National on Cloister, took the three mile chase on Gamecock, the Liverpool hero in 1887, and Chancery won a two mile chase for William Nightingall, the father of 'Saturday Specialist' Walter. Nightingall jun trained at Epsom and turned out many winners in the pink and chocolate colours of Sir Winston Churchill.

In 1892 Lingfield staged a four and a half mile chase, rather ambitiously styled 'The Grand National Chase'. The winner was Rosaline, partnered by Captain Percy Bewicke, the champion amateur in both 1891 and 1892. The 'Royal favour' noted by Bayles came in 1894 at a flat race meeting attended by the Prince of Wales and although Lingfield managed to establish two important races in the thirties, the Derby and Oaks Trials, the track has never aspired to any equivalent events over fences and hurdles.

Nonetheless, the level of prize money has always been reasonable and the easy nature of the course tempted many of the equine stars to an agreeable workout before a big race. Troytown, the National winner in 1920, and the great Manifesto, dual winner in 1897 and 1899 preceded Easter Hero, Golden Miller, Prince Regent, Devon Loch, Halloween and Mandarin on the Lingfield stape.

Even Steve Donoghue was happy to take a rare ride over hurdles in his early days, finishing a poor fourth when claiming the 5lb allowance on Labadens, 6/4 favourite for the Surrey Handicap Selling Hurdle.

EASTER HERO, LETCOMBE REGIS, BERKSHIRE,1931.

Greater glories were awaiting Steve in the glamorous sphere of flat racing, but a more skilful hurdles jockey, George Duller, rode many winners at Lingfield, including Easter Hero who was warming up for his first Cheltenham Gold Cup in the Crowhurst Hurdle on 14 December 1928.

Fred Wilmot was Clerk of the Course during Lingfield's heyday in the 1930s when the classic trials were founded, but he retired in 1939 and it was one of the racing's finest impresarios, Sir John Crocker Bulteel, who saw the track safely relaunched following military occupation during the war.

Soon afterwards Peter Beckwith-Smith, a member of the founding family of Lingfield, took charge of the leafy course with the then delightfully Wodehouseian telephone number 'Lingfield 9' which always reminded the author of Blandings Castle, although that fictitious exchange was 'Loose Chippings'.

With the economic misery of the seventies, Major Beckwith-Smith was forced to decide that Lingfield was no longer viable for a private family concern. The bookmaking firm of Ladbrokes purchased the course for £500,000 and were allowed to operate after some head-scratching by the Home

# Lingfield

Office mandarins who were not easily persuaded that the 'old enemy' should be allowed to run a racecourse. However, refusal would have meant closure and the new Clerk of the Course, John Hughes, was not a man to compromise with any employer, so reluctant consent enabled Hughes to run the track with all his flair, enthusiasm and ingenuity. This latter quality was much in evidence when Southern Television, at the time holders of the independent television franchise for the area, agreed to cover three races from an evening meeting in August 1977. Frustrated by Jockey Club planners who refused to grant a night fixture, Hughes neatly thwarted bureaucracy by starting an 'afternoon' meeting at 4.00, thus putting the last three races into Southern's schedule, and the programme went ahead with the author combining the roles of paddock commentator and Southern's 'Mystery Tipster'; punters noted a singular lack of success so far as the tips were concerned.

Ladbrokes sold out to Ron Muddle in 1982 and it was he who carried out the improvements which included the much-needed drainage work and a re-alignment of the bend into the straight. Muddle in turn passed ownership to Leisure Investments for £7,000,000 in 1988, but fifteen months later a boardroom row involving the resignation of the chairman left Lingfield on the market once again and the course was sold to the Courtwell Group in early 1990.

Unhappily Courtwell, orginally a hosiery firm, met serious financial difficulties. The company's shares slumped from ten pence to one half penny in four months and at the time of writing the atmosphere is not a happy one in which to celebrate Lingfield's centenary.

In 1903, the nearby Dorman's Park Hotel was advertised as 'a magnificent hostelry . . . one and a quarter miles from the paddock . . . and there is a motor garage', thus proving that Lingfield has always looked to the future (doubtless the garage had a rack for the man with the red flag to rest his warning symbol). Let us hope that before these words have been printed a lasting future can be assured for what was racing's most elegant minor course.

# LIVERPOOL

*'Woe worth the chase, woe worth the day,*
*That cost thy life, my gallant grey.'*
'Nimrod' (Charles Apperley)

'**O**UR readers who have paid particular attention to the observations we have frequently made on the subject of popular recreations will not be surprised that we do not on this occasion partake of the enthusiasm with which the great steeplechase, as it is styled, seems to have inspired our townspeople. It was no doubt a very exciting spectacle, but we no more be reconciled to it on that account than we are to cockfighting, bullbaiting or any other popular pastime which is attended with the infliction of wanton torture to any living being. That these steeplechases are of this nature will hardly be denied even by those who are most ardently attached to such sport'.

'In ordinary hunting the sportsman can choose his ground and avoid those perilous leaps which might endanger his own life and that of his horse, but in these steeplechases the most formidable obstacles are artificially placed in the course which the horse must take and the almost certain result is the death of some of the noble animals thus wantonly urged on to their own destruction'.

'With these views . . . we need scarcely add that we have heard with alarm and regret that it is in contemplation to establish steeplechasing annually . . . in this neighbourhood. If any such design is seriously entertained we trust that some means will be adopted to defeat it. We would not decapitate them (the owners) but we would compell them . . . to go through the purgatory of a steeplechase with sturdy drivers at their heels to urge them over hedge and ditch . . . and when they arrived (at the finish) they should do penance in white sheets or horse clothes in the church until they confessed their iniquities and promised to be more merciful to their animals'.

So propounded the Editor of the *Liverpool Mercury* on the day after the third Grand National, then known as the Grand Liverpool Steeplechase, and run on Tuesday, 26 February 1839. One hundred and fifty years later, headlines in the *Sporting Life* and the *Racing Post* had a distinct flavour of déjà vu; 'Jockey Club probes safety of National' proclaimed the Life, under the heading 'Action as outcry grows over fatalities'. The Post editorialised on 'An ugly National truth which can be ignored no longer' and the local RSPCA superintendent, a veteran of nineteen Nationals, bitterly inquired 'Does it (the National) cease to be a spectacle if horses don't die?'

Two horses had been killed in falls at Becher's Brook and one, Brown Trix, fell back into the brook into which Captain Becher had crept when his mount fell in the 1839 race, thus naming the most notorious fence on the Liverpool circuit. Becher survived the ducking, but another horse, Dictator, met his death, after falling badly and being severely injured at a water jump. Ruthlessly remounted by his jockey, Carlin, Dictator fell and broke his back at the next obstacle, one of countless brave animals destined to die in the name of the National.

Controversy has never been a stranger to Liverpool, either to the city, the racecourse or the Grand National which, like the Derby, has been much imitated but never equalled.

In 1839 James Whyte described Liverpool as 'an important town, which ranks first after the metropolis with 'docks . . . on a scale of almost unparalled magnitude.' Attractions, apart from the racecourse at Aintree, then about six miles to the north-east of the town, included three theatres, a Diorama and a music hall.

The author is too young to remember the Diorama, an early form of cinema where clever lighting gave the illusion of movement to a still picture, usually a famous painting, but he does recall getting 'the bird' at the Empire music hall where the audience, traditionally garbed in stained raincoats, were impatient to see the nude chorus girls swimming in a giant fish tank.

Liverpool was first known as a thriving fishing village in the year 1200 and was granted a charter by King John many centuries before the slave trade, which also incorporated the textile industry, became the foundation of the city's early nineteenth century prosperity. The export-import tech-nique was simple. The Liverpool 'slavers' carried cargoes of finished Lancashire cotton goods to Africa, exchanged them for negroes who were then transported in the hold to America and traded for raw cotton for import to Liverpool and thus re-started the cycle, as the fresh slaves picked the cotton to feed the rapacious Lancashire textile industry. William Lynn was happy enough to cater for the rich cotton merchants at his popular Waterloo Hotel and was renowned as 'the best fish-cook in the world'. He was also a keen sportsman and a co-founder of the Waterloo Cup. He combined his sporting and catering interests when he rented the grandstand at nearby Maghull race-course and supplied the hungry and thirsty punters who patronised the flat race track opened by John Formby in 1827; doubtless cooked fish was a standing dish.

Racing had been recorded in the Liverpool area as early as 1576, when a silver bell worth £6.13.4d was competed for at Crosby over a four mile course, and there are records of a three day meeting at Ormskirk in 1765, but by 1786 both meet-ings had petered out from lack of support.

John Formby's course at Maghull was laid out on land purchased by his father-in-law from the Earl of Sefton. Lynn was a member of the Maghull committee in 1828, but the standard of racing was not high and Lynn had plans of his own based on the success of a steeplechase course founded at St Albans in 1830 by a fellow hotelier, Tom Coleman.

Steeplechasing had originated in Ireland,

in 1752, when a match was recorded between Mr O'Calloghan and Mr Edmund Blake over four and a half miles of country from the church of Buttevant to the spire of St Leger church. By 1803 the Irish hunts were organising 'regular steeplechases' for the prizes of a hogshead of claret, a pipe of port and a quarter cask of rum.

In England the first recorded steeplechase had taken place in Leicestershire in 1790. The eight mile course was from Barkby Holt to the Billesdon Coplow and back. The winner was Mr Charles Meynell, son of the local Master of Foxhounds, with Lord Forester second and Sir Gilbert Heathcote third. It seems that Sir Gilbert's mount 'was rather fat' and that a Mr Needham of Hungerton, doubtless with a financial interest in the fortunes of Lord Forester's mount, which was favourite, offered his lordship the opportunity to save a hundred yards by taking a short cut through Needham's garden.

By 1825 the sport had become a popular amusement amongst the hunting fraternity who for many years had prepared for the chase 'before a good blazing fire at six a.m., a splendid buttock of beef or a venison pasty, with chocolate, besides a jug of old October'; and Lynn decided to emulate Coleman's commercial success at St Albans.

Much to Formby's publicly expressed chagrin, Lynn did a deal with Lord Sefton's heir, Lord Molyneux, and leased the land adjoining Maghull in July 1828. The property adjoined the village of Aintree, named in

the reign of Henry III after the original landlord, William Aintree. Aintree left a daughter who subsequently married Thomas Maghull, and the marriage of an heiress from this family to Ralph Molyneux led to the creation of the Viscountcy of Molyneux in 1628, which became the Earldom of Sefton in 1771.

Although at first limited to flat racing, Lynn's plans for Aintree were ambitious. A stand erected in 1829 for this inaugural meeting was four stories high and incorporated spacious cellars for the storing of Lynn's wines which were served in two twenty-eight feet drawing rooms, one for ladies the other for gentlemen enjoying a respite between races which could be observed from the ninety-one feet principal room over looking 'the raceground', or from the balcony extending for the length of the building.

For a time, racing at Liverpool alternated between the two courses, with the Spring Meeting at Maghull and the July and October events run at Aintree, but Formby could not compete with Lynn's superior entrepreneurial flair and the Racing Calendar recorded in Races to Come for 1835 that 'The proprietors of the Aintree and Maghull courses have made an arrangement by which the races at both meetings will be run on the former course'.

At the October Meeting in the same year, Lynn experimented with hurdle races for the first time, and the Formby Stakes, a mile and a half flat race for three-year-olds which had been a feature at Maghull, was run for the last time with that title. This was probably a gesture to Lynn's former partner; the following season the race became the Aintree Stakes.

So racing at Maghull came to an end in 1836 and Lynn was free to frame his first steeplechase. Originally, steeplechasing had been just that, running over a straight four or five miles from one church to another or 'steeple to steeple'. Tom Coleman's St Albans course made the obelisk at West Park, Silsoe, the turning point after two miles and the field started and finished at the same place before spectators anxious to know where their money had gone.

Realising that chasing was a spectacle which could appeal to a wider public than that necessarily confined by the sophisticated sport of flat racing, Lynn took a leaf out of Coleman's book and ensured that the punters attending his inaugural four mile chase over twenty fences and two hurdles could witness both the start and finish of the race. The conditions of Lynn's 1836 race specified that the contestants should carry twelve stone and be ridden by 'gentlemen', a stipulation probably intended more as a courtesy than to have any basis in reality. As Ivor Herbert and Patricia Smyly point out in *The Winter Kings* (1968) it would have been hard to define a gentleman rider in the 1830s and, most jockeys, even those with a handle or a title to their name, demonstrably rode for hire. Eleven years on, Adam Lindsay Gordon summed it up in *How We Beat The Favourite* –

*A gentleman rider? Well, I'm, an outsider*
*But if he's a gent, who the mischiefs a jock?*

There were ten runners for what can be fairly described as the prototype of the National and the The Duke ran out the winner in the capable hands of Captain Becher before a huge crowd including, as one observer noted with surprise, 'a high proportion of the middle-class'. It is hard to understand the astonishment, since although the lucrative slave trade had been abolished in 1807 there were ships amounting to 162,000 tons registered on Merseyside, principally for trade with The Americas.

There was plenty of money about and William Lynn scented a killing. He set about revising the conditions for 1837. The 1836 race had carried added money of £80 to a sweepstake of £10 each, with the proviso that the winner was to be sold for £200 'if demanded'. This stipulation was removed as Lynn realised that he must move up-market and that a seller would never achieve the status he wanted for his brainchild.

The town of Liverpool gave £100, and thus the 1837 race carried £180 added money, again to a sweepstake of £10, with weight-for-age conditions; four-year-olds were to carry 11st, five-year-olds 11st 7lb and six-year-olds and over were burdened with 12st. Lord Molyneux was appointed as umpire, and his duties were to choose the

LIVERPOOL GRANDSTAND, 1830.

course, make sure that the riders understood the layout, and to act as starter.

The last duty was not too onerous as only four horses took part. Lynn had made a rare error of managerial judgement which was perhaps indicative of things to come and had chosen to run on the day following Tom Coleman's 'Grand Annual' at St Albans which had been founded in 1832 and was then the top steeplechase in Britain. The Liverpool field suffered accordingly and even The Duke's regular jockey Captain Becher was absent in Hertfordshire. Consequently, Mr Henry Potts, a family friend of one of the horse's joint owners, Jonathan Williamson, rode The Duke to victory and ensured himself a permanent niche in the annals of the Turf.

In 1838, the town of Liverpool withdrew financial support in the face of mounting criticism from animal welfare groups, headed by the Society for Prevention of Cruelty to Animals. This society formed in the wake of the Ill Treatment of Horses Bill which had been sponsored by the M.P. for Galway 'Humanity' Martin and passed by Parliament in 1823. The prime targets of the bill were ruthless coachmen, carters and farmers, and many thought it hypocritical that 'gentlemen' whipping and spurring tired horses over walls and fences should escape prosecution in the name of 'sport' although in theory the provisions of Martin's bill applied equally.

It is a sad reflection that this is still the case today, although in recent years the Jockey Club has done much to mitigate the ill-treatment of horses while racing.

Lynn's answer was to lower the height of the Trial Fence, a six foot bank with a fringe of thorn which had halted the entire field in 1837. Coleman's St Albans 'Grand Annual' was declining in popularity, The Duke was a runner, with the intrepid Becher back in the plate, and ten horses faced Lord Molyneux' flag. The Duke was 2/1 favourite, but the old horse broke down in the final stages to become the National's first casualty. Sir William also went into the history books as the first Irish trained winner and his jockey Alan M'Donough was the first owner-rider to triumph. But for both The Duke and William Lynn, the sun was setting.

In 1839, the excitement was almost too much to bear. The opening of the rail link between Liverpool and Manchester coupled with the rapid spread of metalled roads pioneered by John Macadam, who barely lived to see the commercial success of his invention, brought unprecedented crowds to Aintree. Hotels were full, and guests were sleeping four to a bed, which must have been cosy. At nine o'clock on the day of the race, Tuesday, 26 February, a contemporary writer recorded 'The road leading to Aintree was crowded with pedestrians . . . pie-men, chimney sweeps, cigar sellers, thimble-riggers and all the small fry of gaming table keepers . . . not a coach or a cab was to be had for love or money . . . half a guinea was offered and refused for 2/6d tickets for a place in the omnibuses. . . . the Grandstand had not accommodation for more than threequarters of the people who presented themselves (at seven shillings for a single ticket and ten shillings for the two

THE LIVERPOOL-MANCHESTER RAILWAY LINK.

days of the meeting) and not an attainable point about the building, even to the very summit of the chimneys, was but occupied. . . . we fancy there could have been not fewer than forty to fifty thousand persons on the raceground.'

Lynn's dream had come true only to turn into a hideous nightmare. Just three days before the race he was forced to announce his retirement and handed the control of Aintree to the Trustees of a syndicate consisting of 1000 proprietorships of £25 each. The Trustees were headed by Lord Stanley and the race committee answerable to them included the Lords Derby and Sefton and that giant of mid-nineteenth century racing affairs, Lord George Bentinck.

Not much went wrong with racing when Bentinck was around; he was a man who made sure that everyone knew their place and, what's more, kept it. The National and Aintree were in safe hands for the foreseeable future but they had destroyed their creator. Lynn's resignation was ostensibly on the grounds of ill-health, but this was almost certainly a nervous breakdown induced by financial failure. He reckoned that he would have had a fortune of at least £30,000 if he had never had anything to do with 'the Race-course concern'. As it was, he bitterly remarked 'Now I have to begin the World over again after thirty years industry'.

Lynn paid all his creditors but although he retained a stake in Aintree and was asked to serve the committee in an advisory capacity, he never had the strength to 'begin the World over again' and died in impoverished obscurity in 1870 supported by the charity of his friends.

This is not intended to be a history of the Grand National, which has been well chronicled over the years, and certainly the 1839 race has received such a welter of publicity, doubtless inspired by the connection in the media mind between the name of the winner Lottery and the chancy nature of the event, that many consider it to have been the first National. It was not, but it did feature two of the outstanding riders of the period; Lottery's jockey Jem Mason and Captain Martin Becher. They could not have been more contrasting figures. The dour Becher was the son of an army officer turned farmer and served behind the lines as a store-keeper in Brussels at the time of Waterloo. He was awarded an honorary commission in the Buckinghamshire Yeomanry (the Duke of Buckingham was a distant relative) and his only military medal was for the not onerous task of parading outside Westminster Abbey at the coronation of another renowned racing character, King George IV.

Always a keen jockey, he was a big fish in a small puddle, riding numerous winners at local meetings in his native Norfolk. In time, his talent was noted by Tom Coleman, who made him first jockey to his string of steeplechasers. By 1829, he was riding at every track in England, carrying Coleman's colours of 'white, red sleeves, black cap' to victory from his base at Coleman's Turf Hotel, formerly the Chequers Tavern, in St Albans.

Becher's favourite party trick was to run around the dining room on the wainscoting without touching the floor and he possessed an ability to imitate animal noises which would have rivalled Percy Edwards.

It was Conrad who failed to clear a brook guarded by strong palings and a rough, high, jagged hedge and hurled Becher into the stream to give the gallant Captain an immortality unequalled in steeplechasing history, as he remarked that 'water was no damned use without brandy'.

However, Becher's most famous mounts were Vivian, on whom he won the Northamptonshire Steeplechase in 1834 and the inaugural Aylesbury chase the following year, and Grimaldi. After winning the St Albans steeplechase Grimaldi dropped dead shortly after passing the post. Becher had one of the animals forelegs pickled which he was proud to show to his friends.

Becher's last race was at Doncaster in 1847, when he fell on the Cantley Common course. He was appointed to the sinecure of Inspector of Sacks for the Great Northern Railway and died in 1864 at the age of sixty-seven. When his possessions were sold off his seven silk racing jackets worn on many a fabled day fetched five shillings between them.

As Michael Seth-Smith says in *The History of Steeplechasing*, Becher more than any other rider is the link between the earliest days of steeplechasing and the emergence of Liverpool as the greatest steeplechase course in the country.

Jem (James) Mason was an elegant, dandified figure, a throwback to Regency days. He always rode in white gloves, and his boots were made by Wren's of Knightsbridge and Bentley of Oxford Street, the former firm constructing the feet and the latter shaping the legs. The Mason family ran a coaching business in the village of Stilton, near Peterborough and famous for cheese.

Despite its proximity to the Great North Road, the business failed and the family moved to Pinner in what was then the county of Middlesex.

Tom Coleman's St Albans racecourse was not far away, and Jem's ability with horses in the hunting field soon drew the attention of a sporting parson of that diocese, the Reverend Lord Frederick Beauclerc. Lord Frederick was a brother of the Duke of St Albans and descendant of Charles Beaucler, the bastard son of King Charles 11 and Nell Gwynn. He owned a soured-up old dog of a horse called The Poet, a reject from the flat who was the despair of his jockeys and regarded racing as his reverend owner would regard purgatory.

Mason first rode The Poet in the 1834 St Albans Steeplechase on a course made a quagmire by persistent heavy rain. The jockey was putting up four stones of lead to make the weight of 12st and The Poet drew first blood by refusing at the initial obstacle. As the Reverend Lord Frederick's eyes turned heavenwards, Mason coaxed The Poet over the fence and, as Ivor Herbert and Patricia Smyly describe, rode 'with magic in his hands and quicksilver in his heels' to steer The Poet to a twenty length victory.

Mason went on to win every important race in the English calendar and became the first international steeplechase jockey, winning a big race in Paris on a horse called St Leger. His association with Lottery was as legendary as Pat Taaffe's link with Arkle a hundred and twenty-five years later, with this sad footnote to ultimate fate of the two great champions; Arkle was painlessly destroyed in 1970 when increasing rheumatism was about to make his life a misery; poor Lottery ended his days pulling a cart in Neasden when he was not being put to the plough.

Jem Mason retired to run a fashionable horse-dealing business in the West End, dying of throat cancer in 1866. Like the former champion jockey John Francome, who is now a colleague of the author in the Channel 4 Racing team, he was expert at putting a horse at a fence 'always bringing him to the jump at the right place and in the right stride'. Tom Coleman's St Albans venture faded away in the teeth of opposition from some well-endowed flat racing at nearby Gorhambury Park, the seat of the Earl of Verulam, a sportsman descended from the distinguished seventeenth century racing buff Sir Harbottle Grimston; and now Liverpool commanded the centre stage of steeplechasing though the course continued to cause controversy. In 1840 the Trustees would have liked to have eliminated the stone wall, but eventually Lord Sefton and his colleagues bowed to pressure from Irish owners to retain an obstacle common enough in Ireland, while reducing the wall to a height of four feet six inches.

The reason for the Irish enthusiasm for this cruel jump soon became plain. There were six challengers from across the water known as St George's Channel, among them Valentine ridden by his owner, Mr Power. This maniacal gentleman had boasted to the whole of sporting Dublin that he would be 'first at the wall' and backed himself accordingly. The wall was towards the end of the first circuit, and Valentine had to set such a blistering pace that only Lottery could live with him. They reached the wall together, but poor Lottery fell and brought down three others in a mêlée as he staggered to his feet, only to be bowled over again. With only five left standing, Valentine still led at the first of the two hurdles in the straight, but not surprisingly ran out of steam to finish third to Jerry, ridden by B. Bretherton.

Valentine gave his name to Valentine's Brook and the wall was demolished in favour of a water jump. Although Lottery was to run again at Aintree under huge weights he was never the same horse. Like Golden Miller nearly a hundred years later, he simply hated the place after his hideous fall.

In 1843 the National became a handicap and the name changed from the Grand Liverpool Steeplechase to the Liverpool and National Steeplechase. In 1847 the race was run as the Grand National Handicap Steeplechase for the first time, and became more or less the National as we know it.

It was also in 1843 that Edward William Topham became Clerk of the Course. The involvement of the Topham family with Aintree was to last for 130 years, not always in happy circumstances. Typically, Topham's first act was to rebuild the wretched wall to satisfy public demand. But, as flat racing plunged into the disreputable mire of the 'Filthy Forties' the sun still shone on steeplechasing, even if the twin shadows of cruelty and corruption were beginning to lengthen over a sport which was unrecognised by the Jockey Club.

Nowhere did the sun shine more brightly than at Liverpool. Stands had been built to complement William Lynn's original and elegant complex; the course was laid out in a style which would alter little until after the Second World War, at least in terms of terrain, and a local paper could report:'On Wednesday last, the town of Liverpool was filled by one of the most brilliant companies that ever graced a provincial meeting. Indeed the whole elite of the sporting circles of England, Ireland and Scotland had made it their rendezvous . . . the grandstand and its enclosure were filled with fashionables. . . .'

The 1843 National winner was Lord Chesterfield's Vanguard, thus completing a double for his jockey, the brilliant but erratic 'Black Tom' Olliver, who had won the 1842 event on Gay Lad. Frequently imprisoned for debt and, on his own admission, off the saddle 'the biggest fool in England' he and Jem Mason dominated the ranks of professional race riders in the mid-nineteenth century and Olliver was to win a third National on Peter Simple in 1853.

The period from the mid-forties to the commencement of the sixties was calm and uneventful, but it was a calm which masked the decline of steeplechasing, and Liverpool, always in the van, could not escape the general downward trend led by

clerks of the course out for a 'fast buck'. There was an eruption of minor meetings; according to Vian Smith in his invaluable *The Grand National* as many as fifteen in March 1857. This may not seem a lot by modern standards but added to the London 'gaffs' at such salubrious venues as Notting Hill and Kensal New Town there were too many races for too few horses.

Many of these tracks were badly organised and when the clerks advertised that the races would be 'All over grass and no ditches' the steeplechase cracks and their riders wisely stayed at home, disadvantaged by the miniature courses. This left the field to lesser animals and to jockeys whose integrity was, to say the least, open to question.

This unhappy situation was not improved when the campaigns of the Crimea and the Indian Mutiny deprived chasing of the kind of genuine amateurs, often commissioned officers, who were starting to provide a much needed backbone for the sport. The Crimean War, waged between 1854 and 1856 with the allied forces of Britain, France, Turkey and Sardinia opposing the might of the Russians, cut a swathe through the young bloods of the nation although as Sir John Astley described in his memoirs, it was still possible to organise a steeplechase behind the lines.

'We, the stewards', said 'The Mate' (as Sir John was often known), who was wounded in the campaign, 'had to clear the course of stones and make the fences . . . we were very lucky in the day and all agreed the sport was first rate . . . we got up a flat race for the Frenchmen, which was clipping fun, they objected to the obstacles, so we found them a flat half-mile, and the winner flogged his horse long after he had past the post.' This lack of sporting ethic displayed by a nation unused to pursuing the uneatable was forgiven when 'We had a large dinner afterwards at a French restaurant in the rear of the Third Division.'

At home the National retained its stature as Britain's premier chase although it was not immune to the odd whiff of scandal. Perhaps the worst example was in 1854, when the warm ante-post favourite, Miss Mowbray, who had won in 1852 and finished second a year later, started to drift dramatically in the market. Rumours of lameness ran contrary to reports that the connections were investing as though defeat was out of the question. Miss Mowbray made the journey from Surrey to Liverpool apparently without injury but was found to be lame half an hour before the start. Her trainer George Dockeray was sure that the horse had been 'got at' and that a blister had been applied without his knowledge. The blister, a treatment for damaged tendons which acts as a counter-irritant, causes pain and induces lameness if needlessly applied.

As in most such cases the culprits were never exposed, but the betting public, faced with the loss of their ante-post bets, had little doubt who the real villains were. In a sordid history stretching from Miss Mowbray in 1854 to Pinturischio, Derby favourite in 1961, bookmakers have often had a lot to answer for concerning well-backed horses mysteriously laid low and unable to give the punters a run.

With the Jockey Club not involved, National Hunt racing desperately needed a ruling body of its own, or even a Lord George Bentinck to conduct a one man crusade against corruption. But the man who had served on the original committee at Liverpool and gone on to reform flat racing in the 'Filthy Forties' had died in 1848; and it was nearly twenty years after that before the National Hunt Committee, which would rule the winter sport for more than a century, came into being.

Following Edward Topham's appointment as Clerk of the Course in 1843, the Topham family took over the management of Liverpool in 1856 and the course went into a rapid decline. The weight range for the National became a nonsense, with many runners set to carry between nine and ten stones. This excluded the best jockeys who could not attempt such weights and consequently the best horses, as their owners were reluctant to allow a weight-carrying horse to run at Aintree only to be beaten for speed by a light-weight on the run-in. *The Sporting Review* came to the conclusion that horses set to receive as much as thirty pounds from the top-weights were 'betting office trash who could not live two miles under 11st 7lb.'

In order to maintain reasonably sized fields Tophams reduced the size of the obstacles into 'trappy little fences' which the correspondent of *The Sporting Review* had difficulty in finding and he reported 'It almost requires a microscope to discover the fences'. It seemed that the course was 'full of ploughed fields and in the back stretch by the canal there seemed to be nothing else'.

Presumably the midget fences suited the tiny ex-flat race jockeys who had caused not a few disasters by taking too many chances at the big, tough obstacles which Lottery and his contemporaries had to negotiate, but that could not be said of George Stevens, who rode five Grand National winners, including Emblem in 1863. This was the year of the marriage of the Prince of Wales and Princess Alexandra of Denmark; the wedding took place on the day before the race and Queen Victoria, although still in mourning for Prince Albert, declared a national holiday. The Aintree crowds decided to make this a two-day affair and vast throngs celebrated for the sporting Prince and his bride at what became known as the Picnic National.

Neither Emblem nor her sister Emblematic, the 1864 winner, could be described as 'betting office trash' although bred for the flat; indeed Emblem won seven times on the level, including a five length victory as a two-year-old at Newmarket. Both mares were owned by Lord Coventry, the ninth Earl, a founder member of the National Hunt Committee which he served until his death in 1930.

By now the Crimean War was over, and chasing enthusiasts could concentrate on a much needed reformation. If there was no Bentinck to hand, there were at least two men prepared to campaign for a properly controlled sport with a ruling body as firm and effective as the Jockey Club was for flat racing. They were W.G. Craven and B.J. Angell. 'Cherry' Angell was the owner of the National winner Alcibiade and Craven was later a Senior Steward of the Jockey Club.

Their campaign had started in 1862, and a prototype committee formed in 1863, which included Lord Grey de Wilton. Although it lacked any legal authority, this self-electing group adjudicated in disputes and their decisions were generally respected. By the end of 1865 the Jockey Club agreed to the formal institution of a separate entity to administer steeplechasing and the first official Committee met in 1866. It was to be hoped that days such as when one owner paraded a broken down carthorse in the paddock to get good odds for his money while the genuine entrant went directly to the start from his home stable were over for good.

In October 1867 the Jockey Club tidied up the loose ends and resolved 'that in future Hurdle races shall NOT be considered as coming within the established Rules of Racing and shall not be reported in the Calendar with flat races.'

There remained only the knotty problem of the definition of a gentleman rider now that gentlemen in the true sense were running the sport. The Committee had proposed in 1865 that 'In all steeplechases advertised for Gentlemen Riders the following qualifications will be necessary – that the riders should be members of the following Clubs.' The Committee went on to list the names of approved establishments, and to include 'officers on full pay in the Army or Navy or persons holding commission under the Crown, or bearing titles in their own right, or by courtesy.'

Needless to say the list of clubs did not meet with the approval of the members of those excluded from the list; one irate letter writer to *Bell's Life*, noting that the Reform Club had been listed but that the Conservative had been omitted, bellowed 'I should like to know why a member of the Reform is a gentleman and a member of the Conservative is NOT.'

However the chief principle at stake was established, namely that those who rode for hire could not be described as gentlemen riders for the purposes of framing races, an arrangement which was ultimately satisfactory for both amateurs and professionals.

*Bell's Life* which had played a leading part in the campaign for a properly constituted ruling body, was ecstatic, and rightly claimed: 'In the good work of endeavouring to bring about a better state of things we were ably supported by a few "good men and true', and the result is a triumphant and gratifying one. With laws to protect it, countenanced by Royalty, and patronized by the leading sportsmen of the day, steeplechasing is no longer the "illegitimate" despised thing

that it was, but now ranks proudly side by side with other ennobling and manly pastimes.'

This particular ennobling and manly pastime was to give the new Grand National Hunt and Steeplechase Committee, in full title, more than a few headaches in the early years, but within a decade contemporary writers were able to compare National Hunt racing favourably with the flat, one even asserting that the game had assumed such proportions 'as to almost menace the position of the sister sport'. In 1875 the prize for the National was almost £2000; the Prince of Wales attended in 1878, and was nearly set alight when loose straw caught fire beneath the specially erected Royal Box; and the shrewdest manager of horses in Britain, Captain James Machell, won three Nationals with Disturbance (1873), Reugny (1874) and Regal (1876).

Machell, whose ability to train and manage racehorses was matched only by his skill as a gambler, also prepared Hermit to win the 1867 Derby, but he was a little slow in placing his commissions for Reugny's National and found that his jockey, Maunsell Richardson, had not only got to the leggers first, but told all his friends as well. The starting price of 5/1 was of little use to Machell and he bitterly informed Richardson that he didn't 'keep horses for Lincolnshire farmers to bet on'. This stinging rebuke persuaded the jockey to give up race riding and go into politics, a decision probably not as eccentric as it sounds for a man experienced in opportunism, deceiving the opposition and last minute changes of direction.

By 1881 the three day March meeting could boast, in addition to the usual flat race programme, the Liverpool Handicap Hurdle over two miles, value £427, and the Sefton Handicap Chase of £257 over two miles and a quarter. This was Thursday's programme, rounded off by a National Hunt Flat Race over two miles and worth £155.

Friday was Grand National day and the then four and a half mile chase, won by Woodbrook in the most appalling conditions, was preceded by the Palatine Handicap Hurdle of £150. Woodbrook waded home through the mangold fields to give jockey Tom Beasley his second consecutive Grand National.

On the Saturday there was the first running of the Grand Annual Aintree Steeplechase over two miles and six furlongs, value £155. This was followed by the Walton Handicap Hurdle for £120, but the most significant race on the card was the first Liverpool Hunt Steeplechase. Run over four miles and a quarter and worth £190, the winner was Seaman, partnered by Mr Harry Beasley, brother of Tom.

Harry Beasley was born in 1850 and rode the 1891 National winner Come Away. Having ridden his last chasing winner at Punchestown in 1918, he continued to ride on the flat until the age of eighty-five, when he was finally persuaded to retire after winning the Corinthian Plate at Baldoyle.

Seaman was to find his own place in the history of Liverpool when he won the National in 1882, ridden by Lord Manners. Apart from being the only peer to ride the winner of the Grand National, statistically at least Lord Manners was one of the most successful amateur riders to vault on to a race-horse, since he also won the Grand Military Gold Cup on Lord Chancellor in the same year from only a handful of rides.

Manners had purchased Lord Chancellor and Seaman from the Irish trainer Henry Linde, who trained at Eyrefield Lodge near the Curragh in Co. Kildare. In the late 1870s and early 1880s, the Irish horse copers had discovered a rich market in the England for the sturdy animals bred on the limestone fields of Eire. Their first target was Liverpool, their second the hunting field and their third the cavalry.

As Clive Graham points out in his pictorial history of the Grand National co-written by Bill Curling, the third option withered with the invention of the internal combustion engine as the tank replaced the horse on the fields of battle, but Henry Linde was a ruthless disciplinarian who learned the value of a rigorous regime as a sergeant in the Royal Irish Constabulary. His horses were thoroughly schooled over duplicates of the Aintree fences erected on his training grounds, and the Beasley brothers Tom, Harry and Willie were top class jockeys who could deliver the goods. Deliver they did, with three Grand National winners, five seconds and a third during the eighties, plus

MANIFESTO.

countless other winners including four victories in the Grand Steeplechase de Paris.

Linde's severe training methods produced a high wastage of horses from the Eyrefield Lodge yard; his 1880 National winner Empress never ran again after her Aintree victory, although she was only five years old, and Woodbrook died within a year of flogging through the mud to win in 1881. Despite her ruined legs Empress survived as a broodmare and her son Red Prince 11 won the Lancashire Chase at Manchester for Linde in 1893.

The decade was notable in three other respects; in 1884 the National winner Voluptuary went on to star at Drury Lane, leaping a water jump every night on the revolving stage in 'The Prodigal's Daughter'; the Prince of Wales had his first runner at Liverpool, The Scot, which was appropriate enough, as Voluptuary had been bred by Queen Victoria; and in 1885 the course was entirely turf, with a heartfelt goodbye to the plough and the mangold fields.

In 1886, W.S. Gladstone was appointed Clerk of the Course in the shadow of the poisoning of Zoedone. The mare, ridden by her owner Count Kinsky, had won in 1883.

Roquefort was the 100/30 favourite for the 1885 National, but Zoedone had been coupled in Spring Double bets with Bendigo, winner of the Lincolnshire Handicap and bookmakers' liabilities were heavy. Like Miss Mowbray, Zoedone was got at between arriving at the course and attempting the preliminary hurdle, then in use as a 'warm up' for the runners. The mare fell at this trifling obstacle but went on to take part in the race, only to come down in agony at Becher's on the second circuit. Again no culprit was unmasked, but there could be little doubt as to where the guilt for the atrocity really lay.

Gladstone was a good and efficient Clerk of the Course and ,set about redeeming the incompetent management of the Tophams during the preceeding years. He railed in the course, revised the National's weight range to make some kind of sense and rebuilt the fences to a standard which, although formidable, was also fair for the competent chaser.

The 'Naughty Nineties' belonged to two stars upon the public stage, one equine and the other human. Manifesto, the Red Rum of his day, ran in the National eight times, won twice, was third three times, fourth once, sixth once and fell on the other occasion. Manifesto won in 1897 and 1899 and in his first victory he was partnered by the amiable if eccentric Terry Kavanagh who slept on a manure heap to lose weight, but it was the more sophisticated George Williamson, who lived in Vienna and was a top rider on the continent, who rode Manifesto in 1899.

Meanwhile the human star glittered in the substantial form of the Prince of Wales, soon to be King Edward VII. The public loved him for his sporting instincts and the royal colours were constantly on display at Liverpool throughout the nineties. The Prince's Ambush II was seventh in 1899 and

AMBUSH II, 1900.

went to post a 4/1 favourite for the first twentieth century National. The punters were in an ebullient mood; the Boers were on the retreat in the South African War, patriotism was the popular theme and Ambush did not let them down, winning by four lengths from Barsac with the gallant Manifesto back in third under the crushing weight of 12st 13lb, giving twenty-four pounds to the winner.

The crowd went wild as the Prince led in Algy Anthony on Ambush, escorted by Lord Derby and his Royal Highness's racing manager Lord Marcus Beresford. Hats were

GEORGE V WATCHING THE 1903 NATIONAL FIELD TAKE THE PRELIMINARY HURDLE.

flung skyward, never to be retrieved; soon Mafeking would be relieved, the war would be over and the Prince of Wales would win the Triple Crown with Diamond Jubilee. The following year, he would be King.

It is interesting to note that F.H. Bayles, writing in 1903, regarded Valentine's Brook as more difficult than Becher's, pointing out that not only was Valentine's fence higher, but that there was a two feet drop on the landing side. Bayles also reckoned that the fence before the water, now known as the Chair, 'takes a lot of jumping'.

Bayles was very critical of the flat race course, observing that it was shaped like a violin case and the six and five furlong courses were practically two sides of a square, going on to add 'it can hardly be placed among our best courses, though it unquestionably is a very popular one'.

The Cup Course was over one mile three furlongs and shared the Grand National start. Eventually a straight five furlong course was laid down to bisect the 'violin case' diagonally, but the remainder of the track remained very much as it was in Bayles's day until flat racing was finally abandoned after the 1976 Spring Meeting.

However in 1903 Liverpool was still supreme in the world of steeplechasing, and even the hyper-critical Bayles described the course as 'good grassland' and the fences as 'beautifully built'.

In 1908 the American-bred Rubio gave a

hint of things to come when winning the National under 10st 51b in the hands of Morgan Bletsoe. Americans had been fascinated with the English Turf since the export of Diomed, the first Derby winner, introduced new blood to the blue grass fields of Kentucky in 1798.

Although his dam was a half-sister to quadruple classic winner Sceptre, Rubio fetched only fifteen guineas at Newmarket Sales in 1899. He won three chases as a five-year-old before breaking down, and in the hope that regular road work would improve Rubio's frail legs, his owner Major F. Douglas-Pennant lent him to the landlord of the Prospect Arms Hotel in Towcester to draw the hotel bus to and from the railway station.

Three years of pulling heavy loads through the streets of Towcester worked wonders both physically and mentally and Rubio galloped home in the National by ten lengths at 66/1.

Global war broke out in 1914 but racing continued at Aintree and in 1915 Jack Anthony won the National on Ally Sloper to make Lady Nelson the first woman to own a National winner. Within months the course had been requisitioned by the War Office and the National transferred to Gatwick as 'The Racecourse Association Steeplechase'. In 1917 it was known as the 'War National Steeplechase' and the final substitute race was run in 1918.

Across the Atlantic two factors were combining to change the face of English steeplechasing. The United States' involvement in the war had brought Europe closer to young Americans, and the Prohibition of the twenties made Paris and London seem even more attractive. As a result the names of Stephen 'Laddie' Sandford, 'Jock' Hay Whitney, Charlie Schwartz and Morgan 'Bam' Blair soon became familiar to English racegoers.

Sandford became the first American owner of a National winner when Captain 'Tuppy' Bennet, the champion amateur

SHAUN SPADAH'S JOCKEY F.B. REES RECEIVES THE CONGRATULATIONS OF THE KING AFTER HIS 1921 VICTORY.

NATIONAL DAY, 1921.

rider, brought Sergeant Murphy home in 1923. Sergeant Murphy was a thirteen-year-old and remains the oldest horse to win this century.

The tremendously tough 'Bam' Blair was an amateur who, like 'Tuppy' Bennet, specialised in backing himself to get round Aintree. He completed the course in 1921 on Bonnie Charlie – after hitting the ground no fewer than four times, thus adding credence to the theory that 'there are fools, bloody fools and people who remount in steeplechases'. He also finished seventh on Jack Horner in 1925 sporting a raw fourteen day old appendicitis scar having sweated off 18lb in the previous forty-eight hours.

Nicknamed 'Bam' after the cry which he uttered in the weighing room as he injected himself with dubious substances before riding, Blair later turned trainer in his adopted

country and won the 1936 Champion Hurdle with Victor Norman. Not surprisingly, his training methods were considered to be unorthodox.

In 1926 Charlie Schwartz, an American stockbroker, bought Jack Horner a few weeks before the National and the horse duly won with the less eccentric guidance of the Tasmanian-born jockey Bill Watkinson. Schwartz offered him a £4000 present or £1000 a year for four years. Having opted for the latter, Watkinson received nothing as he was killed in a fall at Bogside three weeks later.

Another enthusiast from 'across the herring pond' was Howard Bruce who brought the Kentucky-bred Billy Barton to contest the National in 1928. Only two of the forty-two runners were still standing as they approached the last, and Billy Barton only

NATIONAL DAY, 1922.

had to stand up to win. Worried by a loose horse, he toppled over and the unconsidered Tipperary Tim came home alone at 100/1. Billy Barton was remounted to finish second, and as half the field had been brought down or baulked at the Canal Turn when Easter Hero straddled the fence, Tipperary Tim's victory gave further encouragement to those owners who reckoned the National a race that anything could win, however moderate, and the fields began to swell to lunatic proportions.

No fewer than sixty five horses lined up alongside Easter Hero in 1929 for his second attempt, their connections undeterred by a charge of £100 to start. The National was easily the richest race in the Calendar, and even fourth prize of £150 was better than the £100 or sometimes less on offer for the winner at a minor meeting.

THE 1928 NATIONAL, WON BY TIPPERARY TIM, THE FIRST FENCE.

Easter Hero's owner in 1928 had been Captain Albert Lowenstein, a Belgian financier who leaped to his death from his private plane over the North Sea, a victim of the Depression which was to reach its height in the Wall Street crash of 1929. The horse was purchased by 'Jock' Whitney and won the 1929 Cheltenham Gold Cup by twenty lengths before starting the 9/2 favourite at Aintree.

But it was not to be. Half a mile from home Easter Hero spread a plate and could only struggle on to be second to the 100/1 outsider Gregalach.

Whitney was to enjoy a successful career as an owner, principally on the flat, but Easter Hero, probably the finest horse never to win the National in an age when it was greatest prize in steeplechasing, was always his favourite and when retired gave Whitney many a good day's hunting in Virginia.

Years later 'Jock' Whitney became the United States Ambassador to Britain. A former top jockey who had ridden many winners for the American but had fallen on hard days and was back in stables 'doing his two' was heard to say of the man who had inherited a twenty-million dollar fortune from his grandfather 'It's the times we live in. Look at poor Mr Whitney, even he's had to get a job now'.

The transatlantic love affair was to continue to colour the Aintree scene for many years, through Marion du Pont Scott, wife of

EASTER HERO.

ried £1270 and the Grand Sefton Chase paid £1255 to the winner. Only the Lancashire Chase of £1570, run at Manchester, and Cheltenham's National Hunt Chase, worth £1266, could compete at a time when the Cheltenham Gold Cup and the Champion Hurdle offered only £670 each.

The quality of the best horses was improving and when Kellsboro' Jack set a record time for the National in 1933 he was more than half a minute faster than Sprig and Tipperary Tim in the late twenties. Small wonder that Golden Miller, the finest steeplechaser of his era, perhaps of all time, had to tackle Aintree with two Gold Cups already glinting in the candlelight on Dorothy Paget's sideboard. Thirty years later the mighty Arkle was not allowed within a hundred miles of Liverpool, and rightly so in the context of the period.

But things were very different in the thirties and the top horses had to mingle with the 'dogs' in downtown Bootle. Golden Miller was owned by a cousin of 'Jock' Whitney, the Hon. Dorothy Paget, daughter of Lord Queenborough. Having inherited an American chain-store fortune, she plunged into racing and soon became a familiar figure in her shapeless overcoat, with cropped hair and a cigarette holder between teeth. At her mansion in Chalfont St Giles she turned night into day to the extent that bookmakers, aware that she slept every afternoon, allowed her to place huge bets long after her horses had run, trusting her not to have found out the results.

film star Randolph Scott, and her 1938 National winner Battleship, Tommy Smith and Jay Trump in 1965, Tim Durant 'the gallant grandfather' who completed the course at the age of 68 after remounting at Becher's, Team Spirit's victory in the colours of Mr J.K. Goodman, to Charlie Fenwick coming home through the mud in 1980 on Ben Nevis and Mr Frisk, the winner in 1990.

The 1930s were the apogee of Liverpool in the world of steeplechasing. The course staged four of the top six races in the N.H. Calendar; the Grand National, worth £9800 in 1930 and the Champion Chase of more than £1500, while the Liverpool Hurdle car-

THE 1933 FAVOURITES IN A NEWSPAPER COLLAGE:
BACK ROW: BALLYHANWOOD, COLLIERY BAND, COUPE DE CHAPEAU,
HOLMES, DESTINY BAY AND SHAUN GOILIN.
FRONT ROW: NEAR EAST, ANNANDALE, FORBA, REMUS, KELLSBORO' JACK (THE WINNER),
BALLESPORT AND GREGALACH.

Golden Miller fell in his first attempt at the National in 1933, but the following year he set a record which has never been equalled when winning the Cheltenham Gold Cup and the National in the same season, covering Aintree's near four and a half miles in a time eight seconds faster than that of Kellsboro' Jack, although burdened with 71b more.

In 1935 Golden Miller won the fourth of his five Cheltenham Gold Cups and lined up for the National as 2/1 favourite. Such minuscule odds about a popular equine hero, the Desert Orchid of his day, did not suit the bookmaking fraternity and the Miller's jockey, Gerry Wilson, was offered a substantial bribe to stop the horse. Wilson promptly informed the connections and the Stewards, but this did not prevent ugly rumours spreading when Golden Miller tried to refuse at the open ditch two fences after Valentine's and, driven on, ejected Wilson from the saddle.

MISS DOROTHY PAGET.

GOLDEN MILLER.

Golden Miller was brought out the following day and refused at the first fence in the Champion Chase. The booing was the ugliest heard at Liverpool, and as Vian Smith reports, some may have been booing from their pockets, but many . . . 'were expressing judgement on all who in the past had destroyed good horses by asking too much, too often'. Unhappily, this lesson remains to be learned today, as the names of Alverton and Dawn Run, amongst others of humbler stock, bear witness.

It soon became clear that Golden Miller, like Lottery all those years ago, had come to hate Liverpool. Although he won his fifth Gold Cup in 1936, he failed in two more Nationals. Fulke Walwyn coaxed him into second place in the 1936 Becher Chase, but reported that 'the old fellow groaned as he touched down over the drop fences'.

The National winner in 1935 was Reynoldstown, who was to complete the double in 1936, but a more significant event for the future of Liverpool was taking place in the boardroom of Tophams Limited as Mrs Mirabel Topham became a Director of the company. This former chorus girl of the musical comedy stage was married to Ronald Topham, a grandson of Edward Topham, the handicapper at Chester who was appointed clerk at Liverpool in 1843. Ronald Topham had become unwillingly involved in a family business better noted for internecine squabbles than good administration when his elder brother, also named Edward, died.

Like many a man married to a woman of formidable temperament, Ronald Topham took the easy option of a quiet life and handed over control to Mirabel, who combined a theatrical charm with a grasshopper mind and a meddlesome style of management which would have made Margaret of Anjou weep with envy. She was destined to bring the pride of Merseyside to its knees, a future unforeseen as Hitler marched on Poland and infants of Liverpool received their Mickey Mouse gas-masks before being bustled off to the safety of the countryside.

As in the first war racing at Liverpool survived the early months and Bogskar won the 1940 race, when the conditions stipulated that all riders must have won five steeplechases under recognised rules in any country in an attempt to eliminate inexperienced amateurs seeking glory. It is interesting to compare this rule of fifty years ago with the latest requirement from the Jockey Club which insists on fifteen wins 'over fences or hurdles', in effect a lesser qualification, since the rider need not have won or even competed in a steeplechase.

In World War Two there was no reprieve for the National or for Liverpool and racing was abandoned for 'the duration'. The Port of Liverpool, in the forefront of the submarine battle for the Western Approaches, suffered dreadful bombing by the Luftwaffe. When peace came to Merseyside life had changed, as in 1918, but this time those at the bottom end of the social pecking order were calling the shots. Clement Attlee came to power at the head of a Labour Government which received a commanding majority but proved ideologically unsuited to the task of rebuilding a Britain bankrupted by five years of war. The resulting shortages of essential building materials did nothing for tired and creaking grandstands or ancient posts and rails and it was a sad scene which greeted the crowds who came to see Captain Bobby Petre of the Scots Guards win on Lovely Cottage in 1946.

But if the storm clouds were rolling back, however slowly, for the nation at large they were gathering for Aintree, albeit at this stage no bigger than a man's hand. In 1949 Mirabel Topham offered Lord Sefton a reputed £275,000 for the racecourse. The Earl and his advisors, who knew a potential liability when they saw one, accepted with alacrity, adding to the contract of sale a covenant providing that the property should in the future not be used for 'purposes other than racing or agriculture'.

Flushed with success at the purchase of this gargantuan pup, Mrs Topham celebrated by adding a fourth day to the Spring

BECHERS, SECOND TIME AROUND IN BOGSKAR'S 1940 TRIUMPH.

Meeting and founded the Topham Trophy over one circuit of the National course, although little was done to improve the facilities for either competitors or spectators.

A major difficulty was the lack of openings through which loose horses could run out, and when the starter pressed the lever and the gate clattered up while a thirty-six runner field was still milling around adjusting girths and tack in 1951, the result was utter chaos and twelve horses fell at the first. It was the falsest of all false starts, and with animals struggling to find a way out, the race became a shambles better suited to the battlefields of the Crimea than a supposedly senior sporting venue. To quote Vian Smith, 'there was a feeling among those within the sport and outside it that such a mess couldn't have happened elsewhere. Blunder and confusion became associated with Aintree from that day.'

Worse was to follow. In 1952, Mrs Topham

elected to squabble with the BBC over the copyright of the radio broadcast which had been a feature of the event since 1927, when Meyrick Good and George Allison gave a running commentary of Sprig's victory to a nation crouched over their 'cat's-whisker' sets. The BBC rightly decided to let Mrs Topham stew in her own juice, and produce her own broadcast. The result was another shambles, with the gateman covering the start, the eventual winner, Teal, being given as a first fence faller, the commentator at Becher's being so stricken with stage-fright that he could only gasp 'up and over' into his microphone without mentioning any horse by name, and the principal broadcaster denied admission to the course on account of a little difficulty with Tattersalls' Committee and a betting dispute.

Another disastrous venture led to the building of a motor-racing circuit in 1954 which had to be abandoned in 1961, and seriously affected the drainage of the flat race course.

Meanwhile the Irish were reaping the benefit of wartime neutrality and, with the Americans forced into decline by penal taxation, dominated steeplechasing in the forties and fifties. Ten of the first thirteen post-war National winners were bred in Ireland, and five were trained across St George's Channel, principally by Vincent O'Brien who claimed three successive Nationals in 1953, '54 and '55 with Early Mist, Royal Tan and Quare Times.

1956 will always be known as Devon Loch's year, although E.S.B. was the winner. The circumstances surrounding the dramatic collapse of Her Majesty Queen Elizabeth the Queen Mother's Devon Loch on the run-in with the National at his mercy have been well chronicled and nowhere better than by his jockey Dick Francis in his autobiography *The Sport of Queens*. The author had the privilege some years ago during the filming of one of the Francis novels of hearing Dick explaining what may or may not have happened to an actor who knew nothing of racing and did not even know that Francis had ridden in the Grand National. As always, the former champion jockey was painstaking and courteous, which was to be expected of the First Gentleman of National Hunt racing.

Relations were restored with the BBC and Liverpool became a television event in 1960. The gladiatorial nature of the course, where only twenty-four of the one hundred starters for the previous three runnings of the National had completed, made it a 'natural' for the stay at home viewer, who is guaranteed to see far more of the contest than any of the eighty thousand spectators on the track. From the comfort of your armchair, with a glass in your hand, it is hard to resist the head-on view of the National field approaching Becher's which Clive James once compared to a battle scene in a paddy field photographed by Kurosawa.

1960 was no exception and the jockey who rode Merryman II to victory, Gerry Scott, did so with a strapped-up collar bone twice

RED RUM AND BRIAN FLETCHER.

CRISP, 1973.

broken in the previous twelve days, a circumstance unlikely to be permitted under today's regulations.

Liverpool's image was not improved when Tim Brookshaw, a fine jockey and former champion who was unfortunate not to have won the 1959 National, in which he finished second on Wyndburgh beaten only a length and a half by Oxo after having no stirrup irons from the second Becher's, because one of them broke, was paralysed from the waist down after an horrific fall on the sharp hurdle track in 1963.

It was this incident and a similar accident which befell Paddy Farrell at the Chair in the 1964 National which led to the foundation of what is now the Injured Jockeys' Fund which does so much to alleviate the suffering of stricken cavaliers fallen on hard times.

It was in 1964 that Mirabel Topham secured the copyright to the name Grand National Steeplechase before announcing her intention to sell the racecourse to Capital and Counties Property Limited for the purpose of building development, having finally realised that the racecourse was not economically viable. Although Lord Sefton successfully gained an injunction to protect the condition of the original sale restricting the use of the land to racing and agriculture, this was later reversed on appeal and in any case it was made clear in the House of Lords judgement that it would be impossible to force the Tophams to continue to promote horse racing at Aintree.

JAY TRUMP WINS THE 1965 NATIONAL FROM FREDDIE.

So began the long and sordid saga which nearly led to the demise of Liverpool. Although the National had enjoyed sponsorship in the early sixties, these benefactors were long gone, along with most of the spectators who preferred to watch the racing from the shelter of their firesides rather than risk the shabby run-down facilities of Aintree. The decline continued as the Autumn and New Year meetings were abolished in 1966. But in 1973, at long last, Mrs Topham found a purchaser in Bill Davies, whose Walton Group of property developers paid £3m for the course. It was the year of the first of Red Rum's record-breaking three victories, with most of the glory going to Richard Pitman and Sir Chester Manifold's brave front-running Crisp who failed by only three-quarters of a length to give twenty-three pounds to the winner, who completed the course in the record time of 9 mins 1.9 secs.

Crisp was trained by Fred Winter, dubbed 'Mr Grand National' by David Hedges in the sixties after Winter had ridden two National winners (Sundew and Kilmore) and trained two more (Jay Trump and Anglo).

But if 1973 was a vintage National, they were hardly vintage days. Bill Davies knew little of horse racing and even less of the skills required to stage the world's greatest steeplechase. However, he doubled the Levy Board's contribution of £10,000 to the prize money and found a sponsor for the 1975 meeting in the form of the News of the World which guaranteed winning prize money of over £38,000.

But financial difficulties continued and were not alleviated by Mr Davies' extraordinary policy of raising admission charges to a rundown track which few people wished to attend in the first place. The following year he tried to obtain £75,000 from the Levy Board to support the course and came up

BECHERS BROOK, BIG BROWN BEAR (ROBERT STRONGE) LEADS.

FRED WINTER'S LIME STREET AND
CARDINAL ERROR EXERCISING BEFORE
THE 1972 NATIONAL.

with the hardly credible proposition of an
'Aintree Derby' on Liverpool's sharp flat
race track, going on to suggest that these
were his conditions for staging the Grand
National.

Not surprisingly, both ideas received short
shrift in Portman Square but Davies found a
potential buyer in Irish property man
Patrick McCrea. The deal fell through and
Davies turned down an offer of £400,000
from the Levy Board which was clearly
inspired by the Jockey Club. At this stage
Ladbrokes, the bookmakers, threw their hat
into the ring with a bid of £1,500,000. In
December 1975 an increasingly impatient
and understandably irritated Jockey Club
gave Davies a deadline of twenty-eight days
to resolve matters, failing which they would
transfer the Liverpool meeting to Doncaster.

His mind concentrated wonderfully, Bill
Davies made an arrangement with
Ladbrokes on 22 December 1975. The deal
gave the bookmaking giants the right to run

the course until 1978 at an annual fee to Davies of £200,000 a year, with an option to renew for a further five years at a fee of £225,000 for the first two years and £250,000 thereafter.

John Hughes, the finest administrative mind in racing, was appointed Clerk of the Course and with customary energy and expertise set about restoring the fortunes of Liverpool which had suffered for many years from managerial ineptitude.

Within three months Hughes and his team, principally Mike Dillon and Nigel Payne, conjured up numerous new sponsors and when Charlotte Brew on Barony Fort went out to make history in the Foxhunters' Chase as the first girl to face up to Aintree's fierce fences, the meeting was worthy of its brave participants and a far cry from the disgraceful dilapidation of the past.

By 1977 flat racing was abolished and a superb three day jumping fixture with rich prizes brought the crowds back to see Red Rum become the first horse to win three Grand Nationals. Apart from his victories in 1973,'74 and '77, Red Rum was second in 1975 and '76 and must rank as the greatest Liverpool horse of all time, giving rise to the joke 'Who was born in a stable and is followed by thousands?' Answer: 'Red Rum!'

In 1979 the death of Cheltenham Gold Cup winner Alverton at Becher's on the second circuit added weight to the theory that the National is no place for a class horse, no matter how well handicapped. Nine runners were put out of the race by loose horses at

MRS MIRABEL TOPHAM.

the Chair, reviving memories of Liverpool's traditional but now much reduced hazards, although the unpredictable nature of a loose animal is beyond the resource of man, even if most horses prefer to run out.

In 1980 Mirabel Topham died at the age of eighty-eight. Though she was not always universally admired, than can be little doubt that she loved Aintree and the National.

Bob Champion's cancer-defeating victory on the broken-down Aldaniti is too fresh in the mind to require further amplification, and by 1982 Liverpool faced its own peril. As the British task force sailed to the South Atlantic to sort out a few problems with

Argentina in respect of an unauthorised occupation of the Falkland Islands which had not been greeted by the local population with any enthusiasm, Bill Davies announced that he wanted £7m for Aintree. The Jockey Club's response was to agree the price on condition that the money was raised by an Aintree Grand National Appeal to the public. The 1982 race went to Grittar and the distinguished amateur rider Dick Saunders, and the event was marred only by the treatment meted out to the moderate chaser Cheers, who gratified his lady rider's wish to be the first woman to complete in the Grand National at very considerable expense to himself. Any professional jockey would have pulled up the exhausted horse several fences out, and the sight of the poor animal being goaded past the post will stay in the author's memory for a long time. Cheers died in a race only 23 days after the National, when he collapsed three fences from home. That race was at Southwell, but he surely left his brave heart at Aintree.

Meanwhile, the public had failed to respond to the Grand National Appeal and the Jockey Club informed Bill Davies in November 1982 that the best he could hope for was £4,000,000, although the deadline was extended to May 1983.

Eventually the unhappy Davies had little choice but to accept £3m for the property and Major Ivan Straker, member of a well-known Northern racing family (Mr Clive Straker won the first steeplechase on the present course at Ayr in 1950) and chairman of the British arm of Seagram, the Canadian whisky firm, took over responsibility for sponsorship from News International, who had supported Liverpool since 1975.

With the course firmly under the control of the Jockey Club, which had been completely vindicated in its determination to resist untoward pressure, the future seemed safe for the foreseeable future. Plans for a new grandstand to be built next to the refurbished County Stand at a cost of £2,800,000 loaned by the Levy Board interest-free are already in hand but one question remains; how safe is the course for horse and rider?

Following two deaths at Becher's in 1989, the landing side of the fence was altered, reducing the acute backward slope of the brook which catches horses out if they land short, the brook itself was filled in to a depth of fifteen inches from the original forty-five, with only one inch of water, and the running rail on the landing side was re-sited to provide the runners with a sight of the course rather than a sea of spectators and photographers.

No horse rated officially at 30 or below may take part in the National and no amateur jockey with less than fifteen wins over fences or hurdles may ride, point-to-point winners excluded, although at the Jockey Club's discretion a rider who has 'current form with a nominated horse', very likely a top hunter-chaser, may go to the start below the fifteen winner limit.

Other questions are unanswered. Does the Grand National remain the world's greatest steeplechase, or has it become a cruel anachronism? Is the huge public interest in the event fired by a sportin spirit or a desire for a vicarious and slightly goulish thrill? As the distinguished journalist Martin Trew pointed out in The Times on the day of the 1989 race, it seems odd for a nation of supposed animal lovers to find such a spectacle attractive.

It is certain the the National, once the pinnacle of steeplechasing achievement, now stands well outside the modern mainstream of winter sport, perhaps as the City of Liverpool is in many ways outside the mainstream of modern English life. It may be appropriate that they should continue to exist side by side in their own unique fashion.

# LUDLOW

AS the Wars of the Roses lurched towards the end of thirty-two years of blood and treachery, the Yorkist King Edward IV enjoyed the rare privilege of dying in his bed in April 1483. By contrast, his quisling brother the Duke of Clarence had suffered a novel form of execution in a butt of Malmsey wine five years earlier.

Meanwhile at Ludlow Castle high above the River Teme the new King Edward V joined his retinue in the bailey of the eleventh century fortress and at the age of twelve set off on the last journey of his young life to claim his throne in London.

Historians will argue forever about the fate of the King and his eleven-year-old brother, the Duke of York, later known as the Princes in the Tower. Whether they met their deaths at the hands of their uncle Richard III or of Richard's conqueror and successor Henry VII will never be known. Both monarchs had the same motive for the destruction of the boys, and the only certainty is that the murderer was Sir James Tyrrel, Master of the Horse to Richard and later Henry's Ambassador to Rome.

Tyrrel was executed by Henry in 1502, after confessing to the murder of the princes, but it is not clear on whose behalf the deed was done. At this point the Tyrrels decided that regicide was an unwise occupation and pursued a less hazardous life on the Welsh lands granted to the late Sir James by Henry VII. A few centuries later, not many miles from those very lands which were guarded in medieval times by the Castle, racing came to the pleasant town of Ludlow.

Officers garrisoned at the Castle had probably run races as early as the fourteenth century on Old Field, Bromfield, where racing takes place today, but recorded sport dates from 27 August 1729, when Mr Coke's bay mare Statira won both heats of a fifty guinea plate 'for six year old horses which have never won a prize of that value'.

Regular meetings continued throughout the eighteenth century and by 1839 James Christie Whyte was able to report a two day meeting in mid-July with mummers from the Worcester company entertaining the racegoers in the evening at the tiny Ludlow Theatre; a genteel Victorian contrast to the cock-fighting which had so dominated the late 1700s that racing could not start before four o'clock; the sport was known locally as 'cocking at the castle'.

About twelve years later National Hunt racing was introduced, starting with modest hurdle events, and this led to the formation of the Ludlow Club, an exclusive institution devoted to the country sports described by John Milton as a 'Wilderness of Sweets'.

By 1874 the Club had established two fixtures, one in October shared with races under Newmarket rules and another in late April, also shared but with the accent very much on the Club events. By 1888 Ludlow races were the height of county fashion, 'everybody who was anybody' kept open house and 'neighbouring hostesses' entertained in marquees as top flight amateur riders of the time, including George Lambton,

'Bay' Middleton, Roddy Owen, Arthur Brocklehurst and Lee Barber fought out the finishes on horses rather less distinguished than their riders.

If one was in the unfortunate position of not knowing everybody who was anybody or indeed a neighbouring hostess, then accommodation could be found at the Angel and Feathers in the town, where you could stable your horse for five shillings including hay and straw.

In 1904, at the time of the construction of the elegant Edwardian grandstand which remains in use today membership of the club was limited to 320, a figure which infuriated no less an observer of the social and racing scene that F. H. Bayles. However it was perhaps this very exclusivity that made Ludlow supreme amongst the Hunt meetings during the period that such fixtures abounded, and so well reflected the words of Whyte Melville:

> *"When autum is flaunting his banner of pride*
> *For glory that Summer has fled,*
> *Arrayed in the robes of his royalty, dyed*
> *In tawny orange and red;*
> *When the oak is yet rife with the vigour of life,*
> *Though his acorns are dropping below,*
> *Through the bramble and brake shall the echoes*
>     *awake,*
> *To the ring of a clear 'Tally-ho!'"*

Having emerged from the 1914-18 War when priceless turf which had lain undisturbed since Edward I conquered Llewllyn

THE 'FEATHERS' HOTEL.

of Wales was ploughed up to help feed a nation, Ludlow took on very much the status that it enjoys today. Some good staying horses have taken advantage of the stiff galloping circuit and the subsequent Grand National winner Tipperary Tim won the Stewards' Handicap Chase in 1925; maybe his mastery of the Ludlow obstacles stood Tipperary Tim in good stead when he was the only runner to complete the course unscathed at Aintree in 1928.

Rich in heritage and wise enough not to race on Saturdays, Ludlow is the perfect refuge for the true National Hunt enthusiast.

# MARKET RASEN

FOR many years the flat tract of common land known as the Carholme was to the Lincolnshire racing enthusiast what the Knavesmire is to York and the Roodee is to Chester. Our forefathers were sensible enough to race on the Carholme in August and September, and the first Lincolnshire Handicap was run on 10 August 1849. Lord Exeter made the journey from his seat at Burghley House to witness the victory of his filly Media.

The Carholme in March, however, is and always has been a very different matter, and only a masochist could regret the passing of the spring Lincolnshire Handicap meeting often conducted to the accompaniment of bonecutting winds and stinging hail.

When the course closed in 1964 and the spring meeting was transferred to Doncaster, Market Rasen was left as the only surviving racecourse under Rules in Lincolnshire, although the Carholme has been laid down as a point-to-point track and plays host to the Burton Foxhounds, the Blankney Foxhounds and the Southwold Hunt, which raced for many years at the old Louth Hunt meeting.

The early years of racing at Market Rasen are shrouded by the mists of time, although meetings in the county were held at Grantham, Lincoln, Spalding and Stamford in the eighteenth century. The first recorded fixture was on 17 March 1859 under the auspices of the Union Hunt. The feature race on the card was the Union Steeplechase, a £3 sweepstake with £30

added, and there was also a three mile event for maiden hunters.

There were several changes of venue and breaks in continuity, but in 1875 the Union Hunt had found a home at Walesby. The Members' Race went to Mr Rippon Brockton on Susan and Brockton completed a double by winning the Market Rasen Open Hunters' Chase on his own horse Marmion. The Hunters' Stakes for maidens cut up to a walk over, and the results of the other races, which were worth less than £20, were not recorded.

The straw colours of Mr Brockton were still in evidence in 1883 when there were two days' racing on 9 April and 1 October. At the April fixture Brockton finished second in the Open Hunters' Chase, but a more significant result was his defeat by a young thruster, Mr Luke Nicholson, in the seller.

At the October meeting, Nicholson wore his cerise and white silks to victory in both the Members' Stakes and the Hunters' Hurdles Stakes, his winning mount in the latter event being the prophetically named Adieu.

For a few years in the eighties there were no fixtures but the meeting was revived by 16 April, 1888. The acting stewards included Sir John Astley, who lived at Brigg Hall near Lincoln and was Tory M.P. for North Lincolnshire from 1874 to 1880. He was also a pillar of the Turf, an intrepid gambler and a Steward of the Jockey Club. Known as 'The Mate' he was one of the most popular and knowledgeable men in racing.

The first event on the Easter Monday card was the Selling Plate of 25 sovereigns for hunters, the winner to be sold for 100 sovereigns, with weight allowances if entered to be sold for less. In fact this made no difference, as all the runners were entered to be sold for £50, and four went to post for the £22.15s prize.

Only two had a chance and were seriously backed. Dryad, third in a similar event at Hethersett three weeks before, and Vixen, also third on her last outing in a non-seller at the Grafton Hunt fixture at Towcester on 2 April. Dryad started at 6/4 on and was ridden by Mr Luke Nicholson, while Vixen was a 3/1 chance and had the services of a professional jockey, Edward Williams.

It must be remembered that a century ago amateur and professional riders met constantly in races and many amateurs, especially one as experienced as Nicholson, were more than a match for those who rode for hire.

The two no-hopers were soon tailed off and, in a tight finish, Vixen prevailed by a neck. An angry crowd descended on Nicholson, who had to be shielded from the mob on his way to the weighing room where the stewards, presided over by 'The Mate', took a similar view to that of the aggrieved punters and reported the amateur jockey to the Stewards of the Grand National Hunt Committee for 'the suspicious riding of Dryad'. Nicholson, 'having failed to give a satisfactory explanation' was warned off all National Hunt courses, a sentence subse-

quently endorsed by the Stewards of the Jockey Club to cover all meetings under their rules.

There was no argument or namby-pamby appeals procedure in those days, and Nicholson's career ended at that moment. He was perhaps unlucky to have the lynx-eyed Sir John Astley sitting in judgement, since a man who was used to sorting out the canny Newmarket tactics of such as Fred Archer, Charlie Wood and George

SIR JOHN ASTLEY.

# Market Rasen

'Abington' Baird was well able to detect of a spot of chicanery at a minor hunt meeting.

The remainder of the afternoon was marred by the death of an aged gelding, Cashier, owned by Mr W.H. Ash and ridden by his son. Cashier was unable to complete the two and a half mile course in the Subscribers' Plate, but an hour later Mr Ash jun felt obliged to pull him out again in the two mile Town Plate, during which Cashier unsurprisingly broke down and had to be destroyed.

However, the day ended on a bright note when the 6/4 on Bran Bread won the Maiden Hurdle Plate ridden by George Williamson, then in the early stages of a career which was to climax with Grand National glory on Manifesto in 1899.

Sir John Astley was also pleased, announcing to the correspondent of the *Market Rasen Mail* the following week 'The assiduous and enterprising committee of this annual spring meeting unquestionably scored on Monday last the greatest success that has been chronicled since the fixture was revived.'

Little was to change for thirty-six years, and when racing at Market Rasen resumed after the First World War, the Town Plate, now a hurdle race, was worth only four pounds more than in 1888. Fields had remained small and the course was limited to the one day April fixture.

In 1924 a group of local sportsmen, headed by Wilfred Cartwright and James Nettleship, decided to lay out a new course on land purchased by the consortium. Two fixtures were granted, the traditional day in April and on Saturday 17 May.

The going was hard for the opening meeting and fields correspondingly small when Bob Lyall won the inaugural event, simply described as a Selling Chase, on the 2/1 on Have a Care. Lyall, who rode Golden Miller to his first victory and won the 1931 Grand National on Grakle, had the distinction of being the first jockey to turn commentator as a member of the BBC team which covered the 1935 National, won by Reynoldstown.

The following year racing took place on three days in April, May and September. Good going produced reasonable fields, and the April meeting was notable for a treble achieved by the father and son combination of Melton and Avril Vasey. Melton was named after the 1885 Derby and St Leger winner, and was champion trainer in the North in 1919, and Avril, who claimed the 5lb allowance when he rode Tally-Ho, Hereford Lad and Roman Fiddle to win on 13 April 1925, went on to a successful training career. The family had a penchant for unusual names; Avril's grandfather was christened Yeoman.

The fare was as modest as was the prize money, although it compared well enough with other minor meetings such as Huntingdon, and the Town Plate, now an optional selling chase, was worth £63. Thus re-established, Market Rasen jogged along agreeably enough until the hiatus of World War Two. Resumption brought huge crowds to racing generally, and the little Lincolnshire course was no exception, with 20,000 visitors crammed into the primitive stands on Easter Monday 1946.

At this time, Victor Lucas was appointed Clerk of the Course. His task was formidable; his inheritance was wooden buildings and a run-down track. Lucas set to and improved the course itself, with separate hurdle and chase tracks, a proper camber and easier turns, incorporated a path within the rails for the ambulance to follow the runners, and provided a landing strip for light aircraft.

There was little he could do for the ancient facilities until funds were available, apart from providing a cafeteria in the 5/- (25p) ring and a fish and chip bar, but his energy was rewarded in the 1960s when two new stands were opened, the second with Levy Board assistance. Lucas also opened a Tiny Tots' Enclosure (without Levy Board assistance) and was one of the first racecourse administrators to position the parade ring within view of the cheaper enclosures.

The efforts and energies of the man who effectively built the course we have today are remembered by the Victor Lucas Memorial Hurdle at the first March meeting, one of seventeen days' racing at a track now popular for its summer fixtures, but still no stranger to the odd spot of controversy, as when Graham Bradley was found guilty of not trying on a horse appropriately called Deadly Going in April 1987.

No doubt Sir John Astley would have nabbed him too, but things have changed since 'The Mate's' day. Bradley was luckier than the unhappy Luke Nicholson and merely missed the first three months of the following season.

## RACE MEETINGS and INFORMATION

| FEBRUARY 29 and MARCH 1 | MARCH 7 and 8 |
|---|---|
| **LINGFIELD PARK** | **HURST PARK** |
| Visit Lovely Lingfield | The best venue for high class Racing |
| Admission Fee: Club—Gentlemen 60/-, Ladies 40/-, Children under 16 years 20/-, Tattersall's 30/-; Public Enclosure, 10/-. All inclusive of tax. | Programme: Triumph Stakes (Hurdle), Grand National Trial Handicap Chase Garrick Handicap Hurdle, Kew 'Novices' Chase. Six races daily commencing 2 p.m. |
| Programme: The Weald Stakes Handicap Chase, Manifesto Stakes (Handicap Chase), The Hever Stakes Handicap Hurdle Race. Six events daily commencing 2 p.m. | Admission Fee: Club (Daily Badges), Gents £3, Ladies £2; Res. Lawn and Paddock, 30/-; Grand Stand, 12/-; Park, 4/2. |
| Travel: Fast trains from Victoria and London Bridge. | Travel: Frequent fast trains from Waterloo to Hampton Court. |
| Application for Club Membership to: Secretary, Lingfield Park, Surrey. Tel.: Lingfield 9. | Application for Club Membership to: Secretary, Hurst Park Racecourse, West Molesey, Surrey. |

| MARCH 1 and 3 | MARCH 8 |
|---|---|
| **WORCESTER** | **MARKET RASEN** |
| Delightfully situated on the banks of the River Severn. | Delightfully situated on the west slope of the Lincolnshire Wolds |
| Admission Fee: Club, £2; Tattersall's and Paddock, 30/-; Silver Ring, 10/-; Course, 4/-. | Admission Fee: Paddock 21/-, Club Enclosure, 10/-, Daily Club Badge, 30/-. Annual Membership 5 gns. (plus cost of badge). Course 4/-. |
| Luncheons obtainable in Club and Tattersall's. | New Club stand with Tea Lounge for exclusive use of Annual and Daily Club Members. Luncheons and Teas available in Enclosures. |
| Travel: Frequent trains from Paddington, Birmingham and the West. | Station: Market Rasen, B.R. (N.E. Section)—15 miles N.E. of Lincoln. |
| Further particulars from Racecourse Manager: Tel.—Worcester 5364. | For further details apply: Clerk of Course, Market Place, Market Rasen, Lincs. Tel.: Market Rasen 2311 |

| MARCH 4, 5 and 6 | MARCH 12 and 13 |
|---|---|
| **CHELTENHAM** | **FONTWELL PARK** |
| Admission Fee: Reserved Enclosure and Paddock, 32/6 (including 15/10 tax); Public Enclosure, 10/6 (including 4/11 tax); Course, 4/6 (including 1/10 tax). | Admission Fee: Reserved Enclosure and Paddock, 27/- (including 13/1 tax); Public Stand and Enclosure, 10/6 (including 4/11 tax); Course, 4/- (including 1/10 tax). |
| Programme: Feature events—Champion Hurdle Challenge Cup, N.H. Handicap Chase, National Hunt Chase (Amateur Riders), Cheltenham Gold Cup. Six events daily. | Programme: Goodwood Handicap Hurdle, Aldwick Handicap Chase, Richmond Handicap Hurdle, Bognor Handicap Chase. Six events daily, commencing 2 p.m. |
| Travel: Race specials from Paddington to the course. From London by road 95 miles. | Travel: Fast trains from Victoria to Barnham. Motoring distance from London, 60 miles. |
| Application for Club Membership to: Messrs. Pratt and Co., 9, St. George Street, London, W.1. | Application for Club Membership to: Messrs. Pratt and Co., 9, St. George Street, London, W.1. |

70

EARLY 1950s RACECOURSE ADVERTS.

# NEWBURY

NEWBURY is probably the finest dual purpose course in the country, and owes its existence to the enterprise of John Porter, a trainer born in 1838 at Rugeley in Staffordshire who survived the ministrations of William Palmer, the family doctor who transpired to be an infamous poisoner, to send out the amazing total of twenty-three classic winners.

John Porter's victories included seven Derbys and during his career Porter trained the winners of 1063 races, worth £720,021. Most of these came from his yard at Kingsclere in Berkshire, but not a few were prepared at Cannon's Heath in Hampshire where Porter commenced training in 1863. Earlier Porter had been head lad to William Goater at Findon and that part of the Downs of Southern England was to play a significant role in the history of Newbury a hundred years later.

At the turn of the century Porter was considering his retirement, and his eyes lighted upon the piece of land which he had ample time to study as his train to London waited for the signals to change on the adjacent Great Western Railway line. He reckoned it would make an ideal racecourse, and went into partnership with the owner of the land, Mr L.H. Baxendale, to build a track. However, the Jockey Club took the view that there were too many courses already and the fixture list was inordinately overcrowded.

The story has it that when his licence to operate was denied John Porter left the Jockey Club Rooms in Newmarket High Street shrouded in gloom only to bump into no less a personage than King Edward VII, engaged in his morning constitutional. Porter had trained eighteen winners for the King when the monarch was Prince of Wales, and told his tale of woe. Edward intervened with the stewards on behalf of his old servant and Porter obtained his licence by return of post.

When the course opened in the presence of 15,000 enthusiastic racegoers on 26 September 1905 for a flat race meeting, it was not the first time that racing had been staged in the area. Meetings were held annually on nearby Enborne Heath in Regency days, and steeplechasing had been organised by local hunts from around 1839.

Eleven months after the opening on 30 October, 1906, claiming rider Ted Lawn steered the six-year-old Eremon to an eight lengths victory over an extended two miles to land the appropriately, if unoriginally, named First Newbury Handicap Chase, worth £147 to the winner. A successful hunter chaser, Eremon was in his first season and went on to win four of his five contests in 1907, including the Grand National. Trained by Tom Coulthwaite at Hednesford, Eremon won the National in a canter after jumping superbly throughout, although his jockey Alf Newey lost an iron at the second and rode the rest of the race without it. Ten days later, Eremon took the Lancashire Chase under a 12lb penalty and all things considered must have been a good thing at Newbury with only 10st.

Also on the card on the opening day were a one and a half mile Juvenile Hurdle, a seller of £94, the Winchester Handicap Chase over three miles and worth £165, the Moderate Hurdle over two miles and with a value of £164, and the Theale Selling Chase of £94. These were good prizes compared to those on offer at the Hooton Park meeting three days later, where the top reward was £130 and the average £64.

Selling races were a prominent feature of National Hunt racing during this period and for many years to come, perhaps reflecting the horse-coping origins of the sport. Even the National Hunt Festival at Cheltenham included four sellers in the 1930s.

However, some of these races were well endowed by the standards of the time and quite a number of good horses competed, although it must be remembered that only the brave or the stupid would bid at the subsequent auction when it became clear that the connections wished to retain the winner. Rubio, winner of the 1908 National, was not ashamed to pick up a £417 selling chase at Newbury en route to his Aintree victory, being bought in for 320 guineas. Of the fifteen sellers run at Newbury between December 1906 and December 1907, nine winners were bought in, four sold and two did not attract a bid.

By 1910-11 four meetings were firmly established; early December, a fixture just before New Year which still survives today and featured the Berkshire Hurdle, which is now run at the Hennessy meeting in November and renamed in honour of Major General Sir Randle 'Gerry' Feilden, a man who did much for modern Newbury; mid-January, and late February meeting which included military races and a Grand National Trial. Although a fine steeplechase course, few tracks could resemble Aintree less than Newbury but the winner of the Trial, Caubeen, started 8/1 joint second favourite at Liverpool. In common with the rest of the field excepting the winner, Glenside, he fell and the Newbury race was Caubeen's only victory that season.

By now some famous names were emerging on the Berkshire course. 'Tich' Mason, six times champion jockey, was in the autumn of his career in December 1910 but still riding winners, albeit in the modest 3-y-o Juvenile Hurdle over one and a half miles worth £87. Up and coming George Duller was only eighteen when he won on Drudge, the even money favourite for the Wroughton Selling Handicap Hurdle on the same day. Duller must have been good value for his 5lb claim that afternoon as he went on to become champion jockey in 1918 and is widely regarded as the finest rider over hurdles ever seen.

Although he was champion jockey in 1910, Ernie Piggott was making a visit from the French and Belgian tracks when he landed the odds on Finchale in the Novices' Chase at the first December meeting for Tom Leader jun. Whether his three Grand National victories on Jerry M. and Poethlyn (twice) or the fact that he was Lester

Piggott's grandfather have brought greater fame to his memory, is debatable; what is certain is that he was one of the best steeplechase jockeys of the early twentieth century and rode over 1000 winners, including 700 in Great Britain.

Also in contention that afternoon at Newbury were Bill Payne sen, champion jockey in 1911 and winner of the Cranbourne Handicap Chase on Usury; and Walter Earl, later to train no fewer than six wartime classic winners for Lord Derby, rode a double. Glenside's rider Jack Anthony, who became champion jockey when still an amateur in 1914, won the first race on Blue Blazes, while at the military meeting, Fulke Walwyn's father and Harry Brown, the last amateur to be champion rider – in 1919 – both rode with distinction.

Racing continued after the outbreak of war in 1914, and the 1914–5 National Hunt season opened at Birmingham on 30 November. the Birmingham going, officially described as 'slippy', was a good reflection of the weather and the Newbury meeting scheduled for 2 and 3 December was abandoned; indeed this was to be the fate of the first three meetings and only the two day fixture starting on St Patrick's Day, 1915 survived.

Although flat racing was staged until August 1916, National Hunt racing ended at Newbury when George Duller steered Nenuphar into the winner's enclosure after the Maiden Four-year-old Hurdle on 18 March 1915. About this time, the newly formed Tank Corps was adopting the motto 'Through Mud and Blood to the Green Fields beyond'. A better summary of conditions in France could not be imagined, except that there were no green fields in those grim days.

Newbury became successively a prisoner-of-war camp, a hay dispersal centre, a munitions inspection depot and finally a tank testing and repair park. However, the track itself and the original buildings designed and erected by the architect W.C. Stephens emerged fairly unscathed, and the turnstiles started to click again on 26 November 1919 as Newbury enjoyed the post-war boom, albeit short-lived and sliding dismally into the General Strike of 1926. It says much for the management of the course that neither the strike nor the economic stagnation of the 30s affected the continuing prosperity of Newbury in the era between the wars when no fewer than 25 courses were forced to close.

National Hunt racing was in full swing on 21 January 1920, and Captain 'Tuppy' Bennet won the opener, the Ilsey Selling Hurdle, on Kosbie. Captain Bennet went on to win the 1923 Grand National on Sergeant Murphy, only to die following a horrible fall at Wolverhampton.

Some familiar names had reappeared, notably Ernie Piggott, who rode two winners at the meeting, and Jack Anthony, successful in the Reading Selling Chase. A comparatively new name among the winning riders was that of Anthony Escott, who became a

EXERCISING AT NEWBURY, 1920.

leading N.H. rider in the decade of cocktails and laughter, although the war years had severely disrupted his career.

The Rees brothers, Dick and Bilby, were also about to unleash their outstanding talents on the 'chasing world'. Bilby, who rode Jimmy Rafter to win the Weyhill Chase at Newbury on 25 February 1920, was destined to live in the shadow of his sibling, but he was a top class jockey who won the 1922 National on Music Hall and partnered Brown Jack to victory in the Champion Hurdle in 1928. Dick Rees' win on Nareesh

in the Juvenile Selling Hurdle at Newbury on 1 December 1920 was one of the 64 winners that made him champion jockey in that year; he was to win the championship four more times in the next seven years and was probably the best all-round rider between the wars.

Of all the racecourses requisitioned for military use during the Second World War, Newbury probably suffered more than most. By 1942 it was a main supply depot for U.S. Armed Forces stationed in the south of England. The turf so beloved of John Porter

The Illustrated SPORTING & DRAMATIC News

SATURDAY, JANUARY 28, 1933.
No. 3098—Vol. CXXXVIII.
Registered for transmission in the United Kingdom.

PRICE ONE SHILLING :
Postage Rates: Inland, 1½d. Canada, 1½d.
Elsewhere abroad, 2½d.

MISS DOROTHY PAGET WITH INSURANCE.

was buried beneath concrete and thirty-five miles of railway lines; the stables were occupied by prisoners of war and the Members' Bar became an officers' mess, occupied by, amongst others, the author's former bank manager.

Racing resumed in the austere atmosphere of post-war Britain, and although plenty of money was available from the gratuity-filled pockets of ex-servicemen, Newbury missed out; as the crowds flocked to Liverpool to see Lovely Cottage win the 1946 Grand National, Geoffrey Freer, one of the best racing administrators of the period, waited patiently for the Ministry of Supply to find a fresh home for the immense collection of military hardware cluttering the course. It was June 1947 before Newbury was released and the task facing Freer was enormous. The man whose motto was 'racing is meant to be fun' was undaunted; slowly the vast sea of cement was cleared and by 1 April 1949 Newbury was open to the public once again.

But while Newbury had 'been away' a significant event had taken place at Sandown which was soon to transform the presentation and financing of racing, and steeplechasing in particular. During the 1947–8 season, BBC Television covered two chases and a hurdle race from the Esher track. It was immediately obvious that National Hunt was a television 'natural', and when the first commercial stations came on the air in the 50s, the time was ripe for sponsorship by firms anxious to advertise their

products less expensively than by simply buying time between programmes. For around £6000 a company could sponsor a top-class race featuring stars human and equine, gain coverage in every national newspaper and at least 15 minutes air-time on television. It seemed appropriate that the products thus advertised should identify with racing's good-living but slightly risqué image, and it is no coincidence that the first sponsors in the field sold beer and brandy.

Colonel Billy Whitbread led the way, as befitted a man who had completed the course in two Grand Nationals in the days when that was no mean feat, with the Whitbread Gold Cup at Sandown. Seven months later Mandarin, carrying the colours of Mme Kilian Hennessy, won the inaugural Hennessy Gold Cup at Cheltenham. The sponsors were Mme Hennessy's Anglo-French family firm whose connection with English racing went back to 1909 when Lutteur III won the Grand National in the Hennessy colours – the last five-year-old to win the race. Lady James Douglas whose home-bred Gainsborough won the wartime Triple Crown in 1918, was another member of the family.

In 1960, for business reasons, the Hennessy was transferred to Newbury, and in 1961 Mandarin won again, in his final season. He was also in his eleventh year, had been fired and yet the Hennessy was only one victory in an amazing swan-song which included the Cheltenham Gold Cup and the finest hour of a courageous career as he won the Grand Steeplechase de Paris at Auteuil with a broken bit and with his patched up legs finally giving out four fences from home. He was a horse of great ability and loved for his battling qualities by the racing public who always take to a 'good little un'. It is appropriate that the Mandarin Chase at Newbury's New Year fixture is named in his honour.

No sooner had one sponsored plum fallen into Newbury's lap, than another, and, as it proved in terms of publicity at least, riper fruit was to follow. Messrs Schweppes, manufacturers of fine Indian Tonic Waters without which gin would taste like mother's ruin, had sponsored the ailing Grand National in 1960 and 1961 without persuading the assertive Mrs Mirabel Topham to allow the firm's name to figure in the title of the race. Although any sponsor who takes on a famous event runs a risk of being overshadowed, he can at least expect to have his name included in the name of the race.

Disillusioned, Schweppes decided to back their own race the Schweppes Gold Trophy, a handicap hurdle over two miles which was the richest race of its kind in the Calendar, but mistakenly, the firm allowed the inaugural race in 1963 to be run at Liverpool, a sharp hurdle track unsuited to the huge field of 42 and disaster struck at the second flight when Stan Mellor sustained a horrible fall from Eastern Harvest.

The winner was Rosyth, trained by former Commando officer Captain Ryan Price at Findon in Sussex and ridden by Josh

FRED WINTER ON DOXFORD
AT THE LAST AT NEWBURY.

Gifford, champion jockey for the first of four times at the end of '63 season.

Rosyth had been a winner on the flat when trained at Newmarket, but was a novice over hurdles, with only one win to his credit, although he had run creditably in the Imperial Cup at Sandown, a tough handicap, finishing fourth to Antiar, and carrying the minimum weight of 10st. Five days later he was pulled out for the Schweppes, again with the minimum burden, and won by a length.

The directors of Schweppes, meanwhile, were wondering why they, the sponsors of the principal race of the day, had to purchase their admission badges. It was the final straw and they took their money, all £7500 of it, to Newbury, where Rosyth and Josh Gifford lined up for their second Schweppes on 15 February 1964.

Rosyth's record since his Liverpool victory had hardly been distinguished. He had finished unplaced in four of five attempts over hurdles, although winning once on the flat, after which he had reportedly broken a blood vessel. Rosyth started at 10/1 with his stable companion Catapult II the favourite in a field of 24, but had no difficulty in winning the race by two lengths from Salmon Spray, who had left him for dead at Sandown only thirty-five days previously. Clearly, the intrepid Captain Price had some explaining to do, first to the Newbury stewards, who promptly referred the matter to the stewards of the National Hunt Committee.

As John Lawrence, now Lord Oaksey, pointed out in the *Sunday Telegraph*, 'Last time out at Sandown, Rosyth finished nearly ten lengths behind Salmon Spray and met him on only 4lb better terms this afternoon. The discrepancy is there for all to see and while there may be perfectly valid reasons unknown to the public for Rosyth's rapid improvement, it is not altogether surprising in the circumstances that his case has been referred to the National Hunt Committee.'

The upshot was that the Committee withdrew Price's licence to train until the end of the season, Gifford was suspended for six weeks and the Schweppes and Newbury received publicity which in any other circumstances would have been regarded as priceless.

After his licence had been restored, Ryan Price won the Schweppes in 1966 with Le Vermontois, again ridden by Gifford, and duly set about a fourth attempt with Hill House, an ex-flat racer owned and once trained by Len Coville, for whom the gelding had won a small race at Newton Abbot. The pattern of events was similar, but varied from the build up to Rosyth's controversial win. Fourth at Kempton, the winner of a £578 race at Huntingdon when easy in the market, fourth at Cheltenham when join favourite for the Mackeson Handicap Hurdle in November and reportedly unlucky in running (although this is not recorded in the Form Book), followed by nearly three months off the course before reappearing at Kempton, when he refused to race. A week before the Schweppes, Hill House finished fourth in the Spring Handicap Hurdle at Sandown, a length and a head behind the second horse Get Stepping, to whom Hill House was giving 6lb.

Set to give Get Stepping 5lb in the Schweppes, Hill House didn't merely reverse the form, he murdered it, winning by 12 lengths from Celtic Gold with Get Stepping out with the washing.

The booing started from the cheaper enclosures before Hill House had reached the last flight and continued to a crescendo as the horse and Gifford were led back in one of the ugliest scenes the author has ever experienced. Hooligans of all classes may disgrace the racecourse nowadays, but these

MILL HOUSE AND JOSH GIFFORD.

were not the thugs who are nothing to do with racing, but genuine racegoers who thought they smelled a very large rat. The Newbury stewards agreed and the referral to the National Hunt Committee was almost a formality. But worse was to come. The routine dope test conducted on Hill House after the Schweppes proved positive for the steroid cortisol.

The fat was now in the fire. Enquiry followed enquiry, and Hill House was subjected to seemingly endless analysis before Price, Gifford and co-owner Coville were finally exonerated by the National Hunt Committee on 8 August. It had taken nearly six months before the stewards finally concluded that Hill House excreted his own cortisol to an abnormal level.

The full details of this sorry saga have been fully documented in Peter Bromley's invaluable biography of Ryan Price *The Price of Success* and in retrospect the case represented a bench mark in terms of legal representation for trainers and jockeys, as well as

OVER THE WATER.

methods of chemical analysis on racehorses.

The publicity surrounding the Schweppes had reached the level of notoriety, but as Oscar Wilde so wisely remarked 'There is only one thing worse than being talked about and that is not being talked about'. In 1967 the £7500 added money plus the £200 replica trophy and the £100 to the winning stable must have been one of the most profitable investments the Schweppes company ever made.

The race was now established as one of the great gambling events of the season, timed perfectly to bring an invigorating

RACING CANCELLED, 1987.

Schweppes pulled out, and the Tote took over sponsorship, but the race had lost its magic spell; a spell originally cast by the wizard of Findon, who went on to a triumphant career on the flat.

Nonetheless, Newbury remains one of the premier National Hunt tracks in the country; and those of us who have been chasing round Britain for more than a couple of decades will not easily forget the flashing if erratic brilliance of The Dikler in his novice days, a graduate from the point-to-point field reversing the trend of 'old faithfuls' who end up wearily flopping round between the flags; Arkle, majestic in defeat as he failed to give Stalbridge Colonist 35lb in the 1966 Hennessy; and Game Spirit, who literally ran his heart out and collapsed and died on his way back to unsaddle after the Geoffrey Gilbey Memorial Handicap Chase in 1977.

Game Spirit has his own race at Newbury, named in his memory and run on Tote Gold Trophy day to remind us of all those gallant creatures who give so much for our fleeting pleasure.

breeze to the doldrums of February. But February can also be a vicious month; following Persian War's victory under 11st 13lb in 1968 eight of the next 18 intended runnings were lost to the weather, and the Schweppes was run only twice between 1981 and 1986.

# NEWCASTLE

RACING probably took place at Newcastle in the early seventeenth century with meetings on Killingworth Moor. The sport was recorded on Town Moor in 1721, but the odd fixture was still held at Killingworth.

Conditions were rough at these venues in both the social and practical senses. At Killingworth the horses and riders had to race without the benefit of the 'cords' which acted as running rails, and the amount of drinking and wenching which took place before, during and after a meeting at either course would have left Errol Flynn asleep at the post.

Quite who was in a condition to take part in the various competitions staged between races is open to question; but there were dancing trials for young ladies, the prize being a gown or 'other clothing', a grinning competition for the older folk with 10lb of tobacco on offer, and an eating contest during which the entrant had to sup six bowls of hot Hasty pudding and butter, the survivor being rewarded with half-a-crown.

In 1731, Thomas Smales recorded in his diary as follows:

June 12  *To Newcastle Races, Very drunk.*
June 13  *Sunday. At Do. Drinking day and night.*
June 14  *Won the Plate. Drinking day and night.*
June 15  *To Durham, soe to Aldbrough. Drinking all night.*
June 16  *To Gilling with Plates; soe home very drunk.*
June 17  *At home very ill.*
June 18  *Extream ill. Note. In this journey spent £15.17s 6d.*

Allowing for nearly two hundred and sixty years of inflation, it was quite an expensive binge. One hopes that the sporting toper recovered from his unsurprising illness, but he was certainly typical of the Newcastle racegoer of the period.

Colonel Thomas Thornton, a hard man to please in the best of circumstances, was far from happy with the Town Moor facilities and described the stands – or rather the lack of them – as 'an erection of coarse boards, which neither protects the company from wind nor weather, and where every squall endangers the necks of the occupiers'.

The Colonel made his tour in 1786 and three years later the civic fathers of Newcastle wisely decided that the Corporation officials in charge of the race meetings were better employed in sorting out the city's drainage problems and appointed William Loftus as Clerk of the Course.

Loftus raised the finance for a proper grandstand on Town Moor by selling silver Life Membership badges at fifteen guineas each. The new stand was opened in 1800 and eighty-two years later, when racing was moved to the present site at High Gosforth Park, was substantial enough to become a seat of learning where the Roman Catholic youth of Newcastle could munch their boiled beef and carrots under the auspices of Bishop Chadwick's Memorial School.

During this time Newcastle's most famous race, the Northumberland Plate, was founded in 1833 and revived the course's fortunes which had again slumped in the early part of

THE GRANDSTAND, 1843.

the century. The track, considered dangerous by some jockeys, was improved and in 1839 stabling and lads' accommodation provided, which was a major innovation for the times.

The credit for the management of Newcastle during the years described by The Druid as 'it's palmiest period' goes to James Radford, then Clerk of the Course. But not even he could have forseen the grim legacy which the 'Filthy Forties' would produce for racing and by the mid sixties the sport at Newcastle was a mire of corruption matched only by the criminals and ruffians who attended the fixtures.

It was clear that Town Moor would have to be abandoned and in 1881 a new company was formed to purchase land and buildings from the Brandling family, well known for their sporting interests and then the landowners of the vast and beautiful estate at High Gosforth Park. 'A nobleman's park' as F.H. Bayles enthused in 1903, going on to point out the advantages of a man-made park course over one laid down across natural ground.

Bayles was also taken with the parade ring adjacent to the paddock 'an essentiality which every paddock should have – viz., a big circular tan track in order to keep the horses in a given place, and prevent the boys wandering broadcast among the people.'

The Clerk of the Course was Miles I'Anson, fourth son of William I'Anson who trained Blink Bonny to win the Derby and the Oaks in 1857 and the man who gave his eldest son, also called William, the famous advice of which Polonius would have been proud: 'If I were you, I would not bet but if you must bet - BET!'

The new venture was an eventual success, in spite of a dearth of punters at the opening on 9 September 1882 when blazing heat kept the shrewd Geordies making money in the harvest fields rather than spending their hard-earned cash at the races, and Newcastle soon became established as one of Britain's premier flat race tracks.

The skilful layout of the course which was praised by Bayles gave a considerable advantage when Major Ian Straker, a director of the Gosforth Park company and a distinguished Northumbrian sportsman, decided to introduce National Hunt racing in 1951.

The steeplechase track was dovetailed into the flat course with a few minor alterations and produced one of the fairest tests in the country. It is also one of the most severe, as the banked turns can be taken at top speed and offer no respite to a tired horse.

By the mid sixties nine National Hunt fixtures had been established, compared to ten on the flat. Presumably inspired by the feathered life on nearby Gosforth Park Lake, the management decided to name their races after a wide range of wildfowl and soon racegoers became familiar with the Dabchick Novices Hurdle, the Coot Handicap Chase, the Crested Grebe Handicap Hurdle and the Widgeon Chase. Other events were credited to the Shoveller and the Pintail but the most important was the Eider Chase, run over an extended four miles and a good Grand National trial.

**HIGHLAND WEDDING OWEN McNALLY UP.**

Highland Wedding won the Eider three times, in 1966, '67 and '69 before winning the National in the final year. Owen McNally had the ride at Newcastle in '66 and '67, while the then 3lb claimer Bob Champion was in the saddle in '69, but it was the Irish jockey Eddie Harty, deputising for the injured McNally, who rode Highland Wedding at Aintree and demonstrated yet again the topsy-turvy fortunes of the jumping game.

Harty was completing a unique double, as he is the only rider to have represented his country the Olympic Three-Day Event (he was ninth in Rome in 1960) and win the National.

1969 also saw the inaugural running of another of Newcastle's successful races, the 'Fighting Fifth' Hurdle. The race is named after the Fifth Regiment of Foot, raised in 1674 during the Third Dutch War in the reign of Charles II, a conflict which led eventually to the succession of William of Orange to the English throne. They were christened the 'Fighting Fifth' by the Duke of Wellington during the bitter Peninsular War against the French between 1808 and 1814 and are now the Royal Northumberland Fusiliers.

The first winner of the 'Fighting Fifth' was Mugatpura, trained by Fulke Walwyn and ridden by Willie Robinson to collect the prize of £4045 at even money. Mugatpura, who won the Scottish Champion Hurdle the previous season, had a fine campaign, winning seven races.

Other good horses to win the 'Fighting Fifth' include three of the finest hurdlers to race in the seventies, Comedy of Errors, Night Nurse and Sea Pigeon, all crowned champion at Cheltenham, and Gaye Brief, champion hurdler of 1983.

As always in this toughest of all sports, there were bills to pay in both equine and human terms. Ekbalco, one of the most exciting horses of his time and described by Chaseform as a hurdler 'who on his day always looked a champion' crashed to his death at the penultimate flight in Gaye Brief's year, and when Newcastle played host to the Whitbread Gold Cup during the rebuilding of Sandown in 1973, the skilful young jockey Doug Barrott died from head injuries sustained in a fall from French Colonist.

Today Newcastle is struggling to emerge from yet another of the sloughs of despond which have dogged racing there for more than two centuries. When the financial restrictions imposed in a fit of panic by those who ran commercial television in the mid-eighties took their final effect, Newcastle were the losers in terms of coverage, which in turn affected sponsorship and nowadays only Royal Ascot can survive without that. However, Channel 4 racing have restored several of the original dates to the T.V. calendar, so let us us hope that the pleasances of Gosforth Park will continue in the traditions of the filly Palmy Days, winner of the Plate in 1904 and a shy feeder. She won the race sustained by her favourite tipple - a pint of 'dog', otherwise known as Newcastle Brown Ale. Palmy Days indeed.

# NEWTON ABBOT

AT one time racing in the West Country of England was rich in venues, many based on the various resorts considered so efficacious for the health. Totnes, Dawlish, Torquay, Buckfastleigh, Newton Abbot and Devon and Exeter all catered for the many holidaymakers, mostly from the Midlands, who flocked to the coast described with more than a little optimism as the English Riviera. The Cote d'Azur it never might be but then as now, racing in Devonshire signalled the start of the season, albeit overshadowed by the last days of the Goodwood summer meeting, with the big autumn fixtures on the flat still to come. Meanwhile, the late summer sun shone

EXCUSE ME SIR, ARE YOU ALRIGHT?

upon the chasing jockeys. Now was a time to relax and to throw a few high-spirited parties at the Globe Hotel, Newton Abbot or the Queen's at Torquay, where the late supper of welsh rarebit was a dish for the gods.

Now only Newton Abbot and Devon and Exeter remain, and the pleasant two or three weeks to be enjoyed as an agreeable prelude to the endless slogs up motorways and through airports which are the lot of the workers on the National Hunt circuit, and for that matter the camp followers too, are no more; but the price of progress was never cheap.

In 1839 James Whyte referred to Newton Abbot in terms which would have left his valet in no doubt that he need not pack the white ducks for an impending visit; '162 miles from London, two days' racing, about the latter end of July.' As ever the eminent Turf historian was right, and it must be said that there is little to recommend the course from the aesthetic view, set as it is amidst the dreary outskirts of the town and on the marshes of the lower reaches of the River Teign. The river is a mixed blessing, supplying water for the relief of the firm ground at the beginning and end of the season for the fixtures which still give Newton Abbot its basic bread and butter, but also threatens the half-a-dozen mid-winter meetings with waterlogging.

National Hunt racing started there in 1880 and continued as a two day hunt meeting in May and September until Charles Vicary took over as Clerk of the Course in 1919. Vicary was a member of the South Devon Hunt, who today enjoy their point-to-point at Haldon, and his father was joint-master at the turn of the century. Vicary commanded the fortunes of Newton Abbot for thirty-four years until dying in harness in 1953 and it says volumes for his ability and enthusiasm that he conquered the often uphill task of preserving the sport in the unpromising confines of Teign Marshes, and essentially founded the popular track that we know today, described by one observer of the author's acquaintance as 'Jolly atmosphere, but decidedly pokey'. This verdict would have confirmed the worst suspicions of James Whyte but, on the other hand, what more could you ask?

# NOTTINGHAM

$I$T may seem a far cry from Nottingham to Nassau, but the master novelist Ian Fleming was characteristically undettered. The heroine of Thunderball, Domino Vitali, bearing her soul to James Bond in the bar of the Nassau Casino after Bond had taken five thousand dollars from her former lover at chemin-de-fer, tells a romantic story from her childhood in which she describes the picture of Nottingham Castle on the reverse side of a packet of Player's cigarettes as 'a doll's house swimming in chocolate fudge.'

You would have to be a smoker aged over thirty to remember that packet, but Nottingham Castle has been around for a little longer – more than nine hundred years as the original fortress was built by William the Conqueror to take strategic advantage of the River Trent, rebuilt in the seventeenth century only to be burnt down by rioters in 1831 prior to the Parliamentary Reform, and restored as the Industrial Revolution brought prosperity to the city producing the famous machine-made lace.

This affluence was naturally reflected at the racecourse, where the sport had been staged more or less continuously since 1689, the first year of the official reign of William III and Mary. One exception was 1831, when the Reform rioters threatened to injure the horses if racing went ahead; the protest was against country gentlemen in holy orders with rich livings who rode to hounds and generally enjoyed a squirearchial existence, and who, to the rioters, represented the Bishops in the House of Lords who had just

JOHN BANKS.

voted firmly against the first Reform Act, which was to receive the Royal Assent in 1832.

All this must have seemed quite irrelevant to James Whyte in 1839, when he informed readers of his *History of the Turf*, 'the races take place about the middle of October, and last three days; the racecourse is situated to the north-east of the town, and is one of the finest and most ancient in the kingdom . . . the grandstand, and handsome brick building, was erected by subscription in 1777.

Besides Her Majesty's Plate of 100 gs., a Plate of £60 is given by the county members, and another of £50 by the members of the town; a Subscription Cup, value 100 sovs. &c., is also run for.'

It was not surprising that the grandstand was handsome, as it had been built in 1777 by the finest architect of the time, John Carr, also responsible for the stands at York and Doncaster, and the building was well patronised in the 1840s when the Nottinghamshire Handicap Chase over two and a quarter miles was an important event in the Calendar.

In 1846 the land on the fringe of Sherwood Forest, where once legendary bowmen robbed the rich to help the poor, was leased for racing to the subscribers who commissioned John Carr and came under the control of the Nottingham Corporation. A second annual meeting was added in 1853.

There was now a spring meeting in early March, usually on the day after the Grand National (the flat racing season commenced in February in the 1850s) and another in late July, both two day fixtures. Many of the top riders were in attendance, including the first listed champion jockey Nat Flatman who rode the winner of the Nottinghamshire Handicap on Typee in 1855 when the race was worth a handsome £640. In that season George Fordham, then in his first championship year and still riding at 5st 7lb, drew a blank from three mounts, but won the Forest Stakes on Louvat on the second day and Captain 'Josey' Little

pleased his many female admirers by getting up by a neck on Hazelnut in the Sherwood Handicap.

The star local jockey of the period was John 'Brusher' Wells, champion jockey in 1853 and 1854. His double at the meeting on Duet in the Bunney Park Two-Year-Old Stakes and Le Julf in the Portland Handicap was a minor contribution to the Warwickshire-born rider's total of wins amassed on the Midlands tracks. Wells was noted for his eccentricity of dress, and thought nothing of riding work in a feathered Alpine hat, Gordon tartan suit and red Morocco slippers, but as Sir Joseph Hawley, for whom Wells rode five classic winners including three Derbies, remarked: 'I don't care how he dresses, he is a good enough jockey for me.'

National Hunt racing commenced in 1867 and was well established by the mid-seventies, sharing the March meeting with races under Newmarket (Jockey Club) Rules. As ever prize money was modest compared to that on offer to the flatracers, and the majority of riders were amateurs, which made life easy for Jimmy Adams.

The George Duller of his day, Adams had been apprenticed on the flat and his skills acquired in that sphere came in useful as racing over hurdles came into vogue. No lover of the Corinthian jockeys, Adams was heard to complain in the Liverpool weighing room after the successive National victories of Lord Manners and Count Kinsky, 'What the 'ell are we coming to? Last year it was a blooming lord, this year it's a furrin' count and next year it'll be an ole woman most likely.' Still gathering his breath following a six length victory in bottomless going on Zoedone, the future Prince Kinsky of Bohemia retorted, 'Yes Jimmy, and I hope that old woman will be yourself.' Adams' pot hunting at Nottingham was emulated in the eighties by George 'Abington' Baird, the Hon. George Lambton and Ted Wilson, twice champion amateur and twice winning jockey of the National on Voluptuary and Roquefort. The former was trained by his brother William at their Warwickshire home.

But by now the writing was on the wall for Nottingham races. The non-conformist conscience element, which had set fire to the Castle and threatened the lives of animals during the Reform riots, re-emerged in 1890 and the Nottingham Corporation, the custodians of Nottingham's two hundred-year-old sporting heritage, disgracefully allowed themselves to be encouraged by 'teetotal friends' to prohibit racing under the utterly inappropriate provisions of the Public Health Act referring to infectious diseases and music and dancing. This self-same conscience, as expressed by contemporary Members of Parliament, will almost certainly ensure that racing on a Sunday is never allowed but in this instance, as James Gill relates in *Racecourses of Great Britain*, 'sweet reason won the day' and two years later the Colwick Racing and Sporting Company set up a new course on the present site at Colwick Park on the banks of the Trent.

The racegoers were free once again to drink, bet, dance to music and even, heaven forbid, to contract an infectious disease if they considered the lady or gentleman worth the risk. However, the early days at the new venue were not easy, as the Midlands tracks lacked the social patronage as vital to commercial success at the time as sponsorship is today.

The course continued to struggle to establish itself in Edwardian times. Free from Victorian repression, the populace enthusiastically embraced the bohemian example of the new king, and a contemporary journalist observed 'What a place Nottingham is! It may be famed for its Goose Fair, but it is also notorious for its ladies of easy virtue. I was taken to several large hotels to see the painted and be-feathered "birds".'

Meanwhile at the racecourse, five meetings and a mixed card were held between March and December, the season then being on an annual basis. by the mid twenties there were three meetings of two days each in February, October and December as Nottingham settled down to become much the course that it is today; in the words of Patricia Smyly in the *Encyclopedia of Steeplechasing*, 'a trainers' course providing mid-week racing chiefly for novice and less than top class horses', going on to point out that a few select events are framed to attract the better animals such as Tingle Creek who won twice at Nottingham in the seventies.

The outcome of the North Street Handi-

STAN MELLOR.

JOHN FRANCOME ON OSBALDESTON.

cap Chase at Newbury on Hennessy Gold Cup day, 27 November 1971, was vintage material for those who are fascinated by the long arm of coincidence. The winner was Orient War, ridden by Stan Mellor in the colours of the bookmaker, John Banks, who beat Osbaldeston, in the hands of John Francome claiming seven pounds, by two and a half lengths.

The thread of events which led to Francome's ultimately unhappy association with Banks was well chronicled at the time; more importantly, both he and Mellor were to ride over a thousand winners with riding styles as different as their personalities.

It is hard to imagine a greater contrast than that between the modest and self-effacing Stan Mellor and the flamboyant Francome, but both were great champions and supreme artists in the saddle. Just over three weeks after the Newbury race, Mellor rode Ouzo to victory at Nottingham in the

# Nottingham

Christmas Spirit Novices' Chase, and thus became the first National Hunt jockey to ride 1000 winners. After 35 more by the end of 1972 he retired, having been awarded the M.B.E. for his services to racing, not only as a rider but on behalf of his fellow jockeys in the spheres of safety standards and the Injured Jockeys' Fund.

Stan Mellor is now a successful trainer, and is remembered at Nottingham by a handicap chase which bears his name at the December meeting, one of ten fixtures throughout the season. The track reverted to Corporation control in 1965, and despite the usual mid sixties financial traumas which afflicted many minor tracks, Nottingham has continued to capitalise on its geographical convenience for northern and southern trained runners alike. Even the fire started by vandals in the roof of the stands was a blessing in disguise, resulting in greater comfort for the punters following refurbishment, and as Martin Trew points out in his *Good Racecourse Guide*, the mushy peas are good; although, in the view of the author, not as good as those served at Ayr.

# PERTH

AT the ducal palace of Hamilton in 1777 a group of Scottish noblemen and gentlemen decided to form a club dedicated to the pursuit of foxhunting. Numbering twelve in all, the founders of the Caledonian Hunt Club included four dukes, three earls and three baronets. It was decided to limit membership of the Club to forty-five, the only pre-conditions being Scottish birth and the ownership of land in Scotland.

It is not surprising that the Caledonian soon became one of the most exclusive sporting clubs in the world. Rule XI stipulated 'No stranger shall be admitted to the meetings under any pretence whatever'. When the club decided to embrace racing as well as hunting, it was necessary to add the rider to Rule XI 'the annual race meeting excepted'.

The annual race meeting was first held at Kelso in 1779 and featured a race for horses which members of the Hunt Club had ridden to hounds that season. At the time there was only one other major course in Scotland, on the sands at Leith, Edinburgh; and Kelso was the home of the Caledonians until 1786 when the growth of racing in Scotland made the Club decide to ballot the courses at Kelso, Dumfries, Edinburgh, Perth, Ayr, Cupar, Stirling, Aberdeen, Hamilton Park and later Lanark for the very considerable privilege of the Club's patronage, both sporting and social.

Racing at Perth was first recorded in 1613, in the reign of King James I of England and VI of Scotland. Ninian Graham, Laird of Garvo, presented a prize of a silver bell for a race run on the original course on the South Inch. Meetings seem to have been intermittent and no sport took place between 1631 and 1714.

In 1734 the Town Council put up the prize money for three £25 races, and when Bonnie Prince Charlie, otherwise Prince Charles Edward 'The Young Pretender', sailed from France in July 1745 to take advantage of the British Army's absence in Silesia fighting the War of the Austrian Succession, it was to Perth races that his supporters came to plot the '45 Jacobite rising, the bustling punters providing perfect cover for the clandestine conspirators.

The Perth Hunt Club took over the meeting in 1784, and moved the course from the South to the North Inch, on land donated by the eighth Earl of Kintoul, and it was here that the Caledonian Hunt Club sponsored the meeting in 1791. The Perth races were promptly awarded the accolade of inclusion in the official Turf returns for Scotland, and the clubmen instructed the local innkeepers to 'have a little good brandy and gin and a stock of malt liquors, particularly a good London porter that has been some time in the bottle.'

The Caledonians were well aware that their august presence was likely to encourage the management of local hostelries sharply to increase their prices, and circulated a list of charges which innkeepers might make to Club members, adding 'Should any imposition take place the Club is determined never to return to that place'.

# Perth

This threat seems to have had little impact on the hosts in charge of Perth's watering holes, and in 1813 the Club expressed 'great dissatisfaction' with the cost of ordinaries (meals at a fixed time) and charges for accommodation, resolving that unless some reduction to the levels paid elsewhere was obtained 'the Hunt would not again go to Perth'.

However, they sponsored a six day meeting in 1818 when Lord Eglinton won the Caledonian Gold Cup with Sans Culottes, and returned for five days' racing in 1826. By now they were the Royal Caledonian Hunt Club, a recognition bestowed by King George IV in 1822 when he visited Scotland and the Caledonians gave a ball in his honour.

In 1834 the distinguished journalist 'Nimrod', otherwise Charles Apperley, opined that the Club 'towers far above all other hunting or racing clubs in Europe' and in 1863 no less an observer of the sporting and social scene than 'The Druid', whose real name was Henry Hall Dixon, recorded 'The entrance fee is 40gns., and the annual fee ten. The ordinary Club meetings are held once a month for six months in the year at the Douglas Hotel in Edinburgh, where a saddle of mutton (blackface, of course), is the standing dish. In short it is one of those grand old fashioned institutions which struck its taproot deep in the last century, and, except in racing, knows no decay'.

'The Druid' was less impressed with the race meeting which was the prime reason for his visit, complaining of poor fields, fixed races and a lack of spectators. He probably overstated the case, but certainly Perth was gaining a reputation as an accident prone 'gaff' track. In 1807 the temporary stand erected for the stewards collapsed shortly after the start of the race, hurling the Duke of Atholl, the Earl of Mansfield and Lord James Murray, amongst other dignitaries, to the ground.

In 1870, Starvation, owned by Lord Eglinton, bolted on the way to the start and mowed down a spectator, having thrown his jockey. Once the race was under way without Starvation, The Nigger ran out at the first turn and rendered several racegoers unconscious while a policeman was severely cut about the head, although The Nigger's rider was uninjured.

Things had declined since the day that George Fordham weighed out at 6st 3lb to win a fifty guinea plate on 6/4 favourite Challow Boy. It was 10 October, 1855, and the eighteen year old jockey was on his way to a total of seventy winners which was to give him the first of his fourteen championships. On the previous day, in the two mile Caledonian Handicap worth £160, Fordham had drawn 5st 12lb to finish second on Wantage, beaten three-quarters of a length by Braxey with Robert I'Anson up.

With 8st 4lb, Braxey was conceding thirty-four pounds for the services of I'Anson, who was on the threshold of a brilliant National Hunt career, and must have done some wast-

176

# Perth

ing to make the weight, as he was over six feet tall. Luke Snowden, who rode three classic winners before his tragically early death at the age of twenty-two, was also in action at the meeting, but top jockeys were in short supply in 1885, when only two runners appeared for the £29 Hunters' Plate on the first day, and another couple for the Hunters Selling Plate of the same value on the second.

Both events were won by Mr J. Craig on Reedness who started at odds-on on each occasion, and as Mr Craig bought Reedness in after the seller for fifty-five guineas, he made the handsome profit of five shillings for his efforts after four miles of race-riding. Even worse he could not get a decent bet.

The standards of professional racing were little better, and the elite Royal Caledonians, justifiably, had seen enough. After their visit in 1890 they withdrew their patronage, noting in the minutes of the monthly meeting in December 1890: 'It was decided that the Hunt should not again visit Perth, and the Secretary was instructed to intimate this resolution to the Secretary of the Perth Hunt.'

These words sounded the death knell for racing on the North Inch, and the fixture petered out with a mixed meeting in 1893. For a while the course was used for events under Pony and Galloway Rules but it was to be fifteen years before steeplechasing put Perth back on the racing map.

The City of Perth stands at the head of the estuary of the River Tay between the meadows of the North and South Inch. The city, once known as St Johnstoun with its Scottish League football club playing now as St Johnstone, was taken and fortified by Edward I in 1298 when the English forces defeated the Scottish rebellion led by William Wallace.

The revolt against English rule was sparked by the abdication of Edward's puppet King of Scotland, John Balliol, in 1296. Balliol was appointed by Edward following the death at Orkney of Queen Margaret 'the Maid of Norway', as she travelled from Scandinavia to claim her inheritance.

John Balliol was crowned, seated on the ancient Stone of Scone, in the Abbey of Scone at Perth where the coronations of Scottish kings had been held since the ninth century. The Stone was removed by Edward I in 1297 and placed under the Coronation Chair in Westminster Abbey, but the Kings of Scotland continued to be crowned in Scone Abbey until James I in 1424.

James was murdered in Blackfriars Monastery at Perth in 1437, a year in which the city had briefly been regarded as the capital of Scotland, and the Abbey was destroyed by a mob of John Knox's reformers in 1559, but four centuries after James's death the Earl of Mansfield built a mansion on the site which he called Scone Palace.

The Palace was surrounded by beautiful parkland, improved in 1805 by the first Earl who, in his quaint aristocratic way, decided that the village, which had grown up over the centuries in the shadow of the Abbey, spoiled the landscape and so he ordered its destruction, leaving only the graveyard and the village cross. The fate of the inhabitants is not known, although they were probably re-housed on some remote part of the estate, but it is certain that 103 years later the sixth Earl of Mansfield permitted the present course to be laid down in Scone Palace Park, and racing at Perth resumed with a two day National Hunt meeting.

The prize money was unexceptional, with most of the races worth no more than £50, but the Fingask Handicap Hurdle and the Perthshire Handicap Steeplechase were both £100 events. The latter was won by Mr Adam Scott's Rashiegrain, ridden by Mr R. C. Pawson.

The Fingask, run on the first day, and the Perthshire, which took place on the second, were still the feature races at the 1911 fixture, on 5 and 6 October; unfortunately, the £60 Mansfield Chase, over three miles, was declared void as none of the three runners was able to complete the course.

The end of the Kaiser's war saw the demobilisation of many a gallant cavalry officer keen to exercise his equestrian skills in the happier atmosphere of the hunting field and the racecourse. One such was Stewart Wight, who served with the Lothian and Border Horse, and although he finished last as a 5lb claiming amateur in the Scottish Military Hurdle at Perth on 24 September 1920 he was to go on to be a successful Corinthian and later a professional jockey, before a training career which included two Scottish Grand Nationals.

Wight trained Lord Joicey's fine mare Bramble Tudor to win nineteen races and as a tutor of jockeys was the 'Frenchie' Nicholson of the North, passing on his skills to such as Dick Curran, Ken Oliver, Reg Tweedie and Tommy Robson.

Although the races were no better endowed financially by the mid-twenties Perth was attracting good fields and top class riders. Bob Lyall, Jack Anthony, Billy Speck and Sam Armstrong were not ashamed to grace Scone Palace Park, along with the leading amateurs Major Jack Wilson, who won the 1925 Grand National on Double Chance, and Billy Whitbread.

The course was now under the control of Sir Loftus Bates, and doubtless much of the new found success was due to his unquestioned managerial abilities. However, even Homer was allowed the occasional nod, and at the September meeting in 1921 he permitted his son, Captain Giles Bates, to officiate as clerk. Unhappily, Captain Bates failed to spot a printers' error in the racecard for the second day which described a three mile chase as being over two miles. The error was compounded by the judge, who was none other than Major John Fairfax-Blakeborough, M.C., soldier, amateur rider, journalist and subsequent author of the definitive work on Northern and Scottish racing, *Northern Turf History*. It may or may not have been pertinent that at the time the gallant Major's principal literary work was *The Life and Habits of the Badger*, but he proceeded to give the result as the runners

J. FAIRFAX-BLAKEBOROUGH

time to declare the proper result, but this did not prevent some bookmakers claiming that they had paid out on the first 'placings'. The Stewards took the view that, if so, they would have to pay again, as the blue flag signalling the weigh-in had not been hoisted, and suggested to Fairfax-Blakeborough that it would be wiser in future to be guided by the Racing Calendar rather than the race-card.

At this time the racecourse stables were quite well appointed, but somewhat unusually situated, above a garage and the horses had to ascend a staircase to the boxes.

After the Second World War Perth came under the control of the McHarg family who have master-minded Scottish racing with such efficiency in modern times, and today it is primarily a holiday meeting, with dates in April, May, August, September and October. The heavy Perthshire soil precludes winter racing, but prevents the going from becoming too firm at the spring and autumn fixtures.

Heady with history and mulled in tradition, Perth is the kind of course that John Fairfax-Blakeborough had in his thoughts when he wrote 'There is somehow a different spirit in the North to that in the South, for in this part of the world the crowd take an interest in the owner and the horse, as well as the bookmaker's ticket in their pocket.'

passed the post after two miles and the 'winning numbers' were duly displayed in the frame.

Leaving the judge's box under the impression that the race was over, Fairfax-Blakeborough stopped to chat with a friend, Captain Henderson, only to notice that the horses were still running. The unhappy judge managed to get the frame lowered in

# PLUMPTON

THE Plumpton course opened in 1884, and the original intention seems to have been to act as a focal point for the area of east Sussex which at that time was fairly rich in training establishments. The experiment was well supported with good fields at all the four meetings held in January, February, April and November 1885. They were one day fixtures and the prize money not spectacular, the £57 for the Plumpton Handicap Hurdle being the best on offer.

It was much the same at the turn of the century, although the fields were sometimes decimated by the heavy going on the poorly drained course which was laid out on the terrain of the Sussex hills described geologically as 'lower chalk'. In fact this is sand dense with clay over a bed of Weald clay more than twelve feet thick, and it is not surprising that the course often rides hock deep to this day.

It was also hard to draw the punters and the venture was losing money when it was taken over by Pratt and Company in 1901. Professional management took Plumpton from a status described by F.H. Bayles as 'ordinary, fifth rate . . . much below many of the recognised hunt gatherings', to a 'very pleasant feature in the world of steeplechasing, which the visitors and residents of the South Coast much appreciate. It is approached from Brighton by road'.

Doubtless the approach was rather easier in 1901 than in 1990 but one cannot stop progress. Messrs Pratt also improved the course, at least from the spectators' point of

COLD DAY, 1984.

A FIELD OF HURDLERS PASSING THE STANDS.

view, by laying out a new hurdle course involving a loop across the right hand side of the track which made it possible to see the start, previously hidden over the brow of a hill. Finally, what Bayles was pleased to describe as 'Quite a recherché little club stand and carriage enclosure' was 'arranged for the comfort of visitors'.

For the comfort of visitors, perhaps, but Plumpton was never a course for the comfort of jockeys. Just over a mile round with four tight turns interspersed with undulations which would be the envy of a Blackpool roller-coaster, it is a rider's nightmare and many good jockeys, including Fred Winter and Dick Francis have declared

the course not to their taste. Francis frequently came to grief at the second fence in the downhill back straight, and ruefully concluded that his bad luck at Plumpton could be attributed to the fact that he was usually poorly mounted; reasoning that the likes of Finnure, Crudwell and Lochroe would have ensured a safe passage for the jockey of whom the punters would say 'Dick Francis never takes chances'.

On the other hand those top class horses, used to the swards of Sandown and Cheltenham, might have found Plumpton a little unusual, rather like Sebastian Coe being expected to race around a prep school hockey pitch and would have

AWAY FROM VIEW.

dumped Dick just as unceremoniously as the lesser lights. After all, they did not know he was the Queen Mother's jockey and in any event Plumpton is very much a specialist's course, suiting the handy, quick jumper.

As at Fontwell, but more so, Plumpton enjoys generous support from patrons travelling down from the metropolis to the station adjacent to the course; so adjacent that a spark ejected from the funnel of the last steam train to travel the line a couple of decades or so ago set fire to the plain fence just before the home turn on the eve of the September fixture, the first of the new season.

Messrs Pratt still administer the course after nearly ninety years, and Isidore Kerman, the distinguished solicitor who has for many years been Chairman of Plumpton and Fontwell Park racecourses, can recall that the first new stand he built at Plumpton cost £50,000 at a track long served by a relic transported from the defunct Northampton circuit.

At Easter 1990, the 85 year old lawyer, who has been owning horses since Bahram won the Triple Crown saw the opening of a new stand costing £850,000, from which the punters can view seventeen days racing a year.

# SANDOWN

ONE suspects that it was not an easy matter to shoulder the responsibilities of a medieval monarch. Apart from the inevitable difficulties with the French, the Scots, the Irish, the nobility and the usual family squabbles, the Church loomed large as a rich, powerful and literate body in a kingdom with a population of illiterate and downtrodden peasants. King Henry II had more trouble with turbulent priests than most, and so it is not surprising that when he founded the Augustine Priory of Sandon at about the time when the knights Fitzurse, Tracy, de Morville and Brito were galloping to Canterbury Cathedral to rid the King of Archbishop Thomas à Becket, he specified that the brothers of the order did not wear robes and concentrated on tilling the land and caring for the poor and the sick.

Thus avoiding political controversy, Sandon Priory prospered on the farmland adjacent to the village of Esher, until the brethren started to quarrel among themselves and the venture failed financially in 1300. A few monks remained, only to die in the plague of 1338, and attempts to revive

SANDOWN PARK, 1875.

the fortunes of the Priory foundered in the holocaust of the Black Death.

Today, crack steeplechasers leap over and brush through a fence alongside the pond where the Augustines caught their Friday fish; all that remains of Sandon Priory, demolished in 1740, when the area by now known as Sandown was only partly cultivated as farmland and the piece called the Warren became a recreation ground for the thousand inhabitants of Esher village.

A hundred and thirty years later the whole estate came up for sale. Various plans were proposed, including a model village and a lunatic asylum, but only Lt-Col Owen Williams was eccentric enough to suggest a racecourse.

In the last quarter of the nineteenth century, few racecourses enjoyed the benefit of enclosures or any of the facilities for racegoers which we take for granted today. The public paid no entrance fee, arrived in carts or on foot, set up stalls and thimbleriggers, drank vast amounts of Daffy (gin) and generally behaved with a distinct lack of charm. It was clearly no place to take a lady and things were little better in the 'Club', generally a roped-off area adjacent to the grandstand where the gentry parked their carriages, ate large picnics, and drank large quantities of port and brandy, matching a standard of behaviour often little better than that of the proletariat.

That was no place to take a lady either, but Owen Williams had revolutionary ideas. Commander of the Blues, high gambler, suc-

cessful racehorse owner and close friend of the Prince of Wales, Williams installed his brother Hwfa (pronounced 'hoofer') as manager of what was to become known as the first of Britain's 'drawing-room' courses. The entire estate was fenced in at a cost of £2000, grandstands built and the spectators' areas clearly defined into public and Club, or members' enclosures with separate ladies' and gentlemen's lavatories, full catering facilities and two complimentary lady's badges for each member.

For all this luxury the public paid half-a-crown for admission and Members paid a handsome annual subscription after a scrupulous vetting to ensure the desirability of the applicant. For the first time. women could go racing and be entertained in complete safety and comfort, and Williams' concept of the Park course changed the face of British racing. Within the next twenty years, as new tracks were opened at Kempton, Haydock, Lingfield, Plumpton, Folkestone and Newbury, all enclosures were modelled on the Sandown 'drawing-room' pattern.

Sandown Park staged its inaugural meeting on Thursday, 22 April 1875. It was a wet and filthy day and few punters showed up in the public enclosure. Those that did saw Fred Archer ride a winner on a mixed card which featured the Household Brigade Cup over three miles, the first steeplechase run at Sandown and won by Lord Douglas Gordon on a horse with the not inappropriate name of Sandy.

Not surprisingly Lt-Col Williams made

sure that there was a strong military flavour about the remainder of the National Hunt races during the three day fixture, including the forerunner of the Grand Military Gold Cup called the Military Steeplechase Cup, a handicap over three miles 'for horses the property of, and ridden by, Officers on full or half-pay of the Army or Navy of any country'.

The winner was Highland Mary, ridden by Lord Marcus Beresford, another great friend of the Prince of Wales. His Royal Highness had only recently registered his colours, and Lord Marcus was to be the Prince's manager during the greater part of the highly successful royal racing career.

The patronage of the future King Edward VII set the seal on Sandown's social success, and the course went on to establish a reputation for high class National Hunt racing over a track where no spectator need miss a yard of the action in an atmosphere of excitement which on big race days resembles a Roman amphitheatre in the days of Nero for excitement even if not for blood-lust.

The Military Meeting originated in 1834 as military races organised by the 5th Inniskilling Dragoon Guards and became established at Northampton in 1841, only to be re-organised by the 17th Lancers in 1843. A variety of subsequent venues found the Grand Military Gold Cup at Sandown in 1877 when Chilblain won in the hands of Mr W.B. Morris, and apart from visits to Rugby in 1880, Aylesbury in 1886 and Aldershot in 1887, the Esher track has been the home of the Grand Military Meeting ever since.

In the absence of the Grand Military proper at Aldershot in 1887, the Esher course staged its own Sandown Military Gold Cup. The usual conditions applied; the horses had to be the property of officers of the Army or Navy on full or half pay, but this was overlooked when the entry of Hohenlinden was accepted. Hohenlinden was owned by the Prince of Wales who clearly did not fulfil the conditions of ownership, and although the horse duly won with Capt. Roddy Owen in the plate, an objection by the second on the grounds of the Prince's ineligibility was bound to succeed and, much to the embarrassment of the stewards, Hohenlinden was disqualified.

Today, the conditions of the race tactfully include horses owned by Colonels-in-Chief, thus permitting National Hunt racing's finest patron, Her Majesty Queen Elizabeth the Queen Mother, to collect the three Grand Military Gold Cups won by Special Cargo and one by The Argonaut.

Roddy Owen made up the 1887 losses two years later on St Cross. Owen was one of the most famous military riders of all time. Commissioned in the East Devonshire Regiment and later serving with the Lancashire Fusiliers, he took up race-riding in 1882 and rode 254 winners from 812 mounts in the next ten years. Second in the 1891 Grand National on Cloister, Owen won at Liverpool in 1892 riding Father O'Flynn, with the discarded Cloister second again. Ambition satisfied, he promptly embarked on foreign service and died of cholera in Egypt in 1896.

The great majority of military races have been won by owner-riders who in theory also acted as trainer, at least until racing resumed after the Second World War, since when most runners have received the benefit of a professional preparation. However the 1891 winner, Hollington, was trained by Joe Cannon at Newmarket. In the February of the following year, Hollington ended the riding career of the man who was to become the master-trainer of the next forty years, George Lambton, with a heavy fall at Sandown.

Hollington's owner, Captain Whitaker, was anxious to win again, but the hot favourite in 1892 was Roddy Owen's mount Why Not, second in the Grand National in 1889 and destined to win in 1894. Acting on Whitaker's behalf, Lambton went down to Danebury to see Tom Cannon, rider of thirteen classic winners and trainer of two more.

Cannon sold Lambton an unraced four-year-old called Ormerod for £2000. The 'unbeatable' Why Not fell in the Grand Military, but the Cannon-trained Ormerod was going easily at the time and, ridden by the top amateur Captain Percy Bewicke, doubtless landed a nice touch all round.

Other famous names of the period who frequently graced the Sandown weighing room were Captain Lee Barber, inevitably nicknamed 'the Shaver', and Arthur Coventry. Barber was rightly described as the Fred Archer of the Military Meeting by George Lambton, who thoughtfully added the rider that Barber was generally better to back on the first day of the meeting than the second, as the gallant captain's fondness for the pleasures of life prevented him from being as great a jockey as he should have been, and he tended to be a little unsteady on day two.

Arthur Coventry was a very different kettle of fish, as elegant and dandy in his private life as he was in the saddle, although he always referred to himself disparagingly as 'the ugliest man in England'. He was educated in the art of race riding by Tom Cannon and Fred Archer reckoned that there was no jockey living who could give Coventry 5lb; the Duke of Beaufort described him as 'the first Gentleman Rider of the day' in 1887.

The twentieth century saw the introduction of the Imperial Cup, first run on 2 March 1907. The prize was £850, a huge reward by the standards of the time and the race remained the most valuable handicap hurdle in the National Hunt Calendar until the inception of the Schweppes Gold Trophy in 1963.

The first winner of the Imperial Cup was Carnegie, owned by the fifth Earl of Carnarvon in the happy days before he fell under the curse of King Tutankhamun, and starting at the handsome price of 20/1.

Overshadowed only by the Grand Military, the Imperial Cup soon became a prime feature of the Military Meeting. It was won by six times champion jockey 'Tich' Mason on Black Plum in 1910, the race was later farmed by the ace hurdles jockey George Duller who rode the 1914 winner Vermouth and went on to win six out of the eleven Cups run between 1920 and 1930.

Perhaps more than any other event the Imperial Cup established racing over hurdles, hitherto considered a rather dull distraction between steeplechases, as a sport in its own right. The race was usually won by specialists at hurdling such as Frank Wootton, who lowered the colours of the invincible Duller when taking the 1924 Cup on Noce d'Argent by a neck from Duller's mount Spinney Hill.

Staff Ingham, Johnny Gilbert and Harry Sprague also displayed their skills in the art of hurdle race riding in later years, when a greater degree of versatility crept into National Hunt riding generally. The author's Channel 4 Racing colleague Lord Oaksey won as the Hon. John Lawrence on Flaming East in 1958 and Brough Scott was successful on Persian Empire ten years later with all the élan he now employs to bustle twixt paddock and weighing room to entertain the viewers.

During the 1914-18 war Sandown reverted to agricultural use, but not before Georges Parfremont had won the three and a half miles Grand International Chase on Lord Marcus in April 1915. The Grand International had been a feature of the inaugural meeting in 1875 when it was over four miles and Parfremont is the only French jockey to have won a Grand National which he achieved on Lutteur III in 1909. Unlike

some contemporary French riders, he liked Sandown and also won the Imperial Cup in 1923 on North Waltham. A high class international jockey, Parfremont was killed in a fall at Enghien a few weeks later.

Between the wars Sandown maintained a relentless up-market approach scorning suggestions of inclusive rail travel and admission, or indeed any dilution of the standards set more than fifty years before. Protests in the popular press complaining of admission charges which were 150% higher than neighbouring Hurst Park fell on deaf ears and Hwfa Williams' principle of making racing popular without becoming populist continued to pay handsome dividends with huge crowds of 40,000 in attendance.

Enforced closure during the Second World War was followed by a period of acute austerity imposed by the Labour Government, which included bread rationing amongst other strictures. As Winston Churchill was not slow to point out, such a measure had not been necessary in the darkest days of the Nazi submarine war against the Atlantic convoys bringing food from America to a beleaguered Britain. Sandown did its bit, and an annual wheatcrop was cultivated on the infield, but the course was soon to play a leading role in the development of postwar racing.

'There never was a harder rider, a better loser or a more popular winner; and although he always valued the race more than the victory and the victory more than the prize, he would not perhaps have disdained the reward he has won – which is a kind of immortality among the English.'

So ran *The Times* leader the day after the memorial service for the late Lord Mildmay, who was drowned in a bathing accident near Mothecombe, his country home in Devon, in May 1950.

Mildmay was not ideally built for a jockey at a height of 6ft 2in, but he epitomised the very spirit of National Hunt racing in the postwar years. In 1936, as the Hon. Anthony Mildmay and riding his father's Davy Jones, he was robbed of victory in the Grand National when his reins broke landing over the second last. Davy Jones, a tubed reject from the flat, was prepared by Mildmay's friend Peter Cazalet at his home at Fairlawne in Kent, where Harry Whiteman held the licence.

This was a friendship forged on the playing fields of Eton and in the modern era in which well known sportsmen seem to spend more time with their lawyers, accountants and agents than they do on the field, course or court, the Mildmay and Cazalet association must seem a quaint evocation of the days when the umpire's decision was final and undisputed, the rules were upheld and taking part was more important than winning.

Mildmay's and Cazalet's dreams of winning the Grand National were doomed to disappointment, but Cazalet rose to become one of the top National Hunt trainers, winning the championship in 1950, 1960 and 1965. Mildmay was amateur champion for five successive years between 1946 and 1950 and was much admired by a racing public who knew that the famous light blue and white hoops were worn by a man risking his neck for love and not for money and who was always out to win.

Peter Cazalet's death in 1973 signalled the end of the era of the old-style patrician trainer, and both he and Mildmay are remembered at Sandown, the scene of so many of their joint victories, by the Anthony Mildmay, Peter Cazalet Memorial Handicap Chase.

The race has been won by such equine luminaries as Roimond, Cromwell, Team Spirit, Linwell, Larbawn and Burrough Hill Lad, but, in the words of John Oaksey in *The History of Steeplechasing*, Lord Mildmay left 'another priceless legacy behind him – one which, in the years since his death, has helped to carry the prestige and popularity of jumping to heights unthinkable before the war.'

When he was a guest at Windsor Castle for Royal Ascot, Lord Mildmay persuaded the then Queen and her daughter Princess Elizabeth to take up National Hunt racing, which with the honourable exception of King Edward VIII when Prince of Wales had been neglected in royal circles since the heady days when King Edward VII and Ambush II won the 1900 Grand National.

Happily for the future of the winter sport, the venture was an immediate success and Monaveen, purchased by Peter Cazalet on behalf of the royal partnership, won his first

GALLAGHER GOLD CUP, 1965. ARKLE LEADS FROM MILL HOUSE AND THE RIP.

race in the colours of Princess Elizabeth at Fontwell Park in October 1949, ridden by Tony Grantham.

The inevitable mixed fortunes of steeplechasing were to follow; Monaveen was killed at Hurst Park attempting to win a second Queen Elizabeth Chase in 1950, and the disaster of Devon Loch in the 1956 National needs no recounting here, but the die was cast. Princess Elizabeth turned her attention to flat racing as she was bound to do on succession to the throne in 1952, but the Queen Mother in her ninetieth year continues to attend meetings in all weathers. No sport could wish a better patron with her enthusiasm undiminished after more than forty years. Republicans, eat your hearts out.

On a more mundane level Sandown pioneered televised racing, a development for which the author is profoundly grateful. The BBC had made overtures to Sandown in 1939 with a proposal to televise the Eclipse Stakes, offering a facility fee of £15. Reasoning that this would not cover the cost of a decent case of port, the stewards rejected the plan, but in the proletarian atmosphere of 1947 the idea received more sympathetic consideration.

Armed with equipment which nowadays looks like an illustrated catalogue for cat's whisker radio, the BBC transmitted two steeplechases and a hurdle race during the 1947-48 season. It was immediately obvious that the 'thrills and spills' of National Hunt racing were natural television material, and although the Reithian non-conformist conscience of the BBC prohibited any mention of betting, without which racing would not exist, television was to change the face of the sport as dramatically as Owen Williams' drawing-room course had done nearly seventy-five years earlier.

The key that unlocked this particular Pandora's box of mixed blessings came with

ULTIMATE WINNER
PRINCE TUSCAN
(QUARTERED CAP)
GIVES LORD OAKSEY AN
UNEASY MOMENT AT
THE OPEN DITCH IN
1973.

LT. COL. PIERS
BENGOUGH AND
CHARLES DICKENS
LEAD AT THE LAST EN
ROUTE TO VICTORY IN
THE GRAND MILITARY,
1972.

the arrival of commercial television in the mid-fifties, and with it the sponsorship of races which became a form of advertising both enjoyable to the viewer and effective for the sponsor. In recent years many observers have felt that the pressures of sponsorship, at least at minor meetings, have led to the tail wagging the dog and many races now bear some very unsightly names,

but all such considerations were in the future when Colonel W.H. 'Billy' Whitbread, himself an intrepid and skilful amateur rider, founded the Whitbread Gold Cup which was sponsored by the famous brewery of which he was Chairman.

It was a bold innovation and many thought a foolish one. The date chosen was late April, 1957 at a time when the National

ARKLE AND PAT TAAFFE.

Hunt season, although meandering on at minor gaffs until the end of May, was generally considered to be over after the Grand National in March. However, the flat racing enthusiasts who came to Sandown on 27 April 1957 were entranced by the one steeplechase on the card as Much Obliged and Johnny East beat Mandarin and Gerry Madden in the inaugural Whitbread over three miles, five furlongs and 75 yards.

Greater glories were to follow, and the Whitbread Roll of Honour includes the names of Taxidermist, Pas Seul, Mill House, Larbawn (a dual winner) Titus Oates, Charlie Potheen (his race was held at Newcastle), The Dikler, Diamond Edge and Arkle.

Other firms were swift to copy Whitbread's example, and in 1964 the Senior Service Trophy, a steeplechase over three

THE QUEEN MOTHER WITH THE GRAND MILITARY CUP, 1986.

miles and 125 yards, was won by John O'Groats ridden by the now successful trainer Paul Kelleway. Modern medical knowledge has ensured the prohibition of the advertising of cigarettes, and it may have been in anticipation of such legislation that the Senior Service Trophy was renamed in the odd way that sponsors have as the Gallaher Gold Cup in 1965.

It was a vintage field for what was to prove a race for the connoisseur; Arkle's old rival Mill House was ridden by David Nicholson and at 11st 5lb received 16lbs from Arkle, and Rondetto (Jeff King) carried 10st 9lb. Queen Elizabeth's The Rip, more romantically renamed from his original registration as Spoilt Union shouldered bottom weight of 10st along with the no-hopers Candy whose jockey put up 3lb overweight, Lira and the 1964 winner John O'Groats.

It was a grey day on 6 November as Arkle and Mill House led the runners down the rhododendron walk and out on to the course to cheers from the crowd packing Sandown's 1903 vintage stands.

Candy led on sufferance until the fourth fence, but as they rounded the turn for home for the first time Arkle and Mill House took command, leaping like equine ballet dancers and drawing bursts of applause as they matched strides over the obstacles and headed away on the second circuit.

Mill House led Arkle over the second water and was three lengths up when they turned towards the straight, but in a matter of strides the race was over; Arkle streaked over the Pond fence to come home alone by twenty lengths from Rondetto with an exhausted Mill House four lengths back in third.

At the weights Arkle had proved himself to be nearly three stones superior to Mill House, but was unperturbed by his exertions and happily snuffled and munched among the fallen leaves outside the weighing room surrounded by his cheering supporters who had raised the roof in a way unheard by the old rafters since Lemberg and Neil Gow dead-heated for the Eclipse in 1910.

Such was the pace that Arkle had beaten the course record by seventeen seconds. It was a superb chase, the finest that the author has ever seen and won by the greatest steeplechaser in living memory. Those who can recall Golden Miller may not agree, but on that cold November day Arkle was seen at his faultless best over one of the most exciting steeplechase courses ever known.

# SEDGEFIELD

IN recent times this jolly country course has acquired a rather unfair reputation for being accident-prone. Perhaps amiable eccentricity would be a better description of Sedgefield's forté, and this was certainly so in the latter part of the last century. Captain J. E. Rogerson, a well known North Eastern sportsman and a great favourite with the Geordie racegoers, was leading a solitary opponent after all the other runners had fallen, when his mount fell at the open ditch, which then as now was the last obstacle prior to a run-in of 500 yards; longer than Aintree's notorious test.

Rogerson appealed to a group of pitmen standing by the ditch, crying 'Come on you chaps, help me to get this horse up, and I shall win this race yet.' 'Nay! Nay! Mr Rogisson' replied one of the men, 'we think a vast aboot ye but we've backed t'other yen so there yours mun lay.'

On another occasion, the jockey Bob Adams and his horse hid behind a haystack on a misty day after completing half a circuit, joining the field for the second time round and running out a clear winner. However, the mist was not quite thick enough to sustain this blatant cheating and Adams and his mount were disqualified; while Bob Ayre, who was reputed to be a great pigeon shot, still managed to ride a winner at Sedgefield, where flat racing had taken place since before 1732, although he had lost an arm in a shooting accident.

Sedgefield first came to prominence as the headquarters of the Ralph Lambton Hunt. Ralph Lambton formed a club, based at the Hardwicke Arms, in 1804 and here, in the words of Major John Fairfax-Blakeborough, 'good fellows – keen hunting and racing men of the three bottle order – who must have had much better constitutions than we in this degenerate age' (1924).

'They could sing and take their black-strap (drinks on credit) till cock-crow and be up in a couple of hours or so as lively as crickets to gallop off the effects. Brave times, those, my master, when there was no wire and no Socialists, both of which are such a menace to sportsmen of this epoch.'

The reference to (barbed) wire was an oblique attack on farmers who had utilised this device, invented by a woman in the late nineteenth century and commercially exploited by the notorious gambler and doper William 'Betcha-a-million' Gates, in place of fencing; wire concealed in hedge or even exposed was treacherous to the eyesight of a horse. So far as the socialists were concerned, Fairfax-Blakeborough was writing during the time of the first Labour Government, presided over by Ramsay MacDonald. To the Major it must have seemed the end of life as he knew it, but happily the sporting instinct is far stronger than the foibles of mere politicians of any colour.

Ralph Lambton was an ancestor of the Earls of Durham, and among the original members of the club were Ralph Brandling, then the owner of Gosforth Park where Newcastle races are staged today, and Robert Surtees, father of R. S. Surtees, the creator of 'Jorrocks'.

# Sedgefield

Originally the Lambton Hunt Club had its meetings in Lambton Park with the races confined to amateur riders. By 1846 the first recorded meetings were taking place at Sands Hall, the home of the Ord family. On April 6 1875 the Sedgefield Hunt Steeplechase was won by Carbineer at 3/1 on, and the Farmers and Tradesmen's Stakes 'for half-bred hunters the property of Tenant Farmers and Tradesmen' was won by Little Bill.

The odds-on Sober John, recorded in the race card as 'late Camelia' obviously found the sex-change too much for him and finished tailed off, while the selling chase, being for less than £20, was not considered worthy of record.

In March 1888 the Hon. George Lambton had little difficulty in maintaining the Durham family traditions when winning the Wynyard Plate for maiden hunters on Sir William Eden's Leap Year. Things were not so simple in the next, the South Durham Hunt Cup, when Lambton's mount Bellringer was a faller. Remounting to finish second to Bob Adams on the odds-on Verdical, with all the others failing to complete, Lambton was delighted to find that Adams had been disqualified for going the wrong side of a marker. The final event on the card, a selling race for horses beaten at the meeting produced an interesting result with Mischief winning from Cigarette and Dick.

By the turn of the century, F. H. Bayles was able to describe Sedgefield as 'one of the very finest of good, sound, thickly herbaged turf, never known to become deep or heavy in the worst of weather. The surface of the gallop is smooth and as regular as a garden lawn. The fences are beautifully built of birch, and not difficult to negotiate.'

In Edwardian times Sedgefield promoted a two day fixture in March. Although it remained a meeting for hunting men, with the Londonderry Challenge Cup for amateurs donated by the Marquis who lived nearby at Wynyard Park, it was now a much more professional affair.

As always George Gunter, Sid Menzies and Bob Chadwick were well among the winners, and still going strong in 1915 when racing was abandoned for the duration of the war.

The post-war resumption was marred by the death of Richard Ord, the Squire of Sands Hall, shortly before the March meeting in 1920. Ord was not only the owner of the estate where racing still takes place today but also a shrewd Jockey Club handicapper. The Ord family connection went back to the days of the Ralph Lambton Hunt, when Sedgefield was known as the Melton of the North.

By the mid twenties Sedgefield had three meetings, including a lucrative fixture at Christmas. Over the years, this has gradually been expanded to twenty-one days so it is one of the busiest courses in the Calendar. A few of the old race names have survived from Victorian times, with events named after the Hardwicke Arms, Wynyard Park, Sands and the South Durham Hunt at a course which provides plenty of opportunities for modest horses; but sadly the author's personal favourite, the Plodders' Handicap Chase, is no more.

# STRATFORD-UPON-AVON

*Let schoolmasters puzzle their brain,*
*With grammar, and nonsense, and learning,*
*Good liquor, I stoutly maintain,*
*Give genius a better discerning.*

THE lines are by Oliver Goldsmith, a playwright who lived and wrote well over a century after William Shakespeare, but no doubt the Bard would have agreed. Shakespeare was probably the original 'schoolboy with his satchel, and shining morning face, creeping like snail unwillingly to school' and he certainly enjoyed his claret in the Blackfriars Tavern while scribbling the text of Richard III for Richard Burbage.

One hundred and fifty years later the title role of Richard III was a favourite of David Garrick, a thespian who mixed in high society and was connected with many luminaries of the Turf, including the twelfth Earl of Derby, founder of the world's greatest race.

Garrick's rendition of Richard's famous cri de coeur 'A horse! a horse! my kingdom for a horse!' was considered to be definitive, and in 1769 his services to the work of Stratford's most famous son earned him election as an Honorary Burgess of the Corporation.

The celebrations included a three day festival and Garrick was swift to agree that a race with the prize of a piece of plate inscribed with Shakespeare's Arms and Falcon Crest should be the centrepiece of the third day of the revels on Friday, 8 September.

A whip-round by the Burgesses raised the £50 for the winner of what was called the Jubilee Cup. Five went to post, and Whirligig, ridden by his owner Mr Pratt,was the winner after three three-mile heats on a course flooded in some places to a depth of two feet.

The flood water came from the Avon adjacent to the course on Shottery Meadow, near the home of Shakespeare's complaisant wife Anne Hathaway. It is hard to get away from the Bard in Stratford, but they managed it for a few hours on 22 September 1755 when a crowd assembled on The Meadow to witness the victory of Mr Campbell's Forrester in a race described as 'A Gentlemen's Subscription of Fifty Pounds'.

This was the first race to be recorded on the site where racing still takes place today. The official description of the course in the mid-eighteenth century reads like the more fanciful excesses of a Surrey estate agent: 'The Course upon this most beautiful Meadow (allowed to be one of the finest in the kingdom) has been altered and made greatly more convenient and agreeable for both Horses and Spectators.

'Indeed there was very little Occasion for Art where nature had been so lavish of her bounties; the Stream of the Surrounding Avon, the verdant lawns, and the rising Hills and Woods form too delicious a scene for Description'.

Unhappily it turned about to be a case of 'though every prospect pleases, and only

DAVID GARRICK.

man is vile'. The local sons of the soil objected to the damage done by the punters and
their horses to crops and fences, and within
nine years of Garrick's triumphant festival
race the sport at Stratford was no more.

When racing was revived fifty-eight years
later in 1836 Stratford became a home of
steeplechasing which it has been ever since.
The first winner was Lady Teazle, named in
honour of Lord Derby's second wife, the
actress Eliza Farren who made the part her
own in Sheridan's 'The School for Scandal'
and thus perpetuated Garrick's theatrical
theme.

Lottery, winner of the Grand National in
1839, came to Stratford on April 17 for his
final race of the season, the four mile Grand
Steeplechase with £60 added to the stakes.
Despite the bay's formidable reputation a
reasonable field assembled and Lottery's
jockey, the elegant Jem Mason, led his colleagues out to walk the course – a very necessary precaution at the time.

So it proved to be on this occasion. The
riders were shortly confronted by a solid and
immovable five-barred gate, and the only
alternative was a massive bullfinch stuffed
with impenetrable thorn.

One of the young riders asked Mason
which he would choose. The dandy replied
that as he was going to the opera that
evening and did not propose to appear in
the crush bar with a scratched face, the gate
would do for him, adding that he dared any
of the others to follow him over.

Mason duly leaped the gate alone, won

CREDIT CALL.

the race at 2/1 on and arrived in London in
time for the rise of the curtain at Covent
Garden.

Stratford did not maintain this status and
by the seventies was really little more than a
hunt meeting, although the Grand
Steeplechase, now renamed the Stratford
Open Handicap Steeplechase and run over
three and a half miles, was endowed with
£100 added money and duly pot-hunted by
Ted Wilson.

The eighties brought further decline, with
a preponderance of sellers. The ubiquitous
Wilson was still cleaning up, now in competition with George Lambton, and the
mediocre fare was to continue for many
years, with two meetings in May and

DIANA (LEFT) AND JANE THORNE.

Gay Sheppard took over as Clerk of the Course in 1949 that Stratford began to flourish again.

Stratford soon became known as the spiritual home of the hunter chaser. The Horse and Hound Cup, run at the end of the season, has been won by some fine horses, including Baulking Green who won twenty-two hunter chases, taking the Horse and Hound Cups of 1962, '63 and '65.

If Baulking Green was king in the sixties, there can be no doubt who reigned in the seventies – Christopher Collins's Credit Call won the Cup in 1971, '72, '73 and '75 and Stratford stage a hunter chase named after him in February.

Gay Sheppard is remembered with another hunter chase during the same month, and John and Nigel Thorne with a race in March. Originally the Nigel Thorne Memorial Cup following the death of John's son in a car crash, the race now commemorates his father as well. John Thorne, for ever associated with Spartan General among many fine home-bred horses famed in the Warwickshire hunting field and father of Jane Sloan and Diana Henderson, died enjoying the life he loved best; riding over fences in the true amateur spirit embodied in National Hunt racing.

November and the best prize on offer the £150 Coronation Cup.

In the early nineteenth century F.H. Bayles, damning with faint praise, recommended the place as a schooling ground and although things were a lot better in the twenties, with improved prize money attracting better horses partnered by leading riders including Billy Speck, Billy Stott, Jack Anthony, Alf Newey, the Goswell brothers and Keith Piggott, it was not until the late

# TAUNTON

JAMES, Duke of Monmouth, the illegitimate son of Charles II and Lucy Walter, was a keen amateur rider and was reputed to have won a 'Chester Cup' although the meeting was more likely to have been at Wallasey rather than Chester. His uncle James II also had a penchant for the Turf, although political problems gave him little time, and certainly politics were dominant in 1685 when Monmouth returned from exile in Europe to try to wrest the throne from James. Setting up his standard at Taunton, the Duke proclaimed himself the rightful King of England and received the plaudits of the citizens of the West Country town and the attentions of twenty young ladies 'in their best clothes and in their brightest beauty'.

History does not record whether or not Monmouth took advantage of the situation in the way in which his father would certainly have done, but it was probably his last happy evening on earth; having moved on to Bridgwater Monmouth's rebel army of yokels armed with pitchforks and scythes was slaughtered by the King's forces at the Battle of Sedgemoor. Monmouth was executed on Tower Hill and Judge Jeffreys was despatched to Somerset to dispense rough justice at the Bloody Assize held at Taunton Castle, while the King amused himself with a race meeting at Winchester.

Today the 12th century Taunton castle still stands and a few miles to south of its brooding walls and their gory memories lies Orchard Portman, a parish on the Shoreditch Road and the home of Taunton races.

Racing has taken place in the beautiful vale of Taunton-Deane since 1802, originally at a site a little closer to the town, but also on the Shoreditch Road. The first venture failed, possibly because of the outbreak of the Napoleonic Wars, and although the handbills for the 1812 meeting desperately tried to provide something for everybody with ordinaries (dinners) and balls for the gentry and 'Single Stick playing for 5gns on each day of the Races' for the proletariat, the result seems to have been nothing for anybody and the meeting was discontinued.

It fell to nearby Bridgwater to pick up the fallen baton in 1813, and racing continued by the River Parrett until Edwardian times, when it was the home of the Bridgwater Hunt meeting. Taunton was revived in 1825, chiefly through the efforts of a Mr J. E. White, and the following year the *Sporting Magazine's* reporter at the August meeting was enthusing: 'At Taunton Races the company was more numerous and brilliant than ever before assembled in that part of the country: some of the equipages were very superb, and the number of vehicles, filled with fashionable company, conferred on the scene peculiar animation: between eight and nine thousand thronged the course.'

As the track was very confined, and little over a mile round, it must have been rather uncomfortable on a hot summer day, but at all events the meeting did not prosper and attempts to stage a successor on meadowland by the River Tone also failed.

IACOBUS D. G. MONUMETHENSIUM ET
BUCCLUCHENSIUM DUX etc.

*Justus Danckers Exc*

THE DUKE OF MONMOUTH.

# Taunton

The sport languished for seventy years until 1927 when the fifth Viscount Portman formed a Racecourse Company to sponsor National Hunt racing on his estate. Given the economic climate of the period, it was not perhaps the best of times to launch a new racecourse, but unlike Chepstow which had opened as a flat course the year before and also staged National Hunt racing, Taunton was not dependent upon the proceeds of industry but catered for the countryman and enjoyed the benefits of Lord Portman's patronage. Strictly speaking it was not a new fixture at all but a revival adjacent to a time-honoured field in the best traditions of English rural life; Taunton races had simply re-found their home.

And at home they have been, barring enemy action, for sixty-three years, providing decent opportunities for modest animals on a curiously sausage-shaped course, which can occasionally cause horses to slip up on the bends in rainy weather.

Although perhaps rather dominated by Martin Pipe's winners from nearby Nicholashayne, and also failing to draw the really top class animals that frequent Wincanton, Taunton at heart is none the worse for either nowadays, with an enjoyable simplicity of ambiance. Perhaps the Duke of Monmouth should have tried a glass of the famous cider, stayed with his merry maids of Taunton, and thus avoided the attentions of the black-masked man on Tower Hill.

# TOWCESTER

AT the Newmarket first October meeting of 1896 a horse trained by the Hon. George Lambton, then in the early stages of a superb career, was beaten a neck by a chestnut mare called Damsel II. The race was a seller, and Lambton's animal was useful. The trainer knew that anything that could beat him was worth buying, and after £450 had changed hands Damsel II duly arrived at Lambton's Bedford Lodge yard. At evening stables Lambton found the mare charging round her box as though demented and dripping with sweat. A long rest restored her condition but she was of no further use on the flat. Lambton sold her on to the crack amateur rider Charlie Cunningham for him to ride under National Hunt rules, but again she was useless and when Cunningham sent her to stud, she produced a dead foal.

It transpired that she had been doped with cocaine, a device used by trainers in America to rejuvenate horses involved in the merry-go-round of race meetings where the same animals raced continually against each other for eight or nine days at a time before moving on to the next venue.

Medication remains a major drawback to the validity of horse racing in the USA. If this seems curious for the most advanced nation in the world, it is totally legal, as it was at the turn of the century in both Britain and America.

Lambton decided to resolve the matter by doping his own horses, telling the Jockey Club of his intentions. The results were spec-tacular, with moderate horses front-running home with eye-balls staring wildly. The Jockey Club were swift to act, and doping was outlawed in 1904, but not before Lord Charles Montague had borrowed Lambton's last bottle of the drug for the Duke of Devonshire's Eclipse winner Cheers to take the Markeaton Plate, watched by a rueful Lambton who had fancied his own Andrea Ferrara in the same race.

All horses doped to win will defeat the pain barrier, and nowadays drugs can be administered with great skill, but it would have been a brave jockey who took the mount on a stimulated steeplechaser in 1903. Accordingly, it is reassuring to know that the Secretary of the Grafton Hunt Meeting held in Lord Hesketh's park at Easton Neston near Towcester was described as 'Mr Thomas Oldham, Chemist'.

Racing first took place at Easton Neston in 1876, to amuse the Empress of Austria who was a house guest for Easter at the home of Sir Thomas Hesketh Bart; the Barony was not created until 1935. In those days racing in the area was concentrated on the course at nearby Northampton, where the Hunters' Stakes of 10 sovereigns was limited to 'Gentlemen, Farmers or Tradesmen' riders and the Farmers' Cup, value 50 sovereigns was open to non-thoroughbred horses, the property of farmers only, regularly hunted with the Duke of Grafton's or Lord Chesterfield's hounds.

Conditions were strict and although the 5lb allowance for horses bred in the 'coun-

PETER SCUDAMORE.

try', i.e., the province of the two Hunts, was attractive, it was necessary to stipulate that 'No licensed horse-dealer will be allowed to enter or start a horse in this race' and the animal's pedigree and qualifications for the race had to be produced to the Clerk of the Course at the time of entrance.

The final event at the meeting, held at the end of March, was a hurdle race sponsored by the local innkeepers for amateur jockeys, over 'two miles, six leaps'. The winner had to pay three sovereigns 'towards the expenses (sic) of the hurdles', which is a bit like asking the Aga Khan to pay for the paint on the rails at Epsom after Mahmoud had won the Derby.

Forty years later racing was formally introduced at Easton Neston as a hunt meeting held on Easter Monday and staged by the Grafton. This hunt now have their point-to-point at Mollington in Oxfordshire, but for many years they sustained steeplechasing at Towcester, long after Northampton closed in 1904.

The future first Lord Hesketh formed the Towcester Racecourse Company in 1928 with a new course laid out to replace the old left-handed track of the Grafton, described in Edwardian times as 'a very interesting little fixture, well supported by the doffers of the coats of colours' and the terrain was considered to be 'very give-and-takeable'.

The new place was give-and-takeable too and is right-handed with one of the toughest climbs to the finishing line in the country. The gradient was made easier in 1939 but Towcester is still no course for the faint-hearted, either equine or human.

The elegant stands built in 1928 serve today, although extended, and are a superb refuge for the genuine chasing enthusiast. It was at this enchanting time-warp of a course that Peter Scudamore rode his two hundredth winner of the 1988–89 season, on 27 April 1989.

# UTTOXETER

RACING in the area of Stoke-on-Trent and Newcastle-under-Lyme has been taking place for many years. Meetings were held at Netherwood in the 1720s and resumed after a fifty year gap in 1774. In the nineteenth century a range of venues included Lamberts Park Farm, Rocester, Bramshall, Stafford, Stone and Pottery, a course set amongst the scattered villages of the ten square miles where the famous Staffordshire crockery was manufactured.

Bramshall was the only survivor when in 1888 it staged a one day fixture supported by the Meynell Hunt on 10 April. The prizes were good for a hunt meeting, and the punters enjoyed a good start, with the favourites romping home in the first three events.

Things went slightly awry in the seller when Mr C. Payne won on an un-named gelding by Nuneham out of Nevada at 3/1, with 6/4 favourite Battue well beaten. This seemed only a temporary setback as Mr Payne on Conway was sent to post at 5/1 for the last race, a Consolation Plate for horses beaten at the meeting, a type of event common during this period.

Conway had finished a good second to Lamlash in the Uttoxeter Plate and his opponents, Battue and Tipperary, were still recovering from their exertions in the seller half an hour earlier.

It seemed that Conway had only to go down and come back, but fortune came to the bookies' rescue as she has a distressing habit of doing on these occasions. Mr Payne, who had already ridden the course twice during the afternoon, elected to take Conway the wrong side of a marker flag and the inevitable disqualification handed the race to Tipperary. Conway had passed the post fifteen lengths to the good and Mr Payne's reception when he returned to weigh in can be imagined.

The Bramshall meeting faded away in the 1890s and was replaced by an ambitious project at Keele Park, the estate of Ralph Sneyd. Mr Sneyd had let his elegant residence at Keele Hall to Grand Duke Michael of Russia and the Countess Torby 'both of whom evinced great interest in the races' and leased the land on which the track was laid out to a company headed by Mr H.V. Boothby. Keele Park opened in 1895 as a National Hunt course, with long term plans for flat racing. The park was five hundred feet above sea level and, as F.H. Bayles pointed out in his classic *Race Courses Atlas of Great Britain and Ireland*, 'with an expanse of hilly landscape, extending for miles in all directions. One would almost discredit that such a delightful aspect was within gun shot of the famous Staffordshire industry propagated by the memorable Josiah Wedgewood, whose daughter was the mother of the great naturalist, Charles Darwin.'

As Michael Caine might observe, not many people know that or perhaps that Darwin's uncle, also Josiah, was largely instrumental in arranging his nephew's voyage on the survey ship Beagle which led to the masterwork *On the Origin of Species.* At all events Darwin's theory of evolution was considerably to outlive Keele Park which was ignored by many trainers who considered the course inaccessible, although there were two stations within a three mile radius, and despite the patronage of the Russian aristos up at the Hall.

A new company was formed to take over the licence and in 1907 racing was resumed on a site beside the River Dove, where Uttoxeter races were staged in 1839. Three fixtures were arranged with two days in May, two in October and one in December.

The opening event, a maiden hurdle with only three runners, produced a shock result when 5/1 shot Bombay, ridden by Mr Tomlinson, defeated the 5/1 on Rose Point, the mount of George Goswell, a leading rider on the Midlands tracks.

Goswell made amends to the punters by winning the next, a seller, on the 5/4 market leader Cuckoo. Also in the frame at the meeting were Owen Anthony, George Gunter and Alf Newey but, surprisingly, these cracks were not amongst the winners. On the other hand, Mr Tomlinson produced Bombay again on the second day, this time in a steeplechase. Incredibly the partnership were again neglected in the ring, starting third favourite at 4/1 before winning by two lengths.

Established in a permanent home at last, Uttoxeter prospered with decent prize money and a good standard of competitors. Of course there was the usual complement of lower grade races, including selling plates, the last type of race in which the horses were obliged to take part in a run-off or 'deciding heat' in the event of a dead-heat.

In fact this practice, which dated back to racing's earliest days, was not abolished until 1930. It seems extraordinary today that two horses should be asked to re-run a two mile hurdle race, but this was the case on April 3 1922, when Regicles and General Reed dead-heated for the Marston Selling Hurdle Race at Uttoxeter. Regicles's rider Ted Lawn was again in the plate for the run-off, but Bob Clark, General Reed's original partner, gave way to Frank Wootton, a top class hurdles jockey. Priced at 5/1 for the original race, General Reed started at 13/8 on for the decider, but broke down and Regicles finished alone before being bought in for 150 guineas.

Having survived the Kaiser's war and the economic slump of the thirties which saw the closure of many minor tracks, Uttoxeter seemed set fair to continue its pleasant if mundane career when racing resumed after the second global conflict, but it was not to be.

The Racecourse Company had owned all but 140 yards of the course prior to 1939, but in 1946 the farmer who owned the vital area attempted to impose an extortionate sum for the lease of this scrap of land. The Company rightly refused to pay the danegeld and racing languished until the Urban District Council broke the dog in a manger deadlock by a compulsory purchase order in favour of the racecourse.

MICHAEL DICKINSON WITH HIS FATHER.

Uttoxeter re-opened on 12 April 1952, but it was sixteen years before a new stand to replace the antique Edwardian model was erected at a cost of £167,000. The standard of sport was much as ever, with the Midlands Grand National, a four and a half mile handicap chase attracting some good, if slightly leg-weary, runners in April.

It was at Uttoxeter in 1967 that Josh Gifford rode a treble and broke Fred Winter's then record of 121 winners in a season, and it was also on the midlands track in May 1989 that the Dickinson family said farewell to racing. Half Decent, trained by Monica Dickinson, was made 13/8 favourite for the Steve Lilley Novices' Hurdle, but there was no fairytale ending for the racing dynasty of Tony, Monica and Michael that had produced a stream of big race winners including Silver Buck, Bregawn, Wayward Lad, Gay Spartan, Badsworth Boy and Browne's Gazette, to say nothing of the first five home in the 1983 Cheltenham Gold Cup and twelve winners across the card on 27 December 1982.

MRS MONICA DICKINSON.

Half Decent could finish only fifth; but then he had a lot to live up to. Perhaps significantly the race was won by Temple Reef, trained by Martin Pipe. It may have been the end of an era but another had already begun.

# WARWICK

THE Midlands town of Warwick is dominated by the brooding castle from where Richard Nevill, The Kingmaker, attempted to mastermind the Wars of the Roses. Warwick Castle, whose foundations were laid in 915 by Queen Ethelreda, has played a continuing role in the rich pageant of English history and the late Norman Castle was built by Geoffrey de Clinton. It was used as a refuge by Henry I when his dissolute son Prince William, who later met his death when drowned in the wreck of The White Ship, rebelled against him, and as the garrison of Henry III during a spot of bother with some ungrateful barons, Warwick Castle is still occupied and beautifully preserved. Even now sporting masochists can visit the torture chambers in the morning and try to go through the card at the races in the afternoon.

It is probable that racing at Warwick started in September 1714, to celebrate the coronation of the new king, George I, who had succeeded Queen Anne on 1 August. The meeting prospered and was well patronised by the rich and the fancy, leading to the

WARWICK RACES, 1845.

erection of a 'commodious' grandstand in time for the October meeting held in 1815 just as the recently defeated Napoleon Bonaparte was settling in to rather less commodious quarters on the south Atlantic island of St Helena, and peace came to Britain which was to last for nearly forty years.

Steeplechasing at Warwick dates from the very earliest days of the organised sport, and a course was laid down in the mid 1840s. In 1847 Chandler made his famous thirty-nine feet leap to clear a brook and four fallen horses en route to victory in the Leamington Hunt Club Steeplechase, and for many years in the nineteenth century the Warwick Grand Annual, sometimes called the Leamington, was a principal race in the National Hunt Calendar.

This happy situation was already on the wane by the seventies, when the nonconformist conscience which was to plague so many Midland meetings during this period raised its head. At the time betting in a public place of any kind, including a racecourse, was strictly speaking illegal but this was widely regarded as one of those rather silly laws which would never be invoked except in the rare case of genuine obstruction or breach of the peace.

Even the Warwick Town Council, advised by the Chief Constable Mr R. H. Kinchant, took the view that it would be senseless to prosecute bookmakers and punters when there were plenty of ruffians at the races to occupy the attention of the police.

Nonetheless a certain Mr Gold, an enthusiastic member of the Temperance Movement, was determined to put an end to betting, racing, drinking and doubtless anything else remotely suggesting enjoyment. Gold's relentless prosecution of racegoers put the races in real jeopardy and following his victory in a shooting contest for which the prize was a barrel of beer, duly poured down the sewer by this staunch upholder of the rights of man who was presumably not amused by the irony of the situation. He was burned in effigy at the racecourse on 28 February.

The matter even became a political issue with the Tories not slow to point out that it was the Liberals, then in power under Gladstone, who had tried to stop the races and prosecute the punters, thus risking the loss of trade generated by the race meetings, and one poster posed the rhetorical question 'Do the races improve Trade and Circulate the Cash?' and ended triumphantly 'Yes, ask the working man.' Consultations with the working man failed to save more than two days of racing at Warwick in 1883, with a hunters' flat race the only National Hunt event on the August card.

However, the appeal did not fall entirely on deaf ears, and in 1885, the year when the third Marquess of Salisbury presided over his newly-elected first Tory administration, there were three meetings and five days' sport, two over the sticks in February, two on the flat in September and a three day mixed affair in November. Many of the big names

WARWICK RACES, 1967.

were there with Fred Archer and George Barrett mopping up most of the flat events as George Lambton, 'Bay' Middleton and Ted Wilson together with Count Kinsky looked after the interests of the gentlemen riders.

The following year the Warwick Races Club Syndicate was formed with the purpose of ensuring that the meeting would never again be subjected to the eccentricities of the early eighties. In 1902 Warwick became the home of the National Hunt Chase, then the premier race in the Calendar bar the Grand National.

By this time the course had nine days' rac-

ing, and although the flagging out of a four mile course required the consent of nearby landowners, as the syndicate held only limited rights to the basic track on Lammas Field, the application to stage the National Hunt Chase made by Robert Pritchard, then Clerk of the Course, was approved by the National Hunt Committee.

The race had enjoyed the hospitality of many venues since its inception in 1860. 'Atty' Persse, then at the height of his fame as an amateur rider prior to his brilliant career as a flat race trainer, won the 1902 National Hunt Chase on Marpessa, and the following season Captain (later Lt. Col.)

Robert Collis triumphed on Comfit. Afterwards a successful trainer at Kinlet in Worcestershire, he prepared Glenside to win the Grand National in 1911.

The course at Warwick had been put down at no small cost to many fine old trees, hawthorn and bramble hedges and great pains had been taken by Pritchard and his course builders to incorporate the famous 'Chandler's Brook'. It was all the more disappointing to the syndicate when the National Hunt Committee decided to experiment with the race at Cheltenham in 1904 and 1905. The Prestbury track was to become the permanent home of the National Hunt Chase from 1911 onwards, but the race reverted to Warwick between 1906 and 1910.

A highlight of this brief interregnum was the victory of Percy Whitaker on Rory O'More in 1908, the year in which Whitaker headed the amateurs' list with twenty-six winners. Whitaker's stepson Peter Roberts won the next two runnings on Wychwood and Nimble Kate respectively, but this was to be the apogee of Warwick's fame under either code of rules.

The syndicate continued in charge but without any prizes within six hundred pounds of the £825 won by Marpessa, the track became a bread and butter course, providing a reasonable chance for the moderate horse to make a modest contribution towards the ever-spiralling stable bills. Things are much the same today but, after all, in the words of John Milton, 'They also serve who only stand and wait'.

Perhaps the glory days may yet return, but even if they do not Warwick has done its bit for National Hunt racing. The syndicate sold out to the Town Council after the Second World War when an Act of Parliament enabled the council to buy the course. The Act also circumscribed the common grazing rights which had long been a bugbear resulting in poor and uneven going, and the course was enclosed, levelled and realigned.

Racecourse Holdings Trust acquired the property in 1967, and nowadays Warwick stages twelve days' jumping, featuring the Warwick National over an extended three and a half miles in January, and the Crudwell Cup, commemorating a fine steeplechaser always associated with Dick Francis and the winner of fifty races including thirty-nine chases. Crudwell also won seven times on the flat and four times over hurdles.

Though Crudwell was one of the dominant horses of the fifties, his exploits in the hands of Francis and later Michael Scudamore did not receive much media hype in that easy-going age when television was 'something to amuse the servants' and he has been overshadowed by horses like Arkle and Desert Orchid. But his record stands and it is much to the credit of Warwick, a course also deep with shadows of the past, that they remember him today.

# WETHERBY

FOR many years Wetherby was considered the headquarters of steeplechasing in the North and it remains so at least to the extent that it is the only course in Yorkshire devoted entirely to the winter sport. It was originally organised at the quaintly named Bottoms before a track was laid out at Linton Springs in 1842. That well known observer 'The Druid' (Henry Hall Dixon) rated Wetherby 'the best in England, bar none' and the course played host to steeplechasing's most celebrated moveable feast, the National Hunt Chase, in 1865.

The winner was Emperor, ridden by the full-bearded amateur crack, Alex Goodman, whose whiskers streamed past the post first in two Grand Nationals, on Miss Mowbray in 1852 and Salamander in 1866. The meeting on 2 and 3 April 1888, was remarkable for a high proportion of fallers in small fields and the disqualification of Mr H. Robinson's bay horse by The Baron out of Miss Sykes, first past the post in the Maiden Plate, 'on the ground of insufficient description'. Presumably the breeding was suspect or the lynx-eyed stewards suspected a 'ringer'.

However as the nineteenth century entered the decade known as the 'Naughty Nineties', the avaricious greed of the tenant farmers over whose land the races were run and who doubtless enjoyed the liberal hospitality of the hunts on race days forced the closure of the Linton Springs course.

Extortionate rent demands from the tenants killed the goose that laid the golden egg and as the landlord, Lord Leconfield, refused to sell Henry Crossley, a local landowner and long-standing member of the Wetherby Steeplechase Committee, stepped into the breach.

Crossley donated the land adjoining the Great North Road where racing still takes place today, the Committee rolled up their sleeves and a crash construction programme produced a course in five weeks, in time for the Easter Meeting in 1891.

Leaving the tenant farmers to contemplate their turnips, Wetherby prospered on the new site and although the facilities were primitive for some time, the sporting crowd came to Wetherby to enjoy a Yorkshire day out in the best traditions of England's premier county and cheer the exploits of local hero Mr R.H. 'Bob' Harper.

Harper was a graduate of the hunting field and gained his early race riding experience in the hurly-burly of the 'flapping' meetings which abounded at the time and, with all their villainy, were good schooling grounds for the ambitious jockey. He rode his first winner at the old Linton Springs track in 1884, on Ranger, and won many more red coat (hunt) races before forming an association with George Menzies, who trained at Coxhoe in County Durham.

Menzies was a shrewd hunting farmer who trained with great skill and their combined talents landed not a few good coups in the 'North Countree' before Menzies got a little too warm, and in 1902 Bob Harper joined forces with George Gunter, who was on the threshold of a top career as a cross-country rider and trained on his own account at Wetherby.

Masterminded by Harper, the stable provided Gunter with a steady stream of winners, and Harper himself rode more than forty in the 1902 season. Gunter rode eleven winners at Wetherby's three meetings alone in 1911, the year before Bob Harper established what is claimed as a record jump on the Wetherby gallops.

His mount Marcolica took off fifteen feet before a hurdle, landed twenty-five feet over it and slid a further eighteen feet before falling and pushing Harper another twenty feet along the ground. This would not have worried Harper, who had fractured both jaws, both legs, both arms and sustained fifty rib fractures in his career, and the total of forty feet certainly beats Chandler's 'official' record of thirty-nine feet at Warwick in 1847. Captain Percy Bewicke reckoned that he made a leap of forty two feet on a horse called Homeward Bound at Plumpton, but again the horse fell; and since Chandler remained upright the record is presumably his.

George Gunter was still riding winners at Wetherby in 1915 but the sands of time were running out and the training gallops were ploughed up during the War. Bob Harper retired from riding and became a starter at Wetherby and Sedgefield, remaining as cool and collected as he had been his days in the saddle. Faced with an unruly field in a maiden hurdle at Wetherby, he found the jockeys reluctant to form a line. Dryly he commented

'Alright, gentlemen; will those of you who are *trying* please come into line?'

By 1920 the owner of the course was Captain F.J. Osbaldeston Montagu and a company was formed to take control from the old Race Committee, over which the long serving Henry Crossley still presided. Various improvements were made to the stand built in 1906, and stabling provided adjacent to the course.

Today with the exception of Chester, where the confirmation of the Roodee and the old Roman city prohibit the provision of racecourse stabling and the sight of the runners ambling to and from track has become almost a tourist attraction, a course without on-site stabling would be unthinkable but this was not so in the nineteen-twenties, when most courses advertised stabling in local hostelries.

Under the guidance of Rowland Meyrick, an inspired Clerk of the Course, prize money was substantially increased. When Music Hall won the Wetherby Chase in 1920, prior to his victory in the Scottish Grand National, he collected £224 for his connections. In 1925, when the race had become a handicap Rathmore won £492. Roman won the Whitsuntide Chase in 1920 for £116; by 1925, the same race was worth £321 to Hawker, who made the long trip from the Epsom yard of former champion jockey Bill Payne.

Along with most philosophies geared to excellence, this policy paid handsome dividends, as the crowds who have flocked for over sixty years to Wetherby's popular Bank Holiday meetings bear witness. Rowland Meyrick is remembered by a £10,000 three mile chase on Boxing Day, and the old Wetherby Handicap Chase won in the fifties by good horses such as Bramble Tudor and Much Obliged, winner of the inaugural Whitbread Gold Cup, is still going strong.

In the 1970s, Wetherby trainer and former jockey Tony Doyle recounted to James Gill, author of the indispensable *Racecourses of Great Britain,* an interesting theory regarding Devon Loch's extraordinary fall on the run-in during the 1956 Grand National. According to Doyle 'It was a million to one chance. Devon Loch got his back hooves in two bits of false ground at the same time. He wasn't jumping any shadows. He was reaching out to balance himself, because he was slipping in a couple of old hoof marks'.

Poor Devon Loch. This prognosis seems as likely as any other and perhaps more likely than most; if only horses could talk!

# WINCANTON

THE origins of Wincanton, which by any standards nowadays would have to be regarded as the premier track in the West Country, are buried in the sands of time. Hunters' races were probably held at around the time when St Albans and Aintree were pioneering the sport in the mid nineteenth century, but there are no records until those of 3 April 1895, when racing under the rules of the Grand National Hunt Committee was staged at the old course on the lands of Hatherleigh Farm.

The prize money was pathetic, and the entries described by one commentator as 'poor in class and in number'. The only saving grace at this Easter Monday fixture was the society of the Duke of Somerset and the Earl of Ilchester, both stewards who attracted ' a large number of the nobility of Wilts and Somerset'. The reporter added 'Although the sport is very slack it is one of the most select gatherings in the western counties'.

Within a few years, the select gathering had obviously told the slackers in the sporting arena to pull their socks up, and the affair was now ' a very interesting one-day meeting . . . . the entries, as a rule, are very good in class and are well contested . . . the fixture is regarded as a little festival'.

Admission charges ranged from two guineas for a private carriage to a shilling for the view from the infield and by the time the First World War broke out in 1914 the meeting had assumed a degree of importance. However, when racing was resumed in 1920, funds were low and, as is so often the case in English public life, a patrician came to the rescue. Lord Stalbridge, who lived nearby at Motcombe House, Shaftesbury, formed a new board to take over the old Race Company. Stalbridge was the eldest son of a younger brother of the Duke of Westminster. His military career in the Boer War and in the Kaiser's conflict was with the 14the Hussars and latterly the Northamptonshire Yeomanry. He was a keen supporter of National Hunt racing and breeding, training and owning horses to his dying day in 1949.

The enthusiasm of Stalbridge, plus a generous injection of the cash generated by the rents on the Grosvenor estates in Westminster, soon restored the scene at Hatherleigh Farm, only for the lease to run out in 1925.

Lord Stalbridge lost no time in persuading the Race Company to purchase Kingwell Farm, where racing commenced on Easter Monday 1927, a few weeks after Thrown In, owned by Stalbridge and ridden by his son, the Hon. Hugh Grosvenor, had won the Cheltenham Gold Cup.

A policy of good prize money and well-framed races soon made the revived Wincanton popular with the trainers and racegoers alike, although it was not until the mid sixties that the course achieved its present status, with top class horses competing for events such as the Terry Biddlecombe Challenge Trophy, the Badger Beer Chase, and the Lord Stalbridge Memorial Gold Cup, for which the perpetual trophy is the

# Wincanton

WINCANTON RACES, 1989.

Grand National Cup won by Stalbridge's Bogskar in 1940.

But perhaps Wincanton nowadays is best known as a trial ground for Cheltenham. Although quite different in conformation, Wincanton, like the Prestbury course, sorts out the men from the boys and many candidates for the Gold Cup and the Champion Hurdle have stretched their pre-Festival wings in the Jim Ford Chase and the Kingwell Hurdle respectively at the February meeting.

It was at Wincanton where the once familiar red and black chevron colours of Sheikh Ali Abu Khamsin were an early feature of racing in the eighties. The first of the Arabs to taste success, he significantly chose to support National Hunt racing more heavily than the flat. He preferred the sporting cut and thrust of winter racing, and soon became a familiar, if shy figure, on the often chilly wastes of Kingwell, travelling from his home nearby. The Sheikh was leading owner three seasons in succession, from 1981–2 to 1983–4 and for a fourth time in 1985–6. His good horses included Half Free, Fifty Dollars More, Bolands Cross, Migrator and the 1983 Champion Hurdle winner Gaye Brief, and his principal trainers were Fred Winter, Les Kennard and the Rimells. For several years the Sheikh retained Richard Linley as his jockey after the first rider at the Winter stable, John Francome declined to ride one of the Khamsin horses.

Sheikh Ali Abu Khamsin wound down his racing interests in Britain in the spring of 1990 to concentrate on commitments in his native country. His slightly incongruous presence amongst the Somerset and Dorset farmers who throng Wincanton will be much missed.

# WINDSOR

PROPERLY known as Royal Windsor, the course certainly deserves the regal prefix. The cliché 'You'll live to regret it' was not one applicable to friends of King Henry VIII who offended Bluff King Hal. Regret, yes; but live, no, and it cannot be mere coincidence that his principal rivals, in the races run at Datchet and on the royal lands now known as Windsor Great Park, Mr Norrys and the Abbot of Glastonbury, were both summarily despatched, Norrys in consequence of a trumped-up charge of adultery with Anne Boleyn and the Abbot 'judicially murdered' during the dissolution of the monasteries.

A monarch of finer sporting instincts was Charles II, who enjoyed the racing at Datchet Ferry so much that he frequently made the detour to Windsor en route to the meetings at Newmarket. Queen Anne preferred her own course at Ascot, but it was at his stud in the Great Park that the Duke of Cumberland, second surviving son of George II, bred the brilliant Eclipse in 1764.

Racing on the present course at Rays Meadows, otherwise known as Clewer Meads, commenced on 5 June 1866. The date was wisely chosen, being the day after Founders' Day at Eton. A local journalist reported 'The assemblage in the stand and on the ground included many of the patrician supporters of racing', and most of them were doubtless parents pleased to relax after a day sitting on a hard chair in a hot tent watching future cabinet ministers grapple with Virgil's 'Aeneid'.

National Hunt racing started with the conventional spring meeting in April the following year, with hunters' flat races and professional hurdle events run over the course, then in the shape of a figure six. In the 1870s this was a mixed meeting, and the leading jockey was Robert I'Anson, son of William I'Anson who trained Blink Bonny and despite being over six feet tall, a stylish rider over hurdles and fences.

In the following decade, a steeplechase course laid down to incorporate a loop at the top end of the 'six' and encircling the paddock, loose boxes and saddling stalls opposite the stands, was host to the Hunt meeting of Mr W. H. Grenfell's Harriers in May and a two day professional card in December.

Perhaps the officials and stewards were still unfamiliar with the new layout in the late eighties when the Clewer Handicap Steeplechase over two miles and a half was started from the two miles and three-quarters pole. The field for this £97 event were three; Louisa, ridden by Willie Moore, a top class Irish jockey who later trained three Grand National winners, Chancery, the mount of Walter Nightingall, and Gamecock, winner of the Grand National and partnered by Bill Dollery.

Chancery and Gamecock fought out the finish and Chancery won by a short head, with Louisa refusing. This may have been a diplomatic refusal by the canny Willie Moore, who was probably the only jockey to notice the incorrect starting post. At all

WINDSOR GRAND MILITARY STEEPLECHASE.

events, Louisa's owner objected and the race was re-run, without Gamecock, and Louisa won easily from the exhausted Chancery, surprisingly made 6/4 on. Gamecock had the last laugh on the second day of the meeting, running out the easy winner of the St George's Handicap Chase, when Louisa, carrying a 10lb penalty for her previous day's victory, was a faller.

As Roger Mortimer points out in the *Biographical Encyclopaedia of British Flat Racing*, a lot of odd things have happened at Windsor. One of the oddest was a bookmakers' strike in 1925. Of course, strikes were in vogue at about that time, and the layers decided to protest against a betting tax imposed by the then Chancellor of the Exchequer, Winston Churchill. Bar profits soared as the races were run in the presence of a few disinterested and frustrated punters standing desolately in the enclosures.

Even odder was the case of the absent steward, and for this the author is again indebted to Roger Mortimer, who tells the tale of the objection at Windsor which was about to be heard when it was realised that Captain W. was missing. A messenger was despatched and in due course returned to the waiting stewards, the grim-faced trainers and the anxious jockeys, with the following: 'Captain W's compliments, and he will be back in a minute; he's on the rails betting on the result of the objection'.

Windsor soldiered on through two World Wars, though quite why this minor delightful gaff should have survived along with Manchester, Stockton, Brighton, Lewes and Newmarket during the 1914–8 conflict is something of a mystery. It owed much to Lloyd George and the Government, who stood firm against the critics in the press and in Parliament who wished for the sus-

FEEDING A NATION AT WAR. SHEEP GRAZE IN 1916.

pension in time of war. The Prime Minister 'saw no reason to stop the very limited programme of racing which they have authorised and which is necessary to maintain the very important industry of horse breeding'.

The Viennese born comedian Vic Oliver was, during the second global conflict, a keen patron of Windsor. As the star of the radio programme *Hi Gang!* with Ben Lyon and Bebe Daniels, and married to the Prime Minister's daughter, Sarah Churchill, Oliver was a household name. He maintained a private stable at Lambourn, where he regularly rode out, and between 1942 and 1947 his red and yellow colours were often seen in the winner's enclosure at Windsor, attended by their owner except on matinée days.

The bitter winter of 1947 brought severe flooding to a course always vulnerable to the elements. John Knight, who had joined windsor in 1937 and eventually took control from the firm of Frail Brothers which had designed the original track in 1865, was not deterred. Although the flood damage cost £10,000, Knight built a new weighing room and offices and only the restrictions of the postwar Labour Government prevented him from replacing the antiquated stands which

COMEDY OF ERRORS (KEN WHITE) AND SEA PIGEON (JONJO O'NEILL) 1976.

have survived for another forty-three years.

Since those bleak days Windsor has prospered, although the standard of racing has never been high under either code. Described by some commentators as 'undeservedly popular' Windsor is packed for the evening meetings staged on the flat throughout the summer and very well attended during the winter.

The place has charm, as an observer not lacking in that quality, John Rickman noted when he said 'the distance from the Members' bar to the Members' stand is not so far as you can throw your hat'.

The Members' bar, known colloquially as the Jam Stick, has been, temporarily at least, out of action; in March 1988 the course was sold to Thomson Investments, and rebuilding work costing the usual mega-bucks is now in hand. The Jam Stick has been much missed as it is a frequent haunt of the author.

# WOLVERHAMPTON

TODAY the word 'glamour' is not one which is easily associated with the Staffordshire town of Wolverhampton. Even the racecourse at Dunstall Park was until 1973, literally clouded with the smoke belching from the huge chimneys known at the Three Sisters, situated close to the five furlong start until their demolition by the Courtauld company.

However, these dark satanic mills did not start to grind until 1916, and in spite of a location in England's industrial heartland, Broad Meadows, Wolverhampton was the place to be for the inaugural meeting on 15 August 1825.

The Meadows, originally marshland called Hungry Leas and owned by Lord Darlington, were drained at vast expense. A grandstand was provided for the 'high classes' and there was the usual proliferation of booths, galleries and caravans providing every diversion from entertainment with a lady of the town to potshots at a row of clay ducks.

One cannot suppose it was the ducks that took the roving eye of Jack Mytton, the

WOLVERHAMPTON RACES, 1846.

222

squire of Halston in Shropshire. Mytton drank a bottle of wine while shaving as a prelude to the six bottles of port he habitually consumed during the day, and succeeded in being expelled from both Harrow and Winchester. This expert at educational pluralism also owned Euphrates, who had the gall to defeat Lord Darlington's Barefoot in the feature race of the day, the three mile Darlington Cup.

Mytton's way of life was not conducive to longevity and he died in the Fleet debtors' prison ten years later, but not before he had won thousands over the victory of Halston in the Chester Cup in 1829.

Twenty-eight years later Dr William Palmer of nearby Rugeley owned Doubt, the winner of the Wolverhampton Handicap. The doctor was an intrepid punter who used his knowledge of drugs and poisons to hedge his bets. Like most doped horses, his winners were usually front runners, and on at least one occasion he went too far. His filly, Nettle bolted on the way to the start of the Oaks in 1855. She had been purchased with the proceeds of an insurance settlement following the murder of Palmer's wife, and Palmer was hanged at Stafford the following year after poisoning his closest friend, John Parsons Cook.

Doubt's victory saved the life of a bookmaker, Fred Swindell – an unfortunate name for a legger. Swindell was ill-advised enough to share rooms at the Swan Hotel with Palmer on the night before the race. Having laid £3,500 to £500 over Doubt with

SIR ALEXANDER STAVELEY HILL.

Palmer, the bookmaker was persuaded by the charming doctor to seal the wager over a glass of poisoned brandy.

If Swindell died the bet would be void. Needless to say, the bookie was far to ill to go to the races the next day and after Doubt had scored a clever half-length victory Palmer hared back to the Swan and administered an antidote in order to collect his winnings.

By 1878, the Darlington inheritance was the Dukedom of Cleveland. The Mayor of Wolverhampton was anxious to continue racing but the Duke demurred, and a piecemeal deal resulted in neither fish, fowl nor good red herring as Broad Meadows became a municipal park with no room to test the thoroughbred.

As the nannies wheeled their infant

WOLVERHAMPTON THE WATER.

charges in basinets around the ornamental park where once George Fordham drove home the winners from 'Tiny' White, the growth of the railways was to play an unintentional part in restoring racing to Wolverhampton. The gradual spread of the tentacles of rail along which the steam locomotives were to chug in the final concept of the Industrial Revolution carried with it the kind of planning blight which the motorways have inflicted on the nation today.

The view from the bathroom window of Alexander Stavely Hill's mansion, Dunstall Hall, was not an agreeable one although doubtless rich in financial compensation. The future Tory M.P. and knight decided to sell up and move to nearby Oxley Manor, conveniently inherited from a cousin and delightfully free from sweaty navvies wielding pickaxes amidst the dust of development across Dunstall park.

When the grime had settled, a two-day National Hunt race meeting was held at Dunstall in October 1886. In spite of poor facilities the event was well patronised and a company was formed to buy the site from Stavely Hill, who was installed as Chairman.

It was intended to open the new course on the completion of the building of proper stands and the Jockey Club granted a date for Easter Monday, 1888. However, as many of us have cause to remember, builders do not always complete their work on time and the estimable Mr Henry Willock who was charged with the task missed his target by date by four months.

Dunstall Park finally got under way on 13 August, 1888, with Tommy Loates, who had

LILY LANGTRY, 1899.

won the last event on the old Broad Meadows course, appropriately enough in the plate on Silver Spur, winner of the inaugural five furlong All-Aged Maiden Plate. For some years, flat racing was to dominate and many of the more glamorous and raffish names of late Victorian society patronised Dunstall Park, including the Chevalier Odorado Ginistrelli, who won the Derby and the Oaks in 1908 with Signorinetta, the product of an equine love match according to her romantic Italian owner, breeder and trainer; Captain Wilfred Purefoy, better known as the mastermind of the Hermits of Druid's Lodge, a secret training establishment on Salisbury Plain where brilliant gambling coups were hatched; and the beautiful Lily Langtry, who contrived in the mid-1880s to find herself simultaneously in the affections of the Prince of Wales, Lord Lonsdale, and Sir George Chetwynd, culminating in fisticuffs between Sir George and the 'Yellow Earl'. Literally not knowing which way to turn, the Jersey Lily became the mistress of the manic millionaire George 'Abington' Baird, who lived near Wolverhampton at Whittington Old Hall, Lichfield and frequently rode at Dunstall Park. Mrs Langtry owned horses under the 'nom-de-course' of 'Mr Jersey' and was not a little upset when she was excluded from Baird's will after he died of dissipation in 1893.

By now some good horses were making the occasional appearance under National Hunt rules, including Cloister, winner of the Grand National in 1883. Generally speaking, however, the fare remained modest along with the paltry prize money which disgraced steeplechasing for so many years. In 1910 a mile and a half handicap on the flat at Wolverhampton was worth £185 and a two-year-old seller paid £100. In the winter, the three mile chasers earned £77 and the selling hurdlers £67 for a two mile trip.

The railway which had so offended the eye of Alexander Stavely Hill was proving useful, with a station at Dunstall Park and a loading and unloading dock adjacent to the track which was invaluable in an age when most racehorses were transported by train. However it was important to stage other attractions on the course, and in June 1910 an aviation meeting took place. This was ambitious stuff, as it was not long since Louis Bleriot had startled the citizens of Kent with the first cross-Channel flight.

Disaster was always on the cards as the pilots tried to manoeuvre their string-bag craft in filthy weather better suited to December and crashes were frequent. On the outbreak of the war in 1914, the Racecourse Company offered the services of Dunstall Park as a flying base, though the offer was declined by the military authorities.

Post-war some famous names were to catch the eye. Harry Brown, champion amateur jockey four times in successive years from 1918–21, was immortalised as Charlie Peppercorn in Siegfried Sassoon's *Memoirs of a Foxhunting Man*.

When at Eton, Brown's housemaster

recorded 'H.A. Brown – an excellent footballer, who tackled hard and ran very fast when ever he happened to be unable to go to Sandown'. Brown rode the winner of the first race at Wolverhampton when the sport resumed in 1919, the year in which he was not only champion amateur but overall champion jockey, a feat not emulated by any Corinthian rider since.

Brown became a director of the Racecourse Company in 1920 and served in that capacity for thirty-eight years. Like Lord Oaksey and Lord Mildmay, the finest amateurs since the Second World War, Harry Brown could only finish placed in a Grand National, riding The Bore into second spot in 1921 after falling at the last and remounting to land his 'monkey' (£500) each way, notwithstanding a broken collar bone.

Ally Sloper, winner on the National in 1915, was still good enough at the age of 10 to take the Walsall Handicap Chase in 1919; Michael Beary, better known as a classic winning flat race rider, rode a treble over hurdles in 1921, and in 1923 Captain 'Tuppy' Bennet won a novices' chase by six lengths on Red Splash.

The following year, Red Splash won the inaugural Cheltenham Gold Cup ridden by Dick Rees, but tragedy had intervened. At the Wolverhampton meeting on 27 December 1923 'Tuppy' Bennet fell from Ardeen during the running of the Oteley Handicap Chase, was kicked on the head and died seventeen days later with a smashed skull. The accident led to the introduction of compulsory crash helmets for all jockeys.

The Oteley Handicap Chase was to produce a happier result when Bruce Hobbs won on Marion du Pont Scott's Battleship in 1936, en route to National victory in 1938. But the war clouds were gathering again and it was a sorry sight which greeted racegoers when racing resumed on the all but derelict Dunstall Park circuit in 1946. Thanks to the energy of Lord Willoughby de Broke, who became chairman of the Dunstall Park Company, the course found its feet again, only to have to fight off a bid during the sixties' property boom to turn the Park into a housing estate. Amazingly, the attempt was made by two bookmakers, Jack Woolf and Wilf Gilbert, both of whom had shareholdings in the company and tried to repay the debt every bookmaker owes to racing by covering the track in concrete.

Happily, the efforts of the leggers were defeated by the Legge family. That was appropriate enough as the Legges had been associated with the course for many years and Martin Legge officiated as Managing Director when Dunstall Park celebrated its centenary in 1987.

Today Wolverhampton usually attracts modest animals on the flat, good class fields in the winter, and affords the racegoer every comfort and facility; it is all due to Sir Alexander Stavely and the planning blight of the Great Western Railway.

# WORCESTER

JACK MYTTON ON BARONET.

THE year 1718 was a time of comparative calm in the turbulent story of English history. 67 years had passed since the Scottish forces of Charles II has been defeated by the New Model Army of Oliver Cromwell and the Act of Union with Scotland in 1707 appeared to have settled the aspirations of the Stuart succession once and for all.

History forgotten, the good people of Worcester assembled at the Pitchcroft meadow on 20 June to witness a race for 'a Saddle and a bridle, £3 value by and Horse Mare or Gelding carrying ten stone, except Bridle and Saddle, the best of three two-mile heats, the winning horse to be sold for seven pounds.' There were also two athletic contests on the card, one for men running for a pair of silver buckles, and another for 'young women' racing for 'a handsome hat'.

If a similar contest is ever mooted at Ascot, the author's wife will be high amongst the five day entries and probably be in with a squeak, but such contests were rare enough even in eighteenth century Worcester. By 1739 horse racing dominated the Pitchcroft, and Mr Middleton's Cato galloped into the record books as the first recorded winner of a 40 guinea plate run on 22 August.

By 1755, the meeting was a four-day affair, and the programme carried a warning to the owners of loose dogs and the proprietors of sketchily erected tents. The former exhortation was ignored, as it is on all too many tracks today and as any racecourse announcer will testify.

By 1759, Berrow's *Worcester Journal* reported 'The Company that appeared upon this Occasion of the Course, at the Ordinaries (dinners) and the Balls was very numerous and genteel. Peevishness and Debate were nowhere to be found; but Cheerfulness, Harmony, and universal satisfaction were everywhere visible. . . . In short our Races now seem to be established beyond a possibility of being shaken. Upwards of Five Hundred Persons were at the Publick Breakfast at Dingley Bowling Green on the Thursday morning and about Three Hundred on Friday morning.'

With all those Ordinaries and balls, it seems a pity that the punters had to wait until 1837 for the invention of Worcester Sauce to accompany their raw eggs at the

well-attended breakfasts; but undeterred by the rigours of the Napoleonic Wars, the 1820s found the rakish Jack Mytton cleaning up in the Gold Cup with Euphrates, and in addition to the usual revelries of Race Week, there was a Steward's Play on Tuesday evening. In 1825 it was proclaimed as a foot-note in Hayes's Only Correct List of Runners 'Mr Green intends ascending in his Balloon from the Saracen's Head Bowling Green on Saturday Evening at 3 o'clock'.

MYTTON TAKES HIS HORSE INTO THE SEVERN.

THE WATER LEAP, 1846.

Let us hope that Mr Green had a decent bumper of claret at the Saracen's Head prior to the take-off in his Montgolfier, since his landing is unrecorded. The Stewards' Play, on the other hand, was a great success, and by 14 March 1844 the bill at the Theatre Royal offered 'the new Drama of "A Maiden's Fame or the Legend of Lisbon", with "The Scape Goat", "A Thumping Legacy" and "Hunting a Turtle"' as curtain-raisers.

The following night 'the popular Drama of "Old Parr" was preceded by "The Captain's Not Amiss", "The Eton Boys", and a sketch with the intriguing title "My Valet and I"'.

These entertainments followed the running of the Royal Birthday Stakes celebrating the twenty-fifth birthday of Queen Victoria. The race had been something of a cracker, with Grand National winner Discount in the hands of his amateur rider

AROUND THE TURN.

Mr Crickmere, who also partnered him at Aintree, winning from Tom Olliver on his 1843 National winner Vanguard. He was a particular favourite of Olliver's and when the horse died he had a sofa made from the old chaser's hide which he named in honour of Vanguard's last owner, Lord Chesterfield; the name has been associated with padded sofas ever since.

Discount's claim to fame lies in the fact that he was the first horse registered in the General Stud Book to win the Grand National. He was subsequently sold for 1100 guineas at Tattersall's, but his ultimate fate is

WORCESTER RACES, MARCH 1990.